My Dear Hindalla Remember Me

Letters from a Lost World

May 1937—January 1940

Marlene S. Englander

Marlene S. Englander

Hinda Zarkey Saul

Translated from Yiddish into English by Hinda Zarkey Saul

Annotations by Hinda Zarkey Saul and Marlene S. Englander

ISBN 9780983130055

Library of Congress
2011935977

Editing, Joanne Fenton Humphrey

Book Design, Ron Humphrey

Windjammer
ADVENTURE PUBLISHING

Windjammer Adventure Publishing
289 South Franklin Street, Chagrin Falls, OH 44022
Telephone 440.247.6610 Email windjammerpub@mac.com

Acknowledgements

With love and thanks to our families and friends who have supported and encouraged us.

M.S.E.

H.S.

Dedication

With much appreciation to Nochum Berman, whose beautiful letters will keep the memory of Jewish life in Šeduva, Lithuania alive.

Table of Contents

How Many First Cousins Do I Have? 6

Reflections by Hinda's Daughter 8

Setting the Stage 10

The Trip, 2010 13

Letters 1—8, 1937 18

Letters 9—19, 1938 50

Letters 20—27, 1939 102

Letter 28, 1940 128

Note from Mrs. Mellman, 1959 132

Epilogue 133

What Happened To 141

Victims 142

Photographs 154

Endnotes 159

Sources and Other References 170

How many first cousins do I have?

As my children were growing up, the Holocaust and genealogy-related questions came up many times. I remember the first time, when my son Ken excitedly came home from first grade with an assignment.

> "Mom, approximately how many first cousins do I have?" he asked, expecting the number to be so large I wouldn't be able to come up with a precise number.
>
> My somber response was, "Approximately none."
>
> "How many maternal grandparents do I have?"
>
> "None."
>
> "Where is your family from?"
>
> "Lithuania, but it was also Poland, and then for a while it was Russia."
>
> "Where and when were you born? Where did you live?"
>
> "I was born in 1922, in Ponevezh,[1] Lithuania, where my parents temporarily lived during World War I, and for a short time after. But we were back in Widze, which was then Poland, by the time I was three. I also lived with my Aunt Goda, Uncle Samuel, and Cousin Yvette when I went to junior high school in Šeduva, which was in Lithuania."

As the years went by, my three children (Marlene, Ken, and Howard) asked more questions, and found that each answered question turned into more unanswered, complicated questions.

We lived in a suburb of Cleveland, Ohio, where most of our friends and neighbors were first generation Americans, and virtually all of them were Jewish. We all had similar ancestral pasts; we had lived, or had relatives who had lived, in Eastern Europe at the onset of World War II. To my children, these countries seemed as far away as the moon, and thinking of me in any other context other than living in the United States seemed incomprehensible to them. They didn't even seem to notice, or be troubled by, my accent. Because I wasn't in a concentration camp, the stories they eventually heard from survivors didn't seem relevant to our family's history. Since I didn't have a number tattooed on my arm, and I was already in the United States when the war began, they wanted to believe that I also wasn't personally affected.

But then I gave them the letters. Three years of correspondence (May, 1937—January, 1940) to me from my friend, whom we just called "Berman," and he signed all his letters to me just with the letter "B." I was a young teenager living in Cleveland, Ohio, in the United States, trying to adjust to a new lifestyle. I was quiet, studious, and conscientious. Berman was in Šeduva, Lithuania, working as a pharmacist in what had been my Aunt Goda's pharmacy. He was nine years older than I, and was adventurous, open-minded, and optimistic. He was always hoping for something a little more interesting and exciting to happen. We corresponded in Yiddish but I translated the letters into English more than fifty years ago. This not only helped me learn and use the English language, but I hoped one day my three children would want to read them—when they were ready—and I didn't think it likely that they would be fluent in Yiddish.

Berman's letters were very important to me as I was adjusting to my new life. The letters describe the life I left behind in a small *shtetl*[2] in Lithuania, contrasting it so vividly to my new life in America —one whose values were different and whose friendships were different. While I was struggling to find my place in a new country, trying to make new friends and learn a whole new language and culture, Berman offered advice, grounding, stability, and reminders of the Jewish values and lifestyle I left behind. My letters to him gave him pleasure and joy. As he helped me with my transition, I was his hope for a better future. We planned that when I turned 21, and could legally file papers on his behalf, I would be the person who could bring him to America, a land of endless opportunities and freedoms. And then, we would be able to see each other again.

When my two older children, Marlene and Ken, recently decided to go on a heritage tour to Lithuania, with side trips to the *shtetlekh* where my ancestors and I lived, I was apprehensive. I had no idea what they would find—how were Lithuanians treating Jews today, and would my children be safe? And I couldn't imagine they would find anything of any family or personal significance. They assured me they would be fine and promised to call when they found something interesting, or when they had questions.

When they returned, Marlene suggested publishing these letters for a wider distribution than just for the immediate family. I am surprised, yet pleased, that there is renewed interest in this lost world I left behind—a time and place that seems to have been forgotten.

I gladly share my translation of these letters in hope that people without the ability to read Yiddish can understand what life was like during that time.

Hinda Zarkey Saul, Recipient of the Letters

Reflections by Hinda's Daughter

Why this book, and why now? That's the question I have been asked numerous times when I have told people about this project. It's not an easy question to answer as it involves multiple fragments of interest simultaneously converging:

> Wanting to tell Berman's story: years of letters from a young man that so beautifully describe life in a small town in Lithuania in the late 1930's, before World War II;
>
> Finding the original Yiddish letters from Berman, which, to me, was an important part of the process;
>
> Working with my mother to annotate the letters, providing endnote explanations to clarify and further expand on portions of the letters;
>
> My childhood memories of learning about the Holocaust and its effect on my mother and her family;
>
> My decades-long interest in genealogy; and
>
> A recent trip to Lithuania, Latvia, and Belarus that allowed me to "walk in the steps of my ancestors" and get a better understanding of what life was like for my mother before she came to America.

With the proliferation of resources accessible, particularly on the internet, combined with the ability of my mother to remember so much and to be able to answer so many questions, it seemed like the perfect time to put it all together.

The Making of the Book

The cornerstone of this book is the letters. Unlike Anne Frank,[3] whose diary is a legend and whose prose embraced the world, Berman's letters are different. This is a young man, not yet 25, experiencing life in his small town in Lithuania. His days seem routine; he writes of books he is reading and movies he is watching that he expects will influence him for many years. He has goals, ambitions, and an immense desire for knowledge. He rarely speaks of the war that seems so far away, yet his letters convey the effect the war is having on everybody. His early letters are hopeful; his later letters are filled with quiet resolve.

After rereading the letters, many years after having read them the first time, I realized just how special they still are. Not only do they shed light on my mother's transition to becoming an American, they are snippets of the life she left behind, a chronicle of the changes forced upon Lithuanian Jews, and a look into the lives of others whose fates are both known and unknown.

What I learned on my trip to Lithuania is that most of the *shtetlekh* were similar: a town square with a church, Jewish homes and businesses "in the shadow of the church," a synagogue, a Jewish cemetery, a school, and a weekly market. Although these letters were from Berman to my mother, similar letters were probably written by others. If one has ancestors who lived in a small town in Eastern Europe in this time period, these letters may, in part, mirror their experiences as well.

If you read Yiddish, you will not need the English translation. In addition, my mother and I annotated the letters to help describe a situation, a movie, a town, a person, or to clarify subject matter. This should enhance the understanding of what the times were like, and also demonstrate how people communicated across national boundaries in a time long before cell phones, email, and even airplanes. The original content of the letters and my mother's original translation remain unchanged.

Included are pictures from my mother's days in Šeduva, her family, and her friends. There are also pictures of Šeduva and Widze from my trip in the summer of 2010.

There are many historical books and reference materials that discuss Lithuania and other places mentioned in the letters. When possible, I used them to verify and document historical facts. For items of a more general nature I chose to use free online sources that would have easy, global accessibility. The bibliography includes not only the sources used in the annotations, but also other books and websites that provide additional information about material covered in the letters or about Lithuania's Jewish history.

Marlene Saul Englander

Setting the Stage: The Cities and the Families

Although the letters can stand alone without much explanation, a brief description of the people and places mentioned most frequently will provide a better understanding of the context and times during which the letters were written.

Widze, Poland and Hinda's Family

Widze (Vidzy) was where most of my mother's family lived. Located about 75 miles (125 kilometers) northeast of Vilna (Vilnius) and near the current borders of Latvia and Lithuania, it was established over 500 years ago, in Lithuania, and was one of the country's four largest market places. Throughout history it was affected by many different wars.[4] In the 1890's, when my mother's parents, Alchonan Zarchi (Zarkey) and Chana Kagan, were born and later married, it was part of the Russian Empire. They moved to Panevėžys, Lithuania, where my mother was born in 1922. By 1925 the family had returned to Widze, and when my mother's two sisters, Gita and Leah, were born (1925 and 1927) it was then part of Poland.

Widze had a Yiddish secular school that offered a six-year curriculum and taught all subjects in Yiddish. It also was used for lectures and artistic performances and had a library, choir, and dramatic program. Widze had a Zionist youth movement to help youths prepare for *kibbutz* life in Palestine as well as programs for those interested in communism and socialism. If interested in continuing formal education after completing the six-year curriculum, one needed to move to a city that had a junior high school. After my mother completed her studies in Widze, she needed to find a junior high school elsewhere in order to continue her education. Coincidentally, her Aunt Goda, Chana's sister, was living in Šeduva, Lithuania. Šeduva had such a school and it was decided my mother would live with Goda's family and attend school there.

The Kagan Family, about 1914

Back Row: (children) Rachel, Isaac, Chana (Hinda's mother) Joseph, Goda

Front Row: (Hinda's grandparents) Zvi-Hirsch, Doba Kagan (nee Himmelfarb)

Šeduva, Lithuania

Šeduva, approximately 160 miles (230 kilometers) from Widze, is a small town in Lithuania. The Republic of Lithuania is a country in northern Europe along the shore of the Baltic Sea. During the 14th century, it was the largest country in Europe. My mother arrived in Šeduva in 1935; she was 12 years old. Šeduva was similar to other *shtetlekh* in Lithuania, Poland, and surrounding countries. There was a synagogue, a rabbi, a Hebrew school, a Jewish public library, and a Jewish cemetery. Jews spoke Yiddish amongst each other but also spoke Lithuanian with their non-Jewish friends, neighbors, and merchants. In 1897, there were 2513 Jews in Šeduva, more than half the city's population. Due to the economic crisis of World War I, there were only 916 Jews in Šeduva (29 percent of the total population) in the early 1920's. The town's Jews earned their living from commerce, crafts, small industry, and agriculture.[5] A large proportion of the Jews belonged to a Zionist group. Šeduva was almost completely destroyed during World War I, and a combination of poor economic conditions, verbal and physical attacks on Jews, boycotts of Jewish businesses, and many emigrations to the United States, Palestine, and South Africa, resulted in a Jewish population of only 800 in 1940.[6]

My mother's plans were to attend junior high school in Šeduva and then either return to her family in Widze or attend high school, most probably in Vilnius, as Šeduva did not have a high school. While attending school in Šeduva she lived with her Aunt Goda, Uncle Samuel Bardon, and their young daughter Yvette, who was 9 years younger than my mother. Goda was a pharmacist and their living quarters were attached to the pharmacy.

Goda (nee Kagan) and husband Samuel Bardon, 1930

Prior to meeting Goda, Samuel, who had been born in Russia, had already immigrated to the United States and was living in Cleveland, Ohio. In 1930, while visiting his older brother in Kovno (Kaunas), Lithuania, he met Goda, and they married shortly thereafter, in Sudarg, Lithuania, where Goda owned a pharmacy. After their daughter Yvette was born, they moved to Šeduva. Samuel, however, wasn't able to find the type of work he wanted in Lithuania, and he persuaded Goda to move back to Cleveland with him. By then, my mother had completed her Šeduva education and it was decided she would go with them to the United States. They left Šeduva in March 1937, departing from Cherbourg, France, on the Queen Mary.

Hinda Zarkey and Yvette Bardon, 1935

Cleveland, Ohio

Cleveland, Ohio, is in the United States of America located on the southern shore of Lake Erie. The United States gained its independence in 1776 and is a constitutional republic. The contiguous land area is 1.9 billion acres and includes most climate types, including deserts, tropical, semi-arid, alpine, oceanic, and polar. Some states are prone to hurricanes and tornadoes. English is the de facto language of the country. It is a secular nation; the First Amendment of the Constitution guarantees the free exercise of religion and forbids the establishment of any religious governance. In 1920, there were 746,841 residents in Cleveland—nearly 10% of them were Jewish. In 1930, there were 901,482 residents in the city limits; including the suburban area, that number increased to 1,202,838.[7] When my mother and the Bardon family arrived in 1937, Cleveland was a leading manufacturing center, specifically steel and automobiles.

Although similar climatically to Šeduva, that is where the similarities end. Cleveland was a much larger city; people walked, or travelled by streetcar. In Šeduva they walked, as nothing was very far away. There was indoor plumbing in Cleveland, and my mother even commented that there was running water in their garage—and she could take a shower, not just a bath! Although there was a sense of community in Cleveland, it wasn't like in Šeduva, where everyone knew everyone else and knew the small details in their lives. Similar to a scene in *Fiddler on the Roof*,[8] when someone bought a new piece of furniture in Šeduva, everyone came to see it. And, when someone in Šeduva received a piece of mail, everyone knew that, too.

The Trip, 2010

Seventy-three years after my mother arrived in the United States, I took a short trip to Lithuania along with my brother Ken, hoping to find answers to lingering questions:

> "Would we find any of the places, friends, or family members mentioned in Berman's letters?"
>
> "What additional information could we find about Berman's family?"
>
> "Could we find the letters my mother wrote to him?"
>
> "Are the stories my mother heard about her family 65 years ago true, and with improved documentation, research, and archival information currently available, could we prove or disprove the stories?"
>
> "Could we find our mother's house in Widze based on a picture she drew for us?"

Visiting Šeduva

When I visited Šeduva on a beautiful, sunny summer day in June 2010, I walked around, almost like a crazed person, hoping that Šeduva had become Brigadoon.[9] With pictures in one hand and a list of residences and businesses along with a 1940 telephone book in the other, I ran from place to place looking for the people I had come to know so well in Berman's letters to my mother. While the rational side of me knew exactly what I would find, the irrational side had me planning to give a huge hug to Berman, who would be working in the pharmacy; seeing Sioma Davidowitz run between working in his father's shoe store and helping Berman in the pharmacy; and finding the still-beautiful, brown-haired Elke Friedlander at her father's butcher shop.

When the sign for Šeduva appeared, I think I actually screamed out, "I can't believe I'm really here!" After a lifetime of hearing colorful stories about my mother's school years, her friends and family, and looking at photos, I could finally see it all for myself. What would I see? I had heard so many stories and created so many images in my mind. I couldn't wait to get started!

Our first stop was City Hall, where I rapidly named names and showed photos that were more than 70 years old to a woman who was in her 30's and didn't speak a word of English. Our tour guide, who had already taken us to seven *shtetlekh* in Lithuania, Belarus, and Latvia in two days, was ready to be done. But I was just beginning! I wanted to walk in my mother's footsteps. I wanted to recreate her last days in Šeduva. I wanted to see the tree that Berman mentioned in a letter; I wanted to see the school where my mother posed with her schoolmates; and I wanted to find some of her schoolmates—Jewish or Lithuanian—people who would remember her and be excited to meet my brother and me.

My mother doesn't specifically remember that much about her actual last days in Šeduva. Why would she remember them any more than I would remember my last day of junior high school? While some may remember parts of a commencement ceremony or a dress they wore, it is unlikely they remember the weather or the flowers in bloom. My mother is no exception. She and I agreed from the very beginning that this book would be totally factual and that we would not embellish anything. Although we could probably guess what her last days in Šeduva were like, we really don't know for sure.

However, as I was putting the photographs together for this book, one particular photo of a party caught my eye; so many of the people whose names are in the letters are in the picture. (My mother's uncle is missing; he likely had already left for the United States.) It is dated 1937, so it would have been one of the last parties before my mother left. Rather than trying to describe her last days, I thought describing these people might best bring their personalities to life, as well as the "personality" of Šeduva.

Šeduva Party, 1937

It's a party, a celebration, or a holiday because everyone is dressed up. There is red wine on the table, and dessert has yet to be served. The child at the center of the table is Yvette. She is about 5 years old. She's surrounded by adults, but doesn't look tired. Perhaps this is a party for her, but maybe not. The party is at her house. Her mother (my mother's Aunt Goda) is a pharmacist and the living quarters are attached to the pharmacy. Since people would have emergencies in the middle of the night, the pharmacist needed to live at the pharmacy; therefore, social gatherings often took place there. My mother remembered the pharmacy being at the corner of two main streets, not at the center of town, but not far, and on a small hill or incline.

Dr. Blumberg is seated in the front row at the far left. He is mentioned for the first time in Letter #8, December 15, 1937. He was one of two doctors in town. He was very popular with the young ladies in Šeduva, although he had a girlfriend, an attorney, in Kovno (Kaunas). What made him special to my mother is that whenever he traveled to Kovno by train, he would think up some algebra problems for her, and she was always so excited and happy to work them out.

Looking at the picture, the two people to the right of Yvette are the Davidowitzes. Zalman Davidowitz owned a shoe store and had a son, Sioma, who was about the same age as my mother. Mrs. Davidowitz was hoping Sioma would be accepted as an intern at the pharmacy. Berman mentions them a few times in the letters.

Mrs. Rabinowitz, a nurse, is seated next to them. Her husband, a banker, did not attend this party. Their young daughter, Shulamit, was friends with Yvette.

Standing at the far left in the back row is Mr. Fish, the principal of the school. Miss Levinson is next to him, and next to her is Bassia Ulfsky. Both women were teachers at the school. Dr. Blumberg's girlfriend, the attorney from Kovno, is next.

Standing next to Yvette is her mother, Goda (my mother's Aunt). Standing next to her are Mr. Kellman, who was also a teacher at the school, and his wife.

Mr. Friedlander, a pharmacist, is next. He was leaving his position at Šeduva's pharmacy and

Berman was replacing him.

Standing next to Mr. Friedlander is Berman, and my mother is in front of him, behind Mr. Davidowitz.

The Šeduva Yizkor Book website[10] includes a list of the pre-war residents of Šeduva. A similar version is also on the *Jewish Homes of Shadova—Šeduva* webpage.[11] This is the list I had with me as I was trying to find the places my mother would have frequented, and the people with whom she interacted—the people to whom she would have wanted to say goodbye.

My mind is transported back to March 1937. It was probably cold and grey, even if the sun was shining—the kind of day you expect when you are saying goodbye. My mother was probably anxious, nervous, but also excited about what is ahead. I remember a photograph of my mother and her schoolmates, all bundled up in front of their school.

Šeduva Classmates, 1937

Under her coat my mother was wearing her school uniform, a long-sleeved brown dress with a black apron over the dress, and a brown cap with a visor.

Hinda in her school uniform, Šeduva, about 1936

I imagine that my mother is wearing that same coat, with the high black fur collar, as she and Berman walk the streets of Šeduva for the last time. People know she is leaving and I imagine them running out of their homes to say goodbye, wishing her well, and making her promise to write, do well in school, and be happy. I am waiting for them to run out of their houses now to greet me and say, "You are Hinda's daughter? How is she? Tell her I said hello. We have missed her." But, so far, no one is running out to tell me I look like my mother; no one is speaking English, or Yiddish, and no one is looking like anyone in the photographs.

As we walk around the old buildings just off the town square, I quickly start referring to the map. But nothing is making sense. My tour guide tells me the streets are not named the same as they were in the 1930's. I just do not know what I am looking at. I see store after store on two separate streets and I know one of them must be the Panevėžys Street on the map. An old building, which which is now supposed to be a cultural museum, appears to be vacant; it was once a leather store. Is this #11 on my list of residences? Is this where Mr. Kamber's leather store was, with his living quarters on the second floor? I am running around so fast, I am missing so much of the scenery. What kinds of flowers did I see? I don't remember. But, I do remember that we heard lots of birds and flies. Did my mother hear birds and insects in March 1937? We see a building that is now a library. I was told a wealthy Jew once lived there. Why didn't I go inside? Was this where Mr. Payim lived? Berman writes about Mr. Payim in Letter #2. Is this where Berman was living when he wrote that letter? I am getting so close…

According to the map, the Friedlander, Davidowitz, and Rabinowitz families all lived near each other. Elke Friedlander, the beautiful daughter of Yudel Friedlander, (no relation to Mr. Friedlander, the pharmacist) was a good friend of my mother's; Sioma Davidowitz would come to work at the pharmacy with Berman; and Shulamit Rabinowitz was a friend of Yvette's. I should also be able to find Moshe Bret's home. He was a wealthy lumber merchant and his oldest daughter was known to be the only girl in town who could play the piano. My mother had a friend named Milke Bret. I wonder if she played the piano?

Where is Shavl Street? The construction supply store owned by Velvel Feifert should be here, as well as a cobbler shop next to Feifert's place. But, I can't tell. I thought this would be so easy, with this wonderful list of residences, but it is not. While so much of the city looks exactly as I imagined it looked in 1937, I am sure much has changed. The roads are paved. Are these even the same roads my mother would have walked on, or are the muddy paths between the homes what would have been the streets all those years ago?

I love every minute in Šeduva, but so far I am not convinced I have found anything on my map or any real clues to the people or places in the letters. Then, we try another street, and THERE IT IS!

Šeduva Pharmacy, 2010

We have found the pharmacy! It is on the corner of two streets, on a small incline, just as my mother had said, and not far from the town square. *Vaistine*, which means pharmacy in Lithuanian, is still written on the building. It's locked; we cannot go in—nevertheless, we have found the place where my mother lived, and there are tears in my eyes.

We go a little farther and we find her school. Our tour guide tells us it is now a sewing factory. I don't think to ask where the school is now, or if there is one. We take more pictures. We take a picture in front of the same tree under which my mother stood with her classmates. (I am holding the photograph so we won't forget.) I have walked in her footsteps. Again, more tears....

Marlene Englander & Ken Saul at Šeduva School, 2010

On her last day in Šeduva, my mother walks hand-in-hand with her friend, Berman. Despite their 9-year age difference, their personalities complement each other: He is adventurous, assertive, and poised; she is careful, quiet, and self-controlled. They have been friends since he started working at her aunt's pharmacy. However, he surprises her with a conversation that would have been similar to the following:

> *"I have come to be very fond of you, Hindalla. I hope that one day soon I, too, will come to America and you and I can spend time together, not just as friends, but maybe something more."*
>
> *Hinda's eyes wouldn't have been able to hide the surprise she felt hearing his words. "Berman, I don't know what to say," she would reply. "I like you, too. I didn't know you had any feelings for me except friendship."*
>
> *"From friendship something deeper may grow, if given the chance," Berman offered. "Don't worry, Hindalla. We'll see what happens when I get to America."*
>
> *"Very well, we'll see what happens in America," Hinda would reply, sounding more grown-up than her years.*
>
> *"Promise me that you'll write to me often, Hindalla. Promise that you will remember me."*
>
> *"Of course I'll write. And you must write me nice long letters every chance you get."*

They likely smile at each other and turn to walk back to the pharmacy.

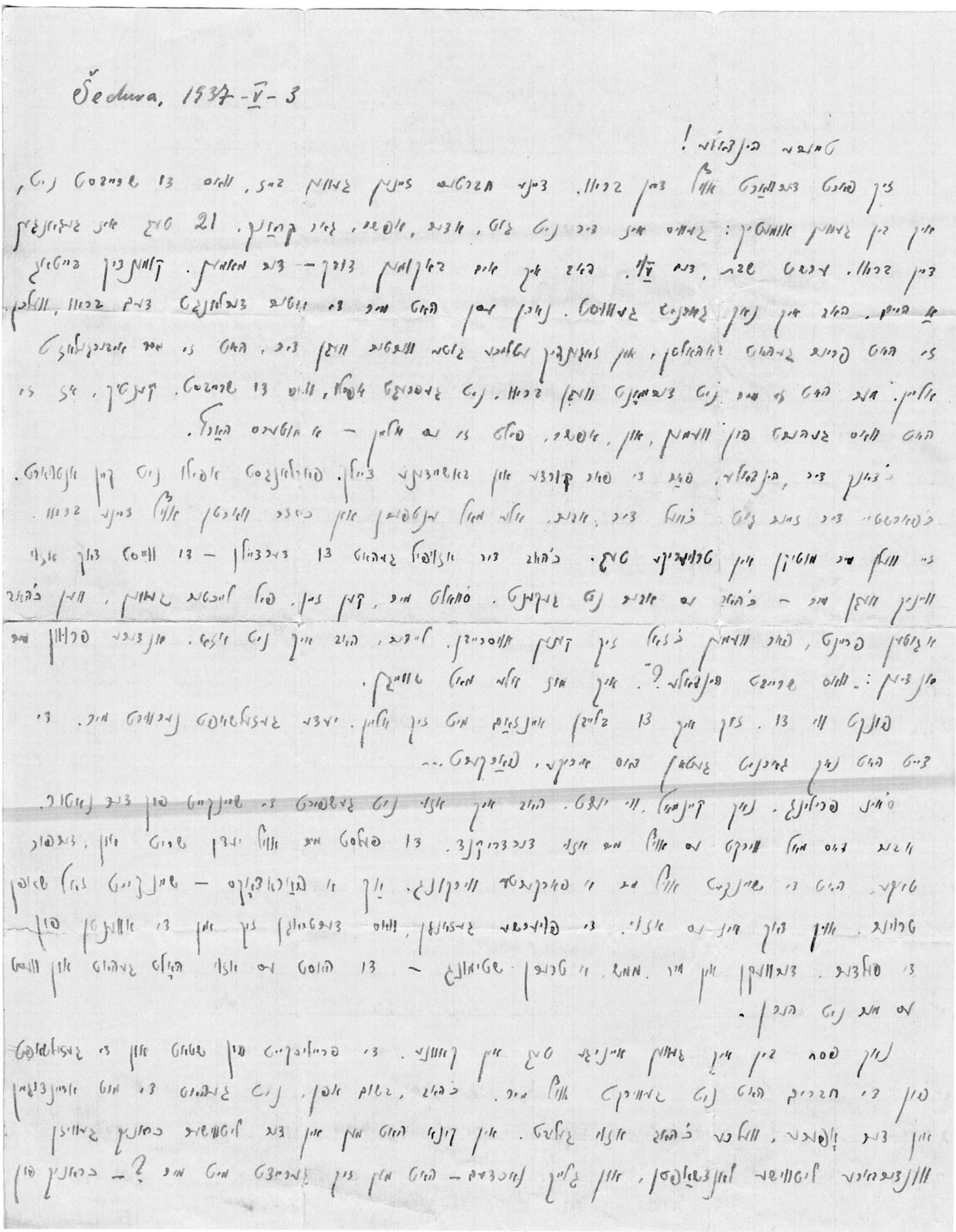

Šeduva, 1937-V-3

טײַערע הינדעלע!

Šeduva, 3/V/1937[12]

(May 3, 1937)

Dear Hindalla![13]

Finally your letter came. Your girlfriends[14] were angry that you hadn't written. I was sad: no doubt you are unhappy or, worse yet, perhaps ill. It took 21 days for your letter to get here. Finally, Saturday, May 1st, I received it via my mother.[15] When I came home in the afternoon I knew nothing. After I finished eating, my mother handed me the letter which she had previously hidden, and saying a few nice words about you, left me to myself. She never mentioned the letter again. She didn't even ask what you wrote. Possibly she might have heard something from someone. Or, perhaps, she might have had a feeling—a mother's heart!

I thank you, Hindalla, for the few short and modest lines. You don't even ask for an answer. I understand you, however, very well. I will always answer you and always await your letters. They will cheer me up on sad days. I had so much to tell you—you know so very little about me—unfortunately, I could not do it. It would have been so much easier for me to have a good friend to whom I could tell everything. Regretfully, I have no one. Others try to start up with me: "What do you hear from Hindalla?" I just keep still. Just like you, I seek solitude... company irritates me. Time has not yet done its job, on the contrary...

It is spring. Never before have I felt the beauty of nature so deeply. But this time it depresses me. I miss you with every step, and that is why the beauty has the opposite effect on me. A paradox—beauty should create sorrow. And still it is so. The songs of the farmers that can be heard evenings from the far-away fields put me almost into a tearful mood—you loved it so much and you will never hear them again.

After Passover I was in Kovno[16] for a few days. The gaiety of the city and the company of my friends did not help to put me in a better mood. I even had no desire to go to the opera, which I always loved so much. In the movies, they showed the beautiful Lithuanian landscapes, and directly after—were they teasing me?—the latest news from America: sports, technique, and advertisements. Two worlds—two opposites; and yet they are so close to me. I could not even enjoy the film.

One thing in your letter pleased me no end—you will continue your schooling. I was, indeed, afraid it shouldn't be otherwise. The sad fate of a Jewish girl again willed that you should break your life a third time.[17] A third time to start everything from the beginning. Fortunately, though, you are endowed with intelligence, ability, and energy. In addition, you are young. In just a short time you will absorb everything in order to become equal with the other American girls your age. I am sure of it. I am also sure that the great opportunities of the free America will help you develop your talent and you will quickly become self-sufficient. You wrote to your girlfriends about your plans. I was very happy to hear about it.

News by me, I am now the manager of the pharmacy.[18] I had no difficulty with the papers. Within two days I received permission to practice. Nobody "bothered" me about my age. I am indebted to a

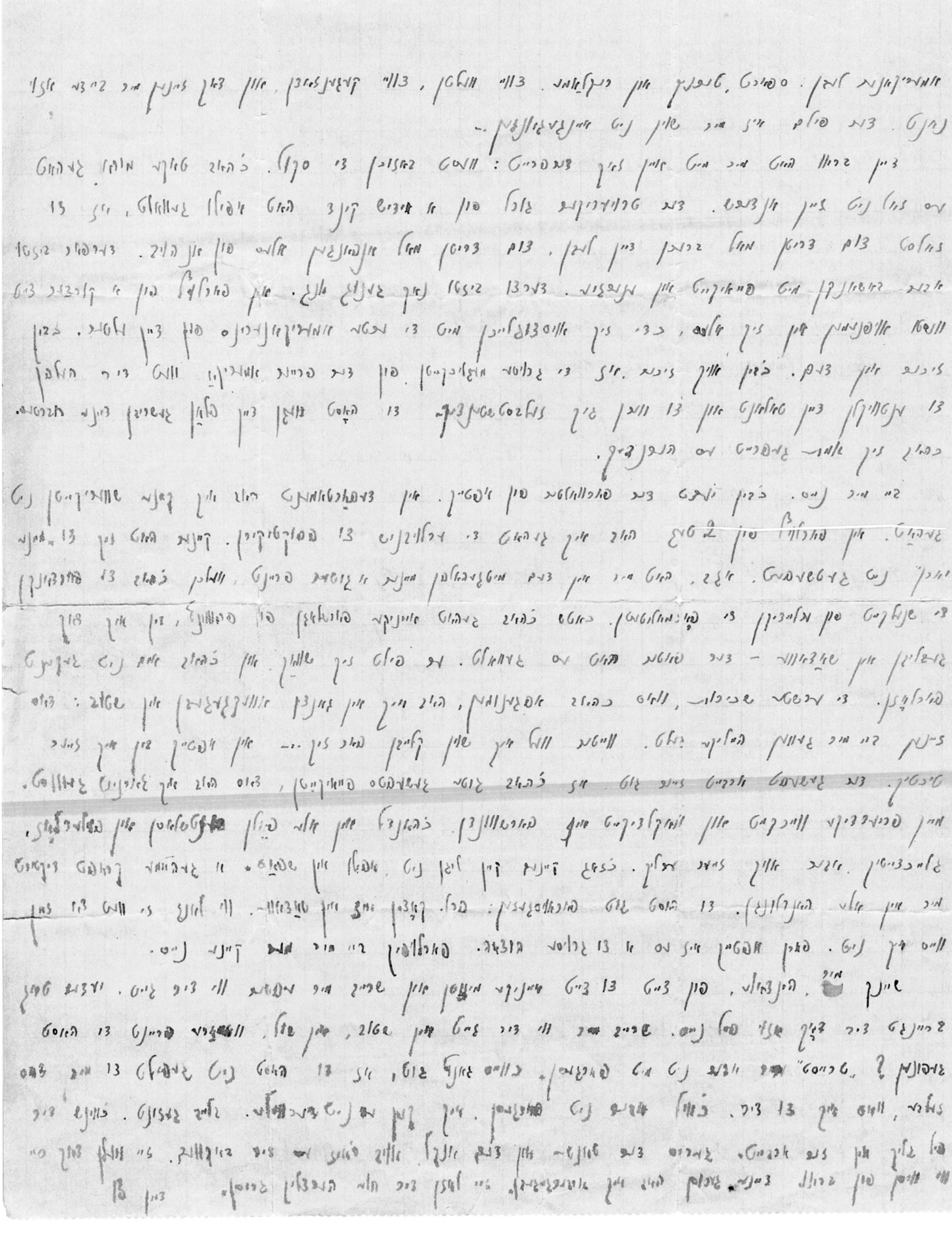

good friend of mine who was very helpful in getting all the formal papers over with so quickly. Even though I had a few offers from the Provinces[19] I chose to remain in Šeduva—my father's[20] desire. He is growing older and I could not leave him. My first wages[21] which I received I turned over entirely to my parents—it was sacred money. From now on I will save for myself... In the drugstore I take my work very seriously. Business is very good. I didn't even know that I possess good business sense. My previous softness and, sometimes, hesitation completely disappeared. I act in all instances with decisiveness and faultlessness, and at the same time with complete honesty. I never tell a lie, not even in fun. A secret force dictates me in all transactions. You predicted correctly, Miss Kotzin[22] is still in Šeduva. How long she will remain here I don't know yet. For the drugstore she is too big an expense.[23] Currently, no more news.

Give me, Hindalla, from time to time a few minutes and write to me often. Tell me about everything. Every day is filled with so much news for you. Tell me how things are at home, in school. What kind of friends have you made? Don't "console" me, though, with forgetting. I know very well that your feelings towards me were not quite the same as mine to you. I don't want to forget, though; I cannot yet.

Stay well. I wish you much success in your school work. Give my regards to your aunt and uncle, if it is convenient for you. They will anyway know about our correspondence.

Your regards I delivered. They, too, send their heartiest regards.

Your

B.

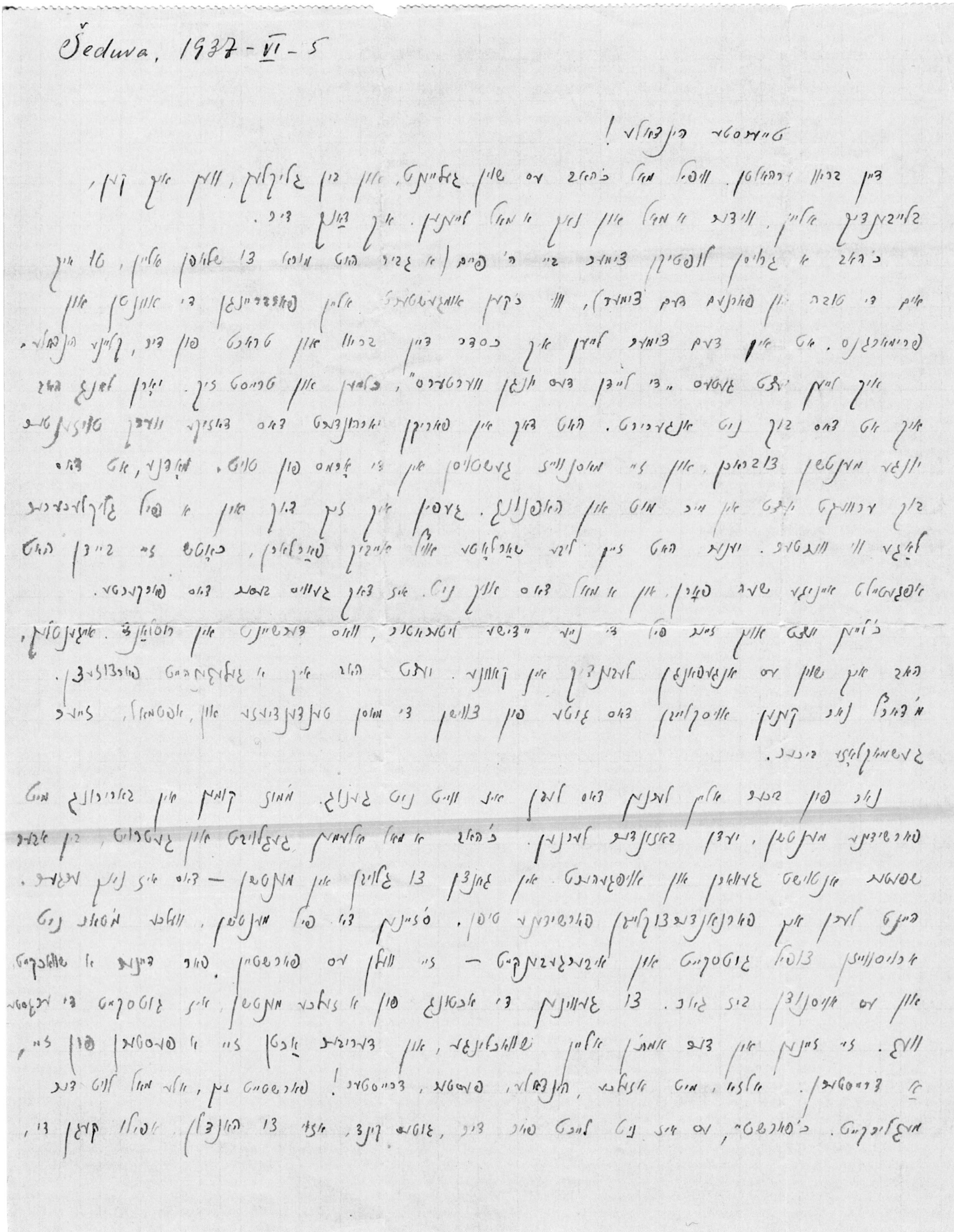
Šeduva, 1937-VI-5

טײַערסטע הינדעלע!

Šeduva, 5/VI/1937[24]

(June 5, 1937)

Dearest Hindalla!

Your letter received. How many times I have read it, and am still happiest, when, remaining alone, I can read it once again. Thank you so much.

I have a large airy room at Mr. Payim's (A rich man is afraid to sleep alone in his house, so I'm doing him the favor and occupy one of the rooms) where I can spend my evenings and early mornings undisturbed. In this room I read and re-read your letter and think about you, dear Hindalla.

I am now reading Goethe's *The Suffering of Young Werther.*[25] I read and console myself. For years I wouldn't touch that book. I recall that in the past century this work affected so many young lives and drove them in masses into the arms of death. It's odd that this book should now give me courage and hope. Am I not much luckier to find myself in a more enviable position than Werther? He lost his beloved Charlotte forever, even though they were separated by just a few hours travel time, or perhaps even less. The opposite is certainly much better.

I also read much of the current Jewish literature that is published in Russia. Actually, I began following it while I was still in college and lived in Kovno. Now I have the opportunity to continue. The only problem is to be able to pick out the good among the very many mediocre, and, often, tasteless, books.

But learning about life from books alone is not enough. One has to come in contact with different people and study each one separately. There was a time when I believed and trusted everybody. I was disillusioned and stopped believing in people entirely—that is even worse. Today I am learning to separate different types of people. There are those whom you cannot show too much kindness and loyalty; they will interpret it as a weakness of yours and will, therefore, take advantage of you. To win the respect of such people, kindness is the worst road. They are truly weak themselves and, consequently, they respect one stronger than they are, more daring. So, with such people, Hindalla, firm and brave! Naturally, always according to the possibility. I understand, it isn't easy for you, dear child, to act that way even against those who you know are using you. Nevertheless, you will have to —life is stronger than we are and upholds its rules. On the other hand, you will most certainly meet people who will answer your goodness and loyalty with the same. Among those choose your friends. You will never be disappointed. Perhaps today's world is at fault that there are so many evil people. Perhaps the character of men could change with different circumstances. I have just recently decided, as soon as I have a little extra money as well as time, to go and see what the heroes of my books look like in real life. With that purpose in mind I am now studying Russian.

The couple days of Shavuot[26] were very pleasant ones for me. An uncle of mine arrived unexpectedly from Africa; he is my father's brother and thirty years from home. During all those years he hardly wrote; now that he is getting on in years, suddenly became lonesome for his relatives and came to visit us. I must confess that I have never met a more interesting person. His youth he spent in the Telshiai

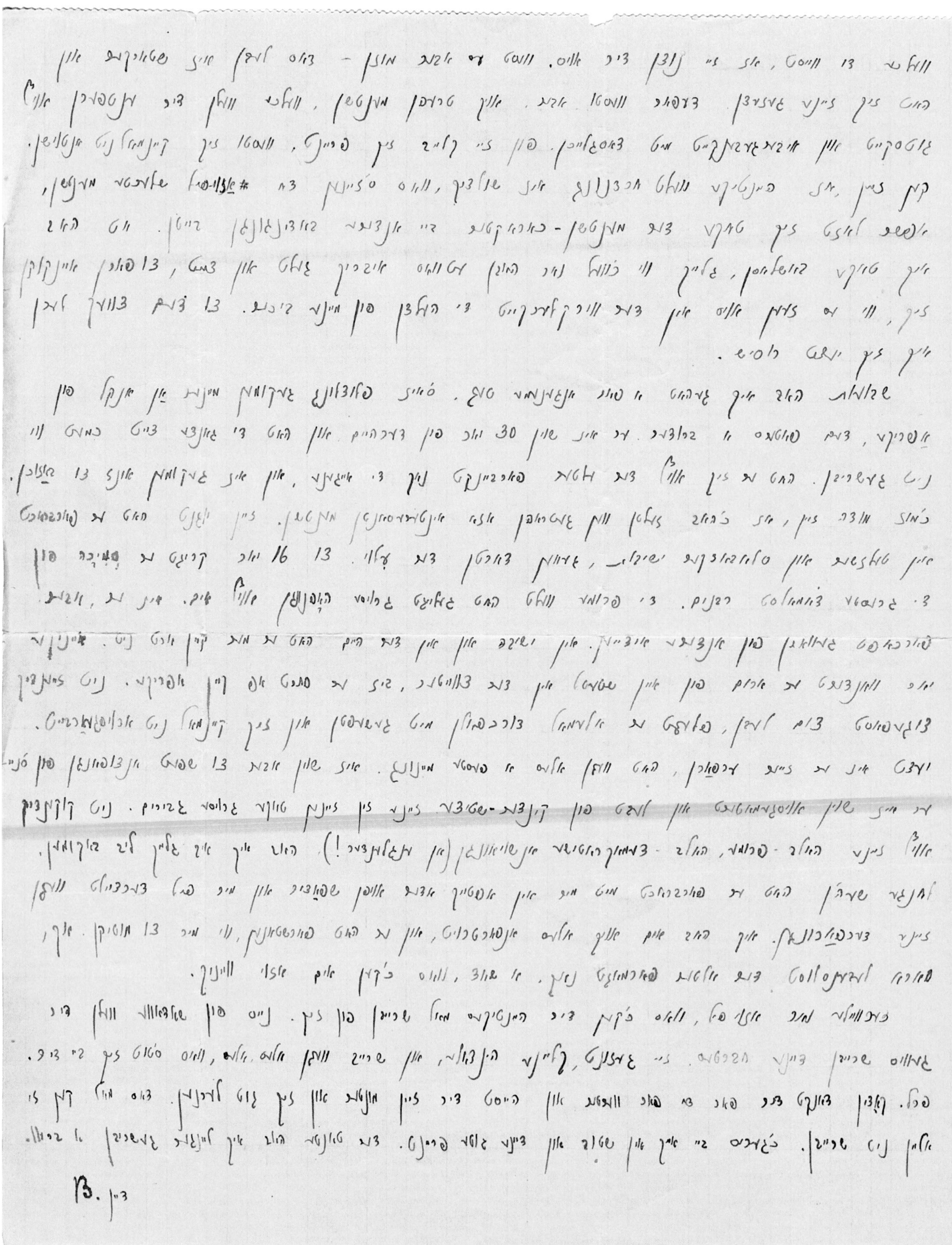

and Slabodka Yeshivahs.[27] He was the genius of his day and became ordained as rabbi at the age of 16. He was the hope of the religious world. However, he got a taste of new ideas and the home and the Yeshivah no longer satisfied him. For a couple of years he wandered from one village to another until he left for Africa. Not being accustomed to the new life, he failed in business, time and again, and never quite "made it." Now he is very experienced, has strong opinions about everything, but it is too late to start all over again. He feels old and tired and lives from children's support. His sons, on the contrary, are very wealthy. In spite of his half-religious, half-democratic outlook (an Englishman!) I immediately fell in love with him. He spent many hours with me in the drugstore or walking and told me of his many, many experiences. I, too, confided in him and he knew how to comfort me. How much love for life that old man still has! I only regret that I knew him so little.

Meanwhile that will be all. Your girlfriends will undoubtedly fill you in about the news of Šeduva. Be well, dear Hindalla, and write me about everything that is happening to you. Miss Kotzin thanks you for the few words and tells you to be cheerful and study well. This time she is unable to write herself. My regards to everyone at home and to your good friends. I have just written a letter to your aunt.[28]

Your

B.

Šeduva, 1937-VI-28

מײַן טײַערע הינדעלע!

איך בין גליקלעך װידער דײַנעם [illegible] בריװ צו לײענען. [illegible] האָט מיר דײַן בריװ װי געטאָן.

[illegible] מיר װי געטאָן די באַשרײַבונג פֿון דײַנע געװעזענע שול-חברות [illegible] צו פֿאָלגן זײ ניט, און

זײ האָבן דיך שוין פֿאַרגעסן. [illegible]

[illegible]

Šeduva, 28/VI/1937[29]

(June 28, 1937)

My Dear Hindalla!

I am most happy again to read a letter of yours. This time your letter was painful to me. I was hurt by the treatment of your schoolmates towards you: they don't miss you and they forgot about you. You shouldn't have expected any more from them. But, why, Hindalla, such a sad, longing mood? Leave that for me. It certainly causes you too much anguish. You have to be cheerful, healthy and strong—you are in the prime of your blossoming youth. Agree, even against your own will, with the advice of your parents and good friends. They mean to do well by you. They, too, acted against their own will. Your leaving for America certainly was the greatest sacrifice for your parents to make. Find consolation in reading and work, and you will find it easier to pass the small "transition-period." I sincerely hope so. In September, when you start school—it certainly won't be any other way—you will surely be more cheerful. It will only take a little time and everyone who is now a stranger will become dear to you.

Such is life, dear Hindalla; now you may feel strange, but you will certainly have a happy future. That will be a consolation for all your friends whom you have left behind.

As I see it, you accomplished tremendously with your English. In such a short time to be able to read English books is no small matter. I am extremely happy. See, my Russian is coming along at a slower tempo, even though I am able to read newspapers quite freely. Still I lack the systematic study. I am also happy that you get to read good Yiddish books. In Šeduva, I would often feel sorry seeing you spend your time on sometimes not entirely useful books, at the time when you were little acquainted with our own and international classics and modern literature. *The Suffering of Werther* I would not advise you to read yet.

Dear Hindalla, this August 1st I will be 25 years old. I never celebrated my birthday, and will probably not do so in the future. At home there is no mention of it. Strangers I don't find it necessary to tell. This time, however, I find myself in need of cheering up. That day will be for me far from a festivity—here the best years have passed and life offered so little, so little. I would like on that day to have just one blessing—from you. Do it for me, my good Hindalla.

By me, my only interest is reading and work. I recently read *The Psalm Jew* by Sholom Asch.[30] A few days I was in "a different world," as you say. After finishing the book, one feels again an emptiness. Last week there was an inspection in the drug store. They found everything in the best order—so my mood was better for the next few days. During the hours when it is very busy I also feel better.

The worst day by me is Saturday; the work in the drug store is slow and I can't find a place for myself. I lost all interest in my friends; the only ones I'm drawn to are those who used to come into the drug store before. I'm drawn to them because they know and respect you, and it pleases me to hear about you, even though I myself keep quiet during such conversations. My opinion about them, Mrs. Davidowitz[31] included, has not changed. But when Mrs. Davidowitz read to me regards from you I was

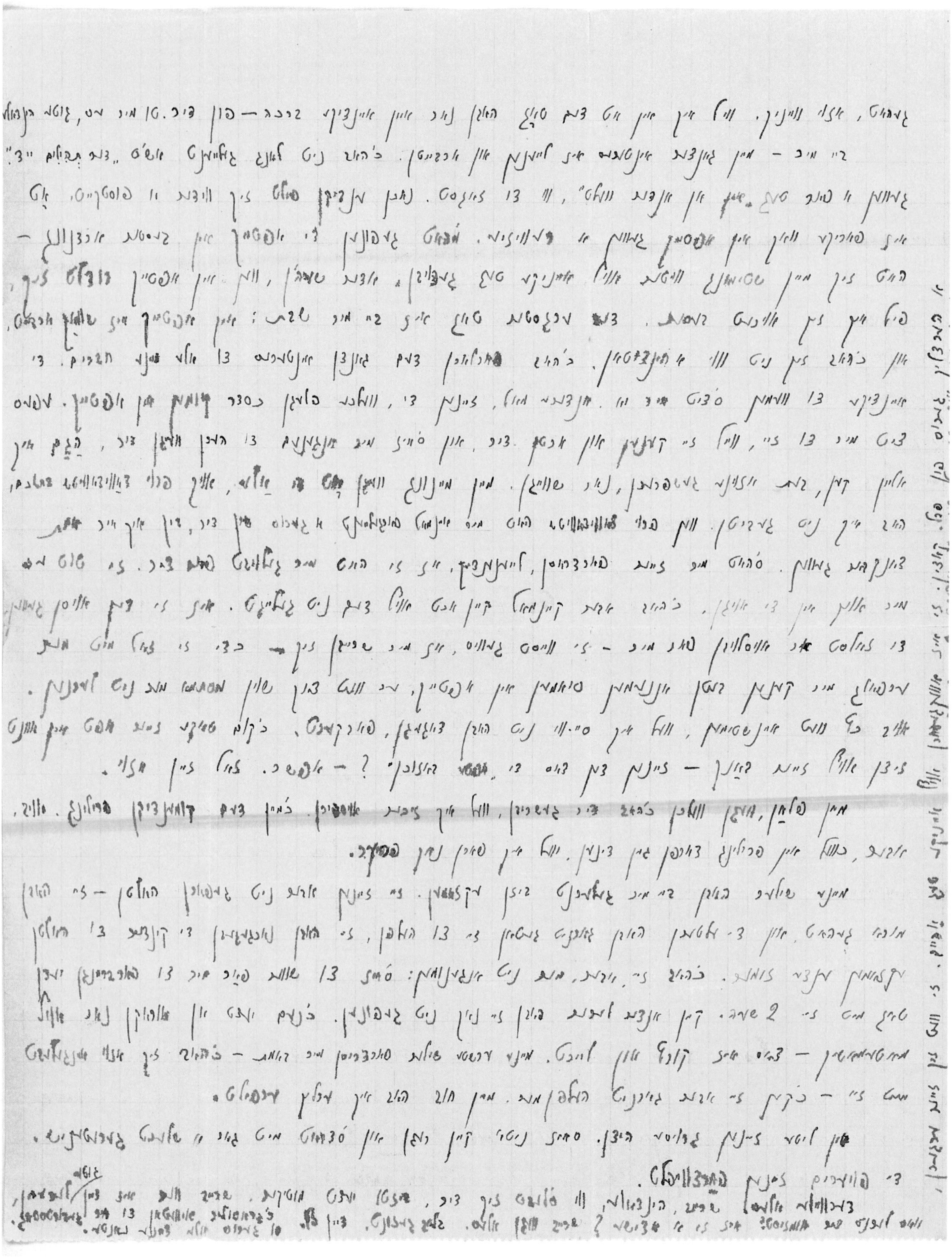

truly thankful. I regretted, though, that she praised me to you. She also does it to my face; I never paid much attention. Now I wonder; was it her intention that you should praise her to me (She undoubtedly knows that we write to each other) so that she would more successfully be able to ask me to register her son as an apprentice at the drugstore? He probably won't go on with his studies. If Mr. Katz[32] agrees, I won't be against it anyway, on the contrary. It is true that some evenings I sit on the bench outside their home—are those the "frequent visits" she is telling you about? Maybe; let it be so.

My plan about which I wrote to you earlier I mean most certainly to carry out; I think the coming spring. If, however I will be drafted into the service,[33] then I will take my vacation sooner.

My students[34] studied with me until the exams, but did not go to take them. They were afraid and the parents did not do anything to make them. They yielded to their requests to postpone it until the end of the summer. However, I did not take them on anymore. It is difficult for me to give up two hours a day with them. In the meantime they have no other teacher. Now I only take on students for math—that is short and easy. I do miss my former students, though—we got along so well. But, I cannot help them any longer. I feel that I fulfilled my obligation honestly to them.

Here, in Lithuania, we are now having our extremely hot days. There is no rain and a poor harvest is predicted. The farmers are desperate.

Meanwhile, that is all. Write to me, Hindalla, how things are with you. Are you now more cheerful? Write to me who that good teacher is who does not take any money from you for lessons?[35] Is she a Jewish woman? Write to me about everything.

Stay well.

Your

B.

I congratulate Yvette[36] on her birthday. Regards to all your friends. Heartiest regards from Miss Kotzin. She went home for a few days. She will be upset that again, this time, she won't be able to write to you personally.[37]

Šeduva, 6/VIII 37.

מײַן טײַערע הינדעלע!

כ'האָב באַקומען אַלעס, וואָס דו האָסט מיר געשיקט. ס'איז געווען בײַ מיר די גרעסטע שמחה
מיט דעם מאָמענט. ווי קען איך דען אויסדריקן מײַן פרייד און דאַנק אין ווערטער?

דײַן וווּנדערבאַר אַרבעט האָב איך אַרומגערעמט מיט אַ ראַם און גלאָז – אַליין געמאַכט עס – און
אויפגעהאַנגען איבער מײַן בעט. אַלעמאָל וועט עס אַזוי הענגען. כ'וועל קיינמאָל ניט מיד ווערן עס פון
נײַ צו באַוווּנדערן און פון נײַ צו האָפן.

אונטערן בילד האָב איך אויפגעשריבן דעם דאַטום פון מײַן געבורטסטאָג און די אַלע באַגעגנסטע
ווערטער פון טאָלסטאָי, מיט וועלכע דו האָסט אַ טאָג אַזאַ, אין אַמאָליקן, אָנגעשאַנגען אין דײַן טאָג-בוך.
ווי משונה'דיק וועט אויסזען שוין אַ שפּעטער דער צוזאַמענהאַנג צווישן בילד און אונטערשריפט.
נאָר איך אַליין וועל עס פאַרשטיין.

דאָס איז די טײַערסטע מתּנה, וואָס כ'האָב ווען ניט איז געקריגן. כ'דאַנק דיר, גוטע הינדעלע.
„גליקלעכע, גליקלעכע אומבאַקערדיקע פאַרשוווּנדענע קינדער-יאָרן! ווי קען מען ניט ליב האָבן, ווי
קען מען ניט טײַער האַלטן די זכרונות וועגן זיי?"

טײַערע הינדעלע, פאַרגאַנגענע וואָך האָב איך, אויב אין אמת, ווידער איבערגעלעבט די גליקלעכע
גימנאַזיע-טעג.

געווען זענען פיר שיינע טעג בײַ מיר. האָב איך באַזוכט אין אונדזער שטעטל מײַנע אַמאָליקע
קלאַס-חברים, מיט וועלכע כ'האָב זיך ניט געזען, זינט מיר האָבן געענדיקט גימנאַזיע. זיי האָבן ווייניק ניט
געביטן. און זיך ווי-עס איז פאַרגאַנגען, ווען זיי זיך אין שטעטל, ווען אין אַ צווישן. טאַקע גלייך
כ'בין עס דאָ זיי געווען! מיר האָבן געהאַט צו רעדן נאָר וועגן די פאַרגאַנגענע גימנאַזיע-יאָרן, וועגן
די אַמאָליקע חברים, וועגן די לערער. אָבער האָבן מיר געפילט, ס'איז אַוועק אַזוי די שענסטע
צײַט פון אונדזער לעבן. ס'איז כאָטש גוט, ווען מ'קען עס אַמאָל דערמאָנען און אָנרופן מיט די, מיט
וועלכע מ'האָט עס דורכגעלעבט.

אונדזערע נײַס בײַ מיר – אַלץ נײַס. און אָפּשטיין די אַרבעט איז מאָנאָטאָניש און ניט צופרידנשטעלנדיק.
כ'וואָלט זייער וועלן בײַטן די שולע און זיך אָפּגעבן אין אַ גרעסערע שטאָט. כ'ווייס, אָבער,
ניט, אויב ס'וועט זיך מיר דאָס אַלץ שנעל אײַנגעבן.

Šeduva 6/VIII/1937[38]

(August 6, 1937)

My Dear Hindalla!

I received everything that you sent me.[39] It was my greatest happiness. How can I express my joy and thanks in words?

Your beautiful work I framed—I made it myself—and hung it over my bed. It will hang there always. I will never tire of it and will always admire it and hope... Under the picture I wrote down the date of my birth and the so appropriate words of Tolstoy with which you began your diary on one of your depressing days. How odd it will look to a stranger the relationship between the picture and the inscription. Only I alone will understand. This is the most precious gift that I have ever received. I thank you, good Hindalla. "Happy, happy, forever vanished days of my childhood! How can you not love them, how can you not cherish their memories?"[40]

Dear Hindalla, last week I truly experienced the happy school days again. I happened to have had a couple free days and decided to travel to a few of our neighboring towns. I visited several of my classmates whom I hadn't seen since we graduated from high school. They did not go on with their studies and managed to obtain employment in their own towns or in towns close by. What a guest I was by them! We had plenty to talk about—about the high school days gone by, about the other students, about the teachers. We all agreed that those were the most pleasant times of our lives. It is good to be able to reminisce occasionally with those with whom you spent those days together.

At present—nothing new. In the drugstore the work is monotonous and not satisfying. I would very much like to change my position and find employment in a larger city. I don't know, however, if that can be accomplished so quickly.

My pharmacy student, Kuklianski's brother-in-law left Šeduva. Since he did not receive any wages by us, he returned to his brother-in-law who had just bought a new drugstore in Alita.[41] I was "attacked" from all over about the registration[42] as a pharmacy student. However, I had already promised Mrs. Davidowitz to register her son, Sioma.[43] Mr. Katz also agreed (Mrs. Davidowitz has a skillful tongue!) and so Sioma is working in our drugstore. He is obedient and quite swift in his work, although far from even a hint of becoming a capable and serious-minded pharmacist. This is probably the best thing I could have done for him.

By us, in Lithuania, the hot days are already over. It's been raining already the second week straight. First the heat, and now the rains, have done much damage to the harvest. In Šeduva, because of the intense heat, there were many fires. The first fire was on Savl Street[44] and the Baers'[45] and Mellmans'[46] homes were both in danger. The other fires were further down on Savl Street, I helped as much as I possibly could. I found myself being very calm, and in no way did I experience the same as I used to in time of a fire. It really surprises me.

Write me, Hindalla, if you have any time left to read Jewish books, and what kind of books do you get. I just finished *By the Dniepr* by Bergelson,[47] and *Without a Home* by L. Kobrin.[48] Perhaps in time

מיין אָפּשטיין-שולער, די וואַנטערס שוועגער, האָט זיך אויסגעקריגן פון שאַדעווער. די אייניגע האָט מיר
דורך דיין געהאָלט נישט באַקומען, איז עס דורכן אונזער צום שוועגער, וועלכע האָט געקויפט אַ
אָפּשטיין אין אַלעסט. מאַיז מיר געפעלן פון אַלע צייטן וואָס צושרייבן צום אָפּשטיין. כ׳האָב שוין,
אויך, געהאָט צוגעזאָגט פראַו דזשאָוויטש אַ נאָמען טיטען. הי׳ כ׳ האָט אויך צוגעשיקט (פראַו ...
האָט זי געגעבן צונעמען). אַזוי אַרום אַרבייט שוין סיטערן אין אָפּשטיין. עס איז אַ פאָלגעדינע אין גאַנץ
פֿלייסיק אין דער אַרבייט. וויכטיג. אָבער אַלעס ווייט פון צו זיין פאַרטיק אין ערנסט. צו וואָס איז
אָפּשטיינקער מאַכט עס אים, מיין זון, נישט שאַטן. סאיז גוט אים דאָס געפֿעלט, וואָס כ׳האָב געקענט טאָן.

די אייניגע אין לעצט. זיינען שוין די היגן אַרבעטער. די צווייטע וואָך, ווי סהאָט נישט אויף 13
באַקומען די היגן, אין יעדער די רעגנס. האָבן פיל שוין אויסגעמאַכט דער הויך-אַרעם געמיינס:
אין שאַדעווער זיינען דער צווייטער, צוליב די גרעסטע היגן, גענומען ערליכע שפּילן אויף שאָלעם גרוס.
דער דער ערשטער שרפה בײַ באַרג. איז טייערע ה׳ מלמונס איז געוואָרן אין געפֿאָר. נאָך צוויי שרפות
זיינען פאָרגעקומען ווייט אויף שאָלעם גרוס. דער די שרפה האָב איך געאַרבעט אין געהאָלפן, ווייל
כ׳האָב נישט געקענט. זיין אָבער געוואָרן מיידל ראַדזין. אין בעטן אַוועק, נישט אַרבעטן דאָס
צוליבער, וואָס כ׳פּלאָג אַלעמאָל איבערצולייגן אין דער צייט פון אַ שרפה. כ׳וואָלט זיך ניט אויסגעדרייט.

שרייב מיר, הינדעלע, אויב ס׳בלייבט דיר צייט צו לייענען יידישע ביכער, און וועלכע ביכער
באַקומסטו? כ׳האָב אַרויסגעשיקט געמאַכט באַקאַנטע „די דאָרפיער" און ל. ראַזערנס „אין די הייך"
וועסט מיט דער צייט געוויס אויך לייענען די צוועלף ביכער, וועסט זיך דערמאָנען אין מיר און, אפשר,
אויך פילן דאָס צוליב, וואָס איך – בעת לייענען.

כ׳וועל שוין מיט אומגעדולד וואַרטן אויף טאָג, ווען דו וועסט אָנהויבן גיין אין הויך-שול. סטודענטקע
ביסט שוין דורך די צייט. דו מוזט מאַכן אַלע באַמיִונגען אָנצוקומען אין שול. דאָן וועסט האָבן – די
בעסטע אויסגערעכנט.

דערווייל אַלעס, וואָס כ׳האָב געקענט דיר שרייבן. שרייב, ווי דו אַרבעטסט און ווי סגייט דיר.
זיי געזונט און מונטער, טייערע הינדעלע. אַלע דיינע נאָענטע לאָזן דיר פיל מאָל גריסן.
איך גריס אַלעמען בײַ אייך אין שטוב. דיין B.

פּ.ס. נעם נישט צום האַרצן, וואָס כ׳האָב „גערעדט מיין האַרץ אויף שוואַרץ". דאָס רעדט זיך
נאָר וועגן טינט... B.

you will read the same books and you will think of me and perhaps have the same feelings as I did while reading.

I'm waiting impatiently for the day when you will start high school. The time is getting closer. You must make every effort to attend high school and that will be your occupation for the time being.

That is all that I can write at this time. Tell me how you are spending your time and are you enjoying yourself. Be well and cheerful, dear Hindalla. All your friends are sending their regards. My best regards to everyone at home.

Your

B.

P.S. Don't consider it a bad omen that I changed my color ink to black. We are only talking about ink...

B.

Šeduva, 8/XII 37.

מײַן טײַערע הינדעלע!

שוין דערטראָגן בין איך ניט אונדזער מזל אַ שטיקל בר-מזל: פּונקט ראש השנה האָב איך ערהאַלטן דײַן בריוו און שנה טובה. כּמעט זײַט אַוועקגעגאַנגען די לעצטע טעג, ניט האָבנדיק פֿון דיר קײן גרוס.

האָניקן טאָג האָב איך זײַער פֿיל געקלערט וועגן דיר. יעדנס, ווען איך שרײַב דיר אַלץ די וואָכע, איז שוין בײַ דיר, זיכער, נאָכן עקזאַמען. האָסט געוויס גוט אָפּגעהאַלטן. און סאָוויס בײַ דיר אַ שמחה. איך גלייב ניט אין דײַנע קדושים (אין פֿרעגן אויך ניט!...). כּ'גלייב, אָבער, אַז די צוהערעניש שוין גענוג די שפּראַך אונדזער קומען אין סקול, איך גלייב אין דײַנע פֿעיִקייטן און אַרבעטזאַמקייט.

בין איך שטאַרק זיכער, אַז ס'האָט זיך געענדיקט גוט אַט דער היסטאָריע, פֿאַר די אַלע ווײַטעריקע טעג. כ'ווינטש דיר פֿיל פֿיל מצליח אין דײַן ווײַטערדיקן לערנען. כ'וואָלט זיך זײַער פֿרייען, ווען דו וואָלסט אויך דאָ זײַן די ערשטע שילערין.

ווי וואָלסטו אָבער אויסקומען מיט צײַט? אַרבעטן אין דער ווירטשאַפֿט און לערנען אין סקול גלײַכצײַטיק. איז דאָך ניט לײַכט. וואָלסט מוזן האַנדלען זײַער ענערגיש. איך, ווען איך דאַנק דיר דאָ ווי רעלבן!

ס'איז זײַער גוט, וואָס דו האָסט די געלעגנהייט זיך לערנען שפּילן פּיאַנע. דו מוזסט אויסנוצן און לערנען זיך סיסטעמאַטיש שפּילן. סאַראַ גליקלעכע איך וואָלט אַ מאָל געווען צו האָבן אַ פּיאַנע אין שטוב. בײַ מיר איז עס אַ שוואַכקייט אַזוי פֿון אַלעמאָל צו פּיאַנע. כ'האָב עס אָבער קײנמאָל ניט געהאַט.

עס פֿרייט מיר, וואָס דו קריגסט דאָרט לײענען אַזעלכע גוטע ייִדישע ביכער, ווי "דער תּהילים-ייִד", "אַ דער וועג צו זיך". און האָב זיך אויך קײנמאָל ניט ענטזאָגט פֿון לײענען ייִדיש, אַפֿילו אין ווײַטן ברען פֿון עקזאַמענס.

ווי גײט עס מיר? ס'לעבט די צײַט פֿון מעשׂים-וואָס אויסצולערנען. ווי ניט גוט עס איז אונדז. כ'לערן צו רעפֿלעקסיע. ספּעל. קריגן האָבן מיר אָנגעטאָן פֿון צײַט-צו-צײַט מיט וואָכעס אָבער ערקלערונגען. איך קום אַלץ מיט אײַך זײַער גוט. די איז זײַער אַ גוטע, אָבער אַ צו האַסטיקע. וואָס געהאַט צום אָנהייבן, איז די נײַעם אויסשטעלן אַלע מײַנע משוגעתן. כּ'האָב, אָבער, אויך זײַער פֿיל פֿון איר געלערנט. פֿיל-ווינטשן האָסטו מיר די ערשטע טאָג זײַער גוט דערקענט.

די צווייטע טאָג סוכּות וועל איך זײַן אין קאָוונע, כּדי צו ערלעדיקן דעם מײַן, וועלכן כּ'האָב פֿאַרגעסן אָנגעשריבן. דעם יאָר וואָס איך בין אין אונדזער מיטלצו, אַ מאָל זיכער. אָנזאָגט מיר צו אַלז פֿון זײַן

Šeduva 8/IX/1937[49]

(September 8, 1937)

My Dear Hindalla!

Still I am sometimes a lucky guy: exactly on Rosh Hashanah[50] I received your letter and New Year's card. I would have been very disturbed during the holidays if I hadn't heard from you. All day I thought about you. Now as I'm writing to you, it is surely after your exams. I'm sure you passed "with flying colors" and you are happy. I do not believe in your cards (colors neither!) I do believe, however, that you mastered enough of the language to start high school. I believe in your ability and perseverance. I am certain that that day, so important to you, ended well. I wish you much, much success in your further studies. I will be happy when you will be the best student there, too.

How will you manage your time, though? To help with the housework and study at the same time is not easy. You will have to be energetic. Oh, if I could help you in any way! It is also good that you have the opportunity to learn to play the piano. Take advantage of it and learn to play systematically. How happy I would have been to have had a piano at home! The piano has been my weakness since way back; unfortunately, I never had one.

I am happy that you have the opportunity to read such good books as *The Psalm Jew*[51] and *The Way to Yourself*.[52] I, too, never refused to read a Yiddish book, not even in the midst of exams.

How is it with me? The time goes without much accomplishment. It isn't good that way. I study Russian a little. Miss Kotzin helps me occasionally with words or explanations. I get along well with her—very well. She is very good-natured, but a little too hasty where the work is concerned. She has to suffer from my idiosyncrasies. But I did learn a lot from her. You sized her up more or less correctly in the first few days.

The second days of Succot[53] I will be in Kovno to wind up the matter which I have started last year.[54] This year I will try a new method, a more dependable one. They promise it will work—I certainly would be pleased. I must confess, though, that I would not really regret too much if it were to turn out otherwise. My parents, on the other hand, would be very upset.

Yes, I gained a friend—Bassia Ulfsky's[55] brother. They settled in Šeduva permanently, together with their mother. They are renting from the Kriegers, where they used to have the Kibbutz Mizrahi,[56] you remember. That is the only family I visit on my days off, and where I feel comfortable. Bassia's brother, his name is Hershel, is older than I am and, "to add insult to injury," is wearing a beard. But he is such a fine person, so smart. I really longed for one like him. It might be that you even saw him—he visited Šeduva a few times. He has quite an extensive library (his own) in several languages. Now I "swallow" his books. In their home I have a chance and the patience to play chess, or rummy, or bridge. (I just learned it.) At times I feel it's not quite as boring as I think.

At the drugstore it is the same work at the same pace as before. From time to time we are visited by one of the bosses. However, I haven't heard from anyone for several weeks. I suspect that Mr. Katz had an appendectomy operation. He didn't want us to know. Sioma has learned his work to a degree

גוט. איך וואלט עס זייער וועלן. איך מוז אבער אודאי זיין, אז ס׳וואלט מיר ניט שאטן פארדריסן, וואיל ס׳וואלט זיך אויסגעלאזט אנדערש. מײַנע זעלטענע וועלן אבער האבן שטענדיק פארדראס.

יאָ, כמעט געקראגן א חשק. דער אלעסקיס ברודער. די האבן זיך געזעגנט און אונטערווייז מיט זייער מוטער. א דירה האבן זיי ביי די קרובים, ווי ס׳איז אמאל געווען דאס קליינע מזרחי. געדענקסט עס געוויס. דאס איז די אמעריקאנער הויז, ווי כ׳קום יעדער אריין און מײַן טאטע זײַט און ווי כאפ זיך גוט. דאכט זיך ברודער, הערשל האסט דו, איז אפילו אלטער פון מיר. און טראגט נאך דו אלע צרות. א גוטער, וואס מיט אזא וואליש און גוטע וואס. אזא קלוגער. נאך אזא אמעריקאנער האב איך טאקע געדריקט. סקאן זיין איז דו האסט איך וואן געזען — עס איז אמעריקאנער מאל שוין געווען און שנעל. ער האט א גאנץ הירש ברילאנטן, און אלעמען, און פארשידענע שפראכן. זאג איך אונדזער מײַנע ביכער. די זיי אין שטאט האבן אין דער געלעגנהייט און געצילט צו מאכן זיך שיין. דאכט מיר אויף שפילן און רעדן אבער ברידער (כאטש זיך עס ניט לייגט אויסגעלאזט). אונדזער מאל דורכט זיך מיר. איך טאקע ניט אזוי לאנגוויליק, ווי כ׳פיל עס.

און אויסערן איז די צייט געשווינד און די צייטן ארויס ווי געווען. פון דעם צו דעם דורכגעלאזט און צו אונדזער שפיל. שוין אבער מען וואלט, ווי כמעט ניט געהערט פון איר. כדין חושד איז עס האט זיך אפגערוקט און א פענצטער. ווייס ניט געוואלט מאמע עס ווייסן. סוף־כל־סוף שוין א גרויס אירדישן און מיר האבן נאך פון איר. דעם טאנץ שרייבן. איז עס וואס פארטרייבן דאנקען איז אונדזער גרויסע, מײַן איך, וואס מאלעט אויך קיינמאל ניט אויפן איין אויסזען, און ער האט שפרינגט דעם געזונט ניט אויסגעלאזן פון חדר...

גוטע וועלטן האב איך עטלעכע מאל אויסגעבן געהערט פון דיר. אויבן לויטער דאן איין עס ניט מאן — די האסט זיך מיט דעם טאטנס איבערגעשיקט אין פאָניאווײַש. א שווער, כ׳פאלג זיך מיט איר דאס אויסגעצייכנט ווען דיר. די האסט דיר פארגעסן און אויסגעשלאפן אויף גאסן.

אט האב איך דיר קיין נײַס דעם מאל ניט צו שרייבן. ס׳איז אידיש, דער טאג דיר ווילסטו נײַס פון דײַנע חברים — וואס ס׳איז פארגעס און ווי ניט. וואס ס׳לעבט אין פאָניאווײַש, און וואס אין ישראל, און וואס — געווען. איך לאז עס, אבער, אלע פאר צו איינעם. די וועלן דיר גריסן וועגן אלע שרייבן.

דעם טאנץ האב איך שוין לאנגע געשריבן א בריוו. כ׳גלייב די האסט עס באקומען. שרייב מיר וועגן דעם. שרייב מיר אלץ אלעס, ווי ס׳גייט דיר. יאָ, דעם מאל וואלט דיך האבן פיל נײַס. שרײַב זיך ניט, אז צו וועלט מיר פארהאקן דעם קלאס "פארהייך", טאמער הינהאלא. וואס מער...

בלײַב געזונט. האב א פרײליכן יום טוב און א גוטן, גליקלעכן יאר. אלע דײַנע ליבסטע גריסן דיר.

איך גריס הערצלעך אלעמען די איין איין שטוב.

[illegible signature]

and is now useful to us. Your aunt's fear that he will chase away customers is without ground. He is never left all alone, and, furthermore, he guards faithfully the commandment of sworn secrecy.

I extended your regards to Garshviene[57] several times. Unfortunately, I cannot do it any more—she and her daughter moved to Ponevezh. Too bad, I used to talk to her often about you. She understood you well and sympathized with you.

This time that is all the news. There is important news for you from your girlfriends; who was promoted and who wasn't; who is studying in Ponevezh,[58] who in Shavl,[59] and who not at all.[60] However, I will leave it to them. They will surely write to you about everything.

I wrote to your aunt recently. I believe she received it. Let me know. Write to me about everything. How are you getting along? This time you will undoubtedly have much news. Don't be afraid of "bothering me" with too much. "Bother me," dear Hindalla, more and more. Stay well. Have a pleasant holiday and a good and happy year. All your dear ones send their regards.

Heartiest regards to everyone at home.

Your

B.

Šeduva, 8/X 37.

מײַן טײַערע הינדעלע!

כ'בין נעכטן געקומען פֿון קאָװנע, װוּ כ'האָב פֿאַרבראַכט אַרום אַ װאָך. און געקומען
בין איך צום סוף שױן, מיט מזל, פֿרײַ. דער מיטאָג, װאָס כ'האָב איבערגעלעבט, [illegible],
װאָס אונדזערע האָבן איבערגעלעבט פֿון [illegible], כאָטש כ'װעל עס קײנמאָל ניט פֿאַרגעסן, האָט זיך
[illegible] די [illegible] פֿון אונדזער.

אַצינד האָט זיך עס געענדיקט. [illegible] געװיס װילסטו [illegible] װיסן.

טײַערע הינדעלע, דײַן בריװ האָט שױן געװאַרט אױף מיר, װען כ'בין געקומען פֿון קאָװנע
און דײַן פֿריערדיקן בריװ האָב איך ערהאַלטן. כ'בין געװען אַזױ גליקלעך — און [illegible]
[illegible]
[illegible]
[illegible]
[illegible]
[illegible]
[illegible]
[illegible]
[illegible]

[illegible]
[illegible]
[illegible]
[illegible]
[illegible]
[illegible]

[illegible]
[illegible]

[illegible]

Šeduva 8/X/1937[61]

(October 8, 1937)

My Dear Hindalla!

I arrived from Kovno yesterday where I spent over a week. And this time thank God, I came back a free civilian. The method which I applied, better I should say, which others applied on my behalf (even though I will never justify it) turned out more effective than the pleas of before. That is how it turned out and I want to report it to you. Certainly, you will want to know.[62]

Dear Hindalla, your letter was already waiting for me when I returned from Kovno. I also received your previous letter. I was so happy—in the other letter you were so cheerful and full of courage: you came just in time to start high school. Now it won't be so boring for you. You'll find interest in your studies. Little by little you will be drawn into the spirit of the American school. I can understand that you won't be satisfied with the American school system, where everything is so noisy and superficial. On the other hand, though, America is the only land where colossal things are accomplished outside the classrooms. And every energetic person has the opportunity to reach heights. And that is why your fate is certainly much better than that of your friends in Poland, and even in Lithuania. In the meantime, it is very good that you are occupied more than half the day in school.

How is it with me? Because of my "rejection"[63] the mood at home is cheerful; and myself, am not too annoyed over it... Certainly, it is much better this way. The holidays I spent working in the drugstore, and I was very happy that I did not have to go anywhere.

Saturdays and holidays are very boring to me. I don't know why. During the week I feel much better. Until recently I would go swimming almost every evening—it was my only pleasure. Now I acquired a ping-pong table and I play with Sioma. It's a wonderful sport! I visit the Ulfskys frequently, where we play bridge. I never imagined I'd be drawn to cards.

The late evening hours I spend reading. I read whatever I can lay my hands on. Occasionally I get hold of some good books. Not long ago I read in Yiddish Lavik's dramatic poem *Abelar and Heloise*.[64] I re-read it a few times. That is how my time passes in Šeduva.

This time, in Kovno, I really had a good time. I saw the Yiddish talkie *Yiddle with his Fiddle*,[65] an American-Yiddish Artists production. I was truly sorry that so much money and effort were wasted on such a tasteless result. Still this film was much better than its earlier Yiddish predecessors. In contrast, I truly enjoyed the second film, *The Good Earth*,[66] book by Pearl S. Buck. It is an excellent reflection of Chinese life. I also went to the opera, *Madame Butterfly*[67] by Puccini. I sat through it with such a heavy heart. Why does the opera affect me so?

That is all for now. But you I am asking to write more; you have more to write about than I do. Be well. Be cheerful and happy and study well.

Heartiest regards to everyone at home. Regards to your girlfriend Yvette,[68] even though I don't know her. Miss Kotzin and all who know you send their regards.

צײַטונגען קריג איך גאַנץ גוטע דורך. זה נישט לאַנג האָב איך געלייענט אין ייִדיש לעבנס
אַקאַדעמישער פֿאָרמאַט „דבֿרים אין הבֿדלות". כ'האָב עס צווייטן מאָל דורכגעלייענט.
עס איז גוט מיר די צײַט אין שווייצלאַנד.

אין וואָכן האָב איך זיך דעם מאָל „פֿאַרגעניגט": כ'האָב געזען דעם ייִדישן טאָן-פֿילם
„ייִדל מיטן פֿידל" — פּראָדוקציע פֿון אַמעריקאַנער ייִדישע אַרטיסטן. ס'האָט מיר זייער געפֿעלן.
אַלס מאָמענט געשפּעסטעט אַ פּאָר פֿיל געזען און מײַ זעלנער דאָרט אין געשמאַקלעכע אידיאָמען. דאָך איז
דער פֿילם פֿיל בעסער ווי די פּראָדוקציע ייִדישע שוישפּילער. דערפֿאַר האָב איך הנאה געהאַט
פֿון די צווייטן פֿילם — „גוטע ערד" לויט Pearl S. Buck's ראָמאַן מיטן זעלבן נאָמען. ס'איז אַן
אויסגעצייכנטע אויסשטעלונג פֿון כינעזישן לעבן.

אין די אָפּערע האָב איך געזען. ס'האָט געשפּילט „מאַדאַם באַטערפֿלײַ" פֿון פּוטשיני. כ'בין
געזעסן די גאַנצע צײַט מיט גרויס פֿאַרגעניגן. פֿאַרוואָס שרײַבסט מיר די אָפּערע אַלײן ניט?
ע. האָסט מיר נאָך אַ פּאָר פֿיל. און זײַ וואָס איך געהערט נישט שרײַבן צו דיר — האָסט
דײַן מאַמע ווײַזן. וואָס זאָל שרײַבן ווי איך.

פֿאָרלויפֿיק געזונט. זײַ מוניטער און פֿרײלעך און לעב זיך גוט.

כ'גריס הערצלעך אַלעמען בײַ אײַך אין שטוב. אַ גרוס אויך פֿון אַלעמען, בײַ מיר
קען מען ניט. פֿיל קושן און אַלע גוטע ווינטשן לאָזן דיר געבן

דײַן B.

P.S. ס'איז זייער שוין אַ גרויל — שרײַבן איך די נײַע וואָס אין די טעלעגראַמע דער פֿאַלשע
נאָך אַ פּאָר אַקטן. וואָס וועט מיר, מיין איך, זײַן אינטערעסאַנט צו וויסן.
B.

Your

B.

P.S. I'll write to your aunt next week—there is some news concerning the drugstore which, I think, may be of interest to her.[69]

B.

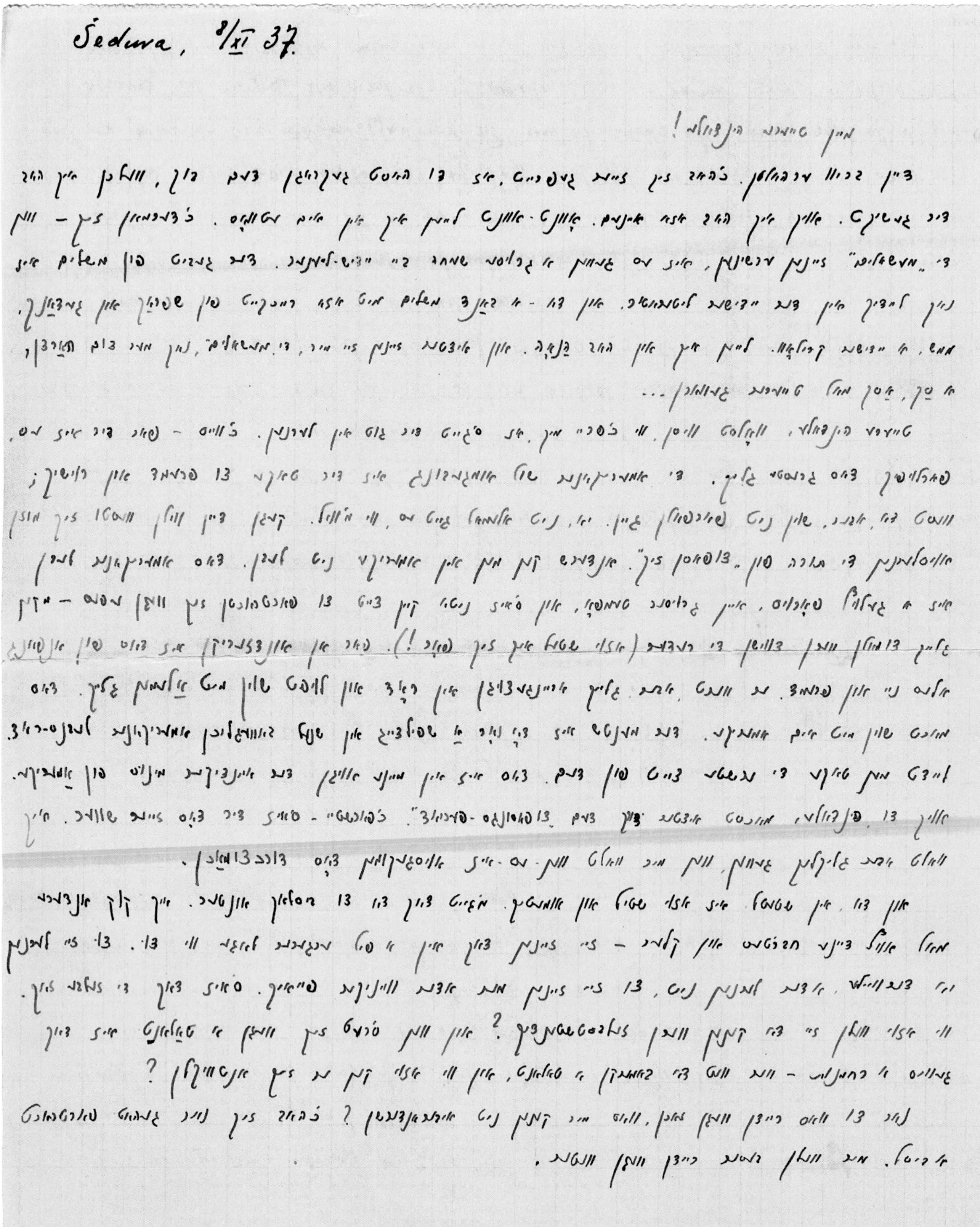
Sedwa, 8/XII 37.

מײַן טײַערע הינדעלע!

Šeduva 8/XI/1937[70]

(November 8, 1937)

My Dear Hindalla!

Your letter received. I am very happy that you received the book which I sent you. I have it, too. Evenings I read it a little at the time. I recall, when the *Fables* were first published what a joy it was for the Yiddish-reading public. The fable territory is still quite barren in Yiddish literature, and here a whole book of fables, with such a wealth of language and thought. Almost a Yiddish Krilov![71] I'm reading and take pleasure. And now *The Fables* are even dearer to my heart, much much more precious...[72]

Dear Hindalla, if you only knew how happy I am to hear that you are doing well in school. I know that for you at this time it is of utmost importance. The American schools are, indeed, strange to you and noisy; you won't get lost there, however. One cannot always have what one wants. Against your better judgment, you will have to learn to become like the others. That is the only way to get along in America. Life in America is a race forward, a fast tempo, and there is no time to stop and reflect—one can get caught within the moving wheels. (That is how I imagine it!) For our people it is all new and strange in the beginning, but soon one gets drawn into the machinery and runs together with the rest. That is what America does to him. The human being is there just like a toy in the fast-moving American wheel of life. That is why one suffers a little at the beginning. That, in my eyes, is the only minus in America. You, too, Hindalla, are going through now the adjustment period. I can understand that it would be difficult for you. I would be very happy, however, if I ever had to go through it myself.

And here, in our small town, is so quiet and depressing. Little by little we go under. Many times I look at your girl friends and think—their situation is so much worse than yours. Whether they study presently or not, whether they are more-or-less capable—it makes no difference. How will they ever attain independence? And where talent is concerned, it is a pity altogether—who will here notice talent? And how will it ever be developed? But why talk about things that one cannot change? I just happened to be thinking. Better we should talk about the weather.

This year our autumn is beautiful: the days are sunny and dry, and the evenings even more gorgeous, but, what?...

You already experienced the first snow in America. It probably reminded you of lonesome snow-covered roads with bent, freshly whitened crosses along the way. You reminded yourself of the warm home and the smell of freshly-baked bread. Such a thing I once experienced when I saw the first snow fall. Every year I remind myself of it, but in no way can I ever experience it again, I see the same roads, the same house, and the same snow—and still not the same—something is missing. It's irritating! That is why the first snow always puts me into a strange mood.

By me, so far, nothing changed. I spend my time as before. I read a little, play cards occasionally. I still have little interest in cards. I play because others are playing. I'd rather spend my free hours alone

מיר האבן היי יאר אזא שיינעם הערבסט: שיינע טרוקענע טעג און נאך שמאלע וואנטן, אבער. וואס ?...

די האסט שוין אויסגעלערנט דעם ערשטן שניי אין אמעריקע. האסט זיך, מסתמא, דערמאנט אין אונזער פארשנייטע

ווינטער מיט אינגעהילטע, פריש אויסגעוואשענע זלאטע ביים וועג. האסט זיך דערמאנט אין די ווארשעווער שטיבער און א ריח פון

פריש געבאקענע ברויט. ערגעץ אזוינס האב איך אליין געזען, ווען דער ערשטער שניי איז געפאלן. אלע

זיינען דערפאר מיד זיך וויגן דערמיט. קען מען, אבער, ווי, בשום אופן, ניט אויסגלייכן. געווען זיך — די גלעזער

ווארעם, די פעלדער שטילער און דער נייגעשניי, און האבן ניט קיין גלעזער - ספארט, ספארט א סך. פארגעקומען א

מאל. שפעט טאג דער ערשטער שניי — א גאר מאדנע שטימונג.

ביי אונדז האט זיך דערוויילע נאך גארניט געענדערט. אויך דער פארברענג איז ווי געוויינטלעך. איך לאז צו ביסלעך,

מיך א קערפל צייטווייז. כ'האב נאך אלץ צו לערנען א קאפן אינטערעס. כ'שפיל, וויל אונדזער שפילן. כ'זיך

געשטעלט שטענדיק צו בלייבן א טרייע שוועסטער מיט זיך אליין, מיט א ברך.

און ניט ווען האבן מיר דא אלץ קינאָ. די קינאָ דאַרפן זיך כמעט אלע מאל. אבער א גוטן פילם זעט מען,

לעצטע, געשען די אונדזער. כ'וואלט זייער וועלן זען „דעם גארטן פון אללאך". אפשר וועל איך זיך ווען דערוואַרטן.

כ'דין דיר אמת מקנא, וואס דו קענסט אפט דאַרפן די קינאָ. כ'פרעג זיך, וואס צו געפינסט אינטערעס

מיט אין קינאָ.

דיינע הרבסט האבן מיר איבערגעגעבן א גרוס פון דיר - זיי האבן געלויבט דיינע א ברוך. כ'האב זיי געבעטן

דיר שרייבן וואס מיר ניט פון שוועסטער. זיי וועלן דיר מיט פון מיר.

יאָ, כ'האב ניט לאנג נאך אמאל געלייענט איבערזעצונג. דער עקר „נעקראַזי". כ'האב עס איבער געשטע פארשטאנט

ווי אמאל אין גימנאזיע. דאן האב איך, אפשר, צו פיל געווען דאווערט פון לערער. ס'וואלט זיין זייער גוט,

הינטער, ווען צו זאלסט עס ווען דורכליינען. ס'איז זייער א לייכטע דראמע. לייען עס אין ענגליש. אינטערעסאנט

וואס איז דיין מיינונג וועגן נעקראַזי.

היינטיקס מאל וויל איך דיר מער ניט שרייבן. ס'האט זיך הערומען א מאדנע גרויל - א שטימונג אזוי.

עס לייזן די גאנצע אלץ, וואס טראגן זיך נאך אלץ דער. מ'האט דיר נאך ניט אונגעמען אין שאַנדזשאַ -

מ'פרעגט זיך אזוי פיל נאך, ווי דיר גייט. אלע ווינטשן דיר 043 געסטע.

זיי געזונט און מונטער און שרייב מיר וואס מער פון זיך. וואָסערע מיינונגען האסטו דערוועגן, ווי ווערט

געלערנט ביי אייך אין סקול, ווי פרעגט מען אלס די אלגעמיין? אלע אלע אינטערעסאנט מיר. דער עקר, אגב,

ווי פארברענגסטו פרייע טעג און נאכן סקול?

איך גריס אלמאן די אייך אין טאג צ

דיין, B.

reading a book. Once in a while there is a movie to see. However, there is seldom a good one. I would very much like to see *The Garden of Allah.*[73] Perhaps it will come here some time. I truly envy you that you can attend the movies often. I am happy that you at least find interest in the movies.

Your girl friends gave me regards from you—they received a letter from you. I told them to write you all the news from Šeduva. They certainly know more than I do.

Oh, yes! I recently re-read the Works of Ibsen, *A Doll's House,*[74] in particular. I understood it better now than when I read it in high school. Then I was, perhaps, influenced by the teacher. It would be nice, Hindalla, if you, too, would read it. It is a light drama. Read it in English. I'm interested in your opinion of Nora.

That is all for now. It turned into a strange letter—I am in that kind of a mood.

Regards from everyone who asks about you. You are not yet forgotten in Šeduva; everyone asks how you are getting along and they wish you the best.

Be well and cheerful and write me more and more about yourself. What grades did you receive? How are the subjects taught? How are you tested? I'm interested in everything, especially how you spend your free days and after school.

Regards to everyone at home.

Your

B.

Šedura, 15/XII 37.

מײַן טײַערע הינדעלע!

דײַן בריוו הײַנט ערהאַלטן. דעם מאָל איז מיר זײער לאַנג אויסגעקומען צו וואַרטן אויף אים.
כ'בין שוין געווען גאַנץ אומרויִק. באַלד איבער אַ וואָך און דער שלעכטער בראָנשטײַנער פֿליגט
מיר יעדן פֿרימאָרגן קאַליע מאַכן מײַן שטימונג. דערפֿאַר אָבער געווען, ווי אַ שטיקל פֿײַער ווערט עס.
דאָך אַלץ עס אַזוי — הײַנט בין איך גאָר אַן אַנדערער.

איך דאַנק דיר פֿאַר אַזוי גענויע אויספֿירן, ווי דיר גייט אין לערנען און ווי דו פֿאַרברענגסט.
כ'האָב זיך אַזוי געפֿרייט, וואָס דו דערציילסט זיך אַלץ אין שקאָלע, [illegible] כ'האָב געוואוסט עס אײַנצוזען
יעדן, וועמען כ'האָב נאָר געקענט, און יעדע מאָל זיך געפֿרייט און דיר געווונטשן ערפֿאָלג אַלעמאָל.
זײַט גוט, כאָטש נישט אַזוי אַמביציעז, וואָס צו געפֿינען אָנגעהויבן און רונדום זיך [illegible] צו. צו שקאָל
און די לערער — פֿאָלג גוט אַלץ דיר.

און וויסטו, וואָס ס'פֿעלט מיר נאָך? — וואָס דו האָסט געוואָרפֿן אַן אַלמאַכן אַלץ לײַענען.
דײַניק. די ווערסט פּראַקטישער. איז דאָך דערמיט צו שאַפֿן זיך און ענערגיע אַלץ אַ מאָדערנע
שפּראַך. [illegible] נאָכקומען. באַוויס, די לעצטע שוין וועלן דיר זײַן די האָליסטע.
אַבער נישט [illegible] מען [illegible] נישט פּראַקטישער שפּראַכן. איך אַליין קען זיך פֿאַר מאָל נישט
אויסהאַלטן אויסער מײַנע שפּראַכקענטעניש צו געוויסער צײַט — ווי איך טאַקע, איז ס'טויג נישט אַזוי.

גערעכנט דאָך געווען מײַן מיינונג וועגן לערנען? גלייב איך אַליין, און אַמעריקע איז לערנען נישט
אַזוי "באַליבט", ווי דאָס די אַנדערע. ס'איז אָבער סימן פֿאַר אַ לאַנג.
נאָר אויך אין אַלגעמיינעם קען לערנען נוצן, דאָן איז עס נישט אַלץ. מען נישט וויסן,
וואָס די צײַט וועט ברענגען.

ס'פֿאַרדריסט מיר נאָר, וואָס דו האָסט אַזוי ווייניק אינטערעסט פֿאַר ייִדיש. אין [illegible] ס'זאָלסטו עס
נאָך פֿאַרשוועכן נישט פֿאַלן — פֿאָלגט דיר שטאַרק דעם לערנען. און דאָס קענסטו זיך נישט פֿאַרלירן.

בײַ מיר איז קיין גרויסע נײַס נישטאָ. אין אַלגעמיין איז איצטער מער אַרבעט, ווי זומער, און דאָס נעמט
מיר אַוועק כמעט דעם גאַנצן טאָג. כ'בין צופֿרידן מיט דעם. איצטער צו דיר, כ'וואָלט מוזן
פֿאַרברענגען דעם ווינטער אין שאַדעווע. כ'האָב פֿריער גאָר נישט געדענקט אַלץ דעם. נישט צו מוזן.
כ'טרייסט זיך נאָר, וואָס צו פֿרילינג וועל איך קריגן אורלויב, מאַכט מיר צופֿרידן. און כ'וואָלט
דאַרפֿן פֿאַרווערקערן מײַן פּלאַן. וואָס נאָך דעם וועט זײַן, קלער איך נישט. דערווײַל לעב איך ממש מיט

Šeduva, 15/XII/1937[75]

(December 15, 1937)

My Dear Hindalla!

Your letter received today. This time I had to wait very long. I was quite concerned. It's been over a week, and the mean mailman would spoil my mood every morning. You are probably right, how a piece of paper can effect. It is so true—today I am like a different person.

I thank you for your exact account of your studies and your free time. I was so happy that you are doing so well in school that I had to tell it to everyone I knew, and everyone was happy for you and wished you success in the future. It is good, though not so American, that you find interest and form ties little by little with the school and the teachers—it will have a good effect on you. And do you know what else I'm happy about? That you found disfavor with Latin. It looks like you may become more practical. Isn't it better to spend time and energy on a modern language, or on something else more useful? I know, the hours of Latin will remain dear to you but one mustn't always yield to impractical weaknesses. I, myself, cannot rise above some of my weaknesses toward some things and I know it isn't the best way. You, undoubtedly, remember my opinion of Latin. I'm sure in America, too, Latin is as "beloved" as it is here. It is a good sign for a country. But if it is useful in college then don't give it up. One never knows what the future will bring. I do regret, though, that you have so little time for Yiddish. Perhaps you shouldn't look for it at this time—it may hinder you in your studies and that you cannot afford.

By me nothing new. In the drugstore there is more work now than in the summer. I am busy all day and am happy about it. I can see now, I will have to spend the winter in Šeduva. I wasn't counting on it. Can't be helped. I console myself that I will have vacation in spring. I was promised, and I will be able to realize my plan. What will be later I'm not giving any thought. In the meantime, I just live for that thought. You know what my "plans" are—I told you about them recently.[76]

In my free hours I "bother my brain" with books on economics. I came upon them by chance, so I have to explore it. Oh, yes, another madness. I had the desire to read *The Good Earth* in the original. I bought the book and with the help of a dictionary I manage quite well. It is much more interesting than the translation. If I have enough patience for a few more books, I will really learn English. That certainly shouldn't hurt.[77]

In Šeduva it is quiet and lonely, as before. Last week we had plenty of snow. It was snowing for three days straight, just like in that folksong. Now, it is finally letting up. It should make for good ice skating. All we need is a good frost. I'm looking forward to it. Except for the weather, nothing in Šeduva changed.

You want to know how the city feels without Dr. Blumberg.[78] Very well. It means, it didn't improve, but no one feels his absence. He was not an honest person. I couldn't tolerate him at times. It looks like others didn't either. You can imagine, he left—still he lived here several years—and seldom anybody remembers him, even more seldom with anything good. He must have deserved it. Others

דעם געדאַנק. ווייסט דאָך אַז ווי מיין „פּלאַן״ דערשטייט – כ׳האָב דיר לאַנגע געשריבן.

און פּראָבירט שרײַבן דרײַ און צוויי די [illegible] מיט עקזאַמענס [illegible]. כ׳האָב מיך צופעליק

געטראָפן. ניי, דאַרף מען מיך צוברעכן.

וואָס, ניט מיט משוגעת. ס׳האָט זיך מיר פאַרוואָלט לייענען „די גוטע ערד״ אין אָריגינאַל. כ׳האָב

געקויפט דעם בוך און מיט דעם הילף פון אַ ווערטערבוך קריך איך עס גאַנץ נישקשה דורך.

ס׳איז פיל אינטערעסאַנטער ווי די איבערזעצונג. אַזוי איך וועל האָבן געדולד צו נאָך אַ פּאָר

ביכער, וועל איך זיך גאָר אויסלערנען אַ ביסל ענגליש. וואָס מע [illegible] ניט שאַטן.

אין שולע איז געבליבן אַזוי און [illegible], ווי געווען. פּאָפּירט האָט אָנגעהויבן ש״ס, צו שפּעט.

„דער שני׳ האָט געשפּילט דרײַ טעג נאָך צווישן״. [illegible] פּונקט, ווי אין יענע פּאָלקס-לידל. [illegible]

עס [illegible]. [illegible] וואָס עס זאָגן, ווי זיך צום גליקן! ס׳דאַרף נאָר וואַרטן אַ פּראָטעסט. כ׳וואַרט שוין אַזוי דעם.

אויסזען וואָס האָט זיך אין שולע [illegible] גאָר ניט געזען.

ביז איצט אינטערעסאַנט, ווי פילט זיך ס׳שטעטל און דער בלומבערג? – זייער גוט. ס׳האָט – ניט

דערווייל געוואָרן, נאָר מ׳פילט ניט זיין פֿעלן. געווען ניט קיין [illegible] דער בלומבערג. כ׳האָב

אים אַ ביסל ניט גלויבן. [illegible], אַליין אונדזער ניט. [illegible] האָב, [illegible]

[illegible] אין [illegible], און [illegible] וואָס עס [illegible] זיך נאָך אין [illegible]. [illegible]

[illegible] פאַרגעסן. [illegible], פון [illegible], [illegible] און [illegible] לאַנג.

מיט די נייע דירעקטאָרים האָב איך זיך [illegible] זייער גוט. זיי זײַנען [illegible], און כ׳פיל זיך מיט

זיי גוטע חברים.

דוכט זיך שוין וועגן אַלעס געשריבן.

שרײַב מיר, הינדעלע, ווי גייט עס דיר? ווי וועסטו פאַרברענגען די [illegible] און ניי-יאָר [illegible]?

וועגן אַלעס אַלעס שרײַב מיר – איך וויל אַלעס וויסן. כ׳האָב דעם מאָל וועלעך שוין אַזוי לאַנג ניט

[illegible] אַזוי דײַן [illegible]. זאָל נאָר מיין [illegible] אַזוי לאַנג ניט זיין, ווי דאָס [illegible].

כ׳גריס האַרציק אַלעמען דאָ [illegible] און [illegible]

זיי געזונט און מוטיק –

דײַן ב.

people remember and mention for many years. With the new doctors I get along very well. They are younger and I feel more of a kinship.

It seems I wrote about everything. Write to me, Hindalla, how you are doing. How are you planning to spend the Christmas and New Year vacation? Tell me about everything—I want to know everything. I hope this time I won't have to wait as long for your answer. I hope it wouldn't take for my letter so long to get to you as the other one.

My heartiest regards to all at your home.

Be well and cheerful.

Your

B.

Šeduva, 18/I 38.

מײַן טײַערע הינדעלע!

איך קום דערװאַרטן אַזױ זײַן בריװ. איך דאַנק דיר זײער. די זאַך, דאָס איך, לױפֿט אַזױ שנעל,
און פֿון מײַן בריװ זײַנען צװײ, װי זיך. זאָגן װאָלטן זיך זײַן.
פֿאַר דעם זײַט האָב איך, אָפֿילו, געהערט פֿון דיר אַ סך גערעדט.
פֿאַראינטערעסירט אױף לאַטינאַמעריקאַנער אַרומגעלאָפֿן מיט אַ שמחה און איר געװוּנטשן אַ „שנה-טובֿה", װעלכע די האָט
געקראָגן פֿון אירע באַװוּסטע שכנים. די האָט זיך אַזױ געפֿרײט, װאָס אַהער זיך דערמאָנט אין איר. איך,
אַבער, האָב גלײַך געזען, װאָס ס'האָט איר ניט טײַערגעמאַכט. איר האָט איך מע ניט געזאָגט. די לאַנגע צײַטן
פֿיל מאָל גערופֿן.
און הײַנט. דײַן אַרבעטגעצײַגן איז געקומען אַ בריװ פֿון דער טאַנטע פֿײַגע. די שרײַבט דאָרט װעגן דיר
אַלײַנע — צו האָסט גרױס דערפֿאָלג אין סקול. ס'האָט מיר פֿאַרשאַפֿט, אַ סך גרױס, אַ סך פֿרײד. פֿאַרװאָס,
הינדעלע, דערצײלסט מיר אַזױ װײניק װעגן דעם?
און װײַסט װיסן, װי דער אַפֿרײַמאַזגן האָט געמײנט װעגן דיר? — אַזױפֿיל דאַנקבאַרקײט און באַגײַסטערונג! ס'װינטשט
מאַל, דאַכט מיר, אַז אַלע דער צײַט האָבן גוטע װינטשן פֿאַר װאָכן-טעג.
אָבער אָבער, הינדעלע, באַנעמט דיר גוטע פֿרײַנט. אַלע װאָלטן װעלן הערן פֿון דיר װאָס מע גוטס. איך גלײב,
אַז אין אַמעריקע האָסט שױן באַװיזן צו האָבן אַ סך גוטע פֿרײַנט, װעלכע װעלן דיר אַלעמאָל זײַן און לײַען.
מײַן פֿאַרװאָס נאָך אַלץ אַזױ אַלײן און נישטאָ? פֿאַרװאָס פֿילסט זיך נאָך אַלץ אַזױ אײנזאַם? ניט
שױן בעסער ניט ס'קען זיך קײנעם ניט אין דיר? — נײן, הינדעלע, פֿילסט זיך אַנדערע מאָל צו קלײן אין דײַנע
אײגענע אױגן. ניט גוט אַזױ.
מיט זיך אין אָרבעט. צו װאָס מײנט אַלע אָנזאָגן יעדע געלעגנהײט, װאָס די גוטע אַמעריקע טראָגט דיר אָנטאָג.
אַלײן אין פֿאָרגאַנג זיך אין גאַנצן אין דער אַרבעט.
שױן אַ פּאָר װאָכן, װי פּרל. קײַזין איז אין פּאַניװעזש. איר שװעסטער איז זײער קראַנק, און די טאַנטע ניט
װײַס פֿון איר שװעסטערס בעט — זיצט אין אײנזאַמקײט פֿאַר די אױגן. דאָך זײַן. די װעט נאָך אַזױ זיך ניט
דאַרפֿן קומען צוריק אין שאַװלי. װען איך מוזן זיצן אין אַנדער געהילף. אַ שאָד, אַזױ גוט זיך געהאַט
צוזאַמענגעלעבט. דערװײַל אַלײן אין אַלײן. ס'איז אַ פֿרעמד מיר װאַנדערנדיק. מיר זײַנען בײדע די שפּעט אין
אָװנט פֿאַרטאָג. כ'האָב זיך, אָבער, קײנמאָל אַזױ גוט ניט געפֿילט, װי אַצינד. ס'פֿאַרדריסט מיר נאָר, װאָס
איך װײס װײניק אָבער פֿאַר זיך: כ'האָב דעם מאָמענט ניט פֿיל געלײענט און געלערנט.

Šeduva 18/1/1938[79]

(January 18, 1938)

My Dear Hindalla!

Your letter arrived—I could hardly wait. I thank you very much. Time, it seems goes so fast, but from one letter to the next is like years. During that time, however, I did have regards from you on several occasions.

Last week our mutual landlady, Lastauskiene,[80] ran in elated showing me a New Year's card which she received from her "former tenants." She was so happy to be remembered. I saw immediately who it was that remembered her but I didn't tell her. She sends her best regards to everyone. And today the Efraimsons[81] received a letter from your aunt. She also writes about you, you are doing well in school. I was truly pleased to hear about it. Why, Hindalla, do you tell me so little of your accomplishments? And you should have heard how Mr. Efraimson talked about you! Such tenderness and esteem! The first time, it seems to me, I ever heard the man say any good word about anybody. Everyone, everyone, Hindalla is your good friend. Everyone wants to hear good things about you. I believe, that in America, too, you must have managed to make many good friends, who will always respect you and love you. So, why, then, still so sad and lonely? Why do you still feel lonesome? Could it possibly be that no one needs you? No, Hindalla, you sometimes think too little of yourself. It is not good that way.

Find courage in your work. See to it that you make use of all the opportunities the good America brings you. I, too, forget myself in my work. For the past few weeks Miss Kotzin had been in Ponevezh. Her sister is very ill and she does not leave her sister's bedside; she is very loyal to her family. It might be that she will not be back in Šeduva for some time and I might have to look for another helper. I am sorry; we got along so well. In the meantime, I am alone. Sioma is a wonderful help. We are both busy till late at night. In spite of all the many hours on duty I've never felt better than I do now. I only regret that I haven't accomplished much on my own behalf. This month I even had very little time to read.

In Šeduva, we had a few evenings of Lithuanian entertainment. I was planning to go to the Scouts'[82] New Years Ball. Unfortunately, I had to be on duty that evening and couldn't go. I wasn't too upset about it.

Before Miss Kotzin left I did manage something important—the Habima Theatre of Palestine[83] was on tour in Lithuania. When they played in Ponevezh, I took advantage of the opportunity and went to see them. They presented Ansky's *The Dybbuk*.[84] It was an evening of complete enjoyment.

We have movies in Šeduva quite often now, and lately even some pretty good ones. A Polish film, *Mazurka*,[85] with Paula Negri was very good. Next week we are supposed to get *Yiddle with his Fiddle*. I did see it not long ago in Kovno and was not very enthused with it. However, I do look forward to seeing it again here. I hope I will be free that evening. It is pleasant to hear the Jewish folk-melodies in a film.

און שוואַרץ זײַנען די צײַטן געווען װעלכע קריסטליכע אַמאָל. אײַנס נאָך דעם אַנדערן פֿון די שלאָסן האָב איך זיך
דערקלערט צו זיך. ליידער איז מיר דעם מאָל אויסגעקומען צו בלײַבן אַליין און אומזיסט און נישט געקענט אַרויסגיין.
קיין גרויס פֿאַרגעניגן האָב איך נישט געהאַט.

אַ דאַנק פֿון קוזין איז אַוועקגעפֿאָרן, האָב איך נאָך אָרגאַניזירט אַ גאַנצע וואָך זיך –
אין טעאַטער איז געווען אַלע די בעסטע פֿון פּאַלעסטינע „הבימה" טעאַטער. די האָב איך געזען און אַלע
אין פֿאַרשטעלונגען. כ'האָב נישט אײַנגעזען די געלעגנהייט און געפֿאָרן צו דער פֿאָרשטעלונג. כ'האָב געזען זיי שפּילן
אויסערן „הדיבוק". ס'איז געווען פֿאַר מיר אַ גאַנץ פֿון גרויסן גענוס.

גאַנץ אָפֿט קומט אין שוואַרצע קינאָ, און די לעצטע צײַט נישט קיין שלעכטע פֿילמס. גוט איז געווען
„מאַזלטאָג" מיט „פּעלאַ נעגרי". די קאָמעדיע וועגן ברענגען מיך צו „יידל מיטן פֿידל". כ'האָב עס געזען, אפֿילו
געזען לינקס אין קינאָ און וואָס נישט געווען, כאָטש איך האָב שוין צו קוקן עס צוויי מאָל.
כ'האָב שוין דעם מאָל צו האָבן אַ טרויער. ס'איז גאַנץ אויסגעמאַכט צו האָבן די יידישע פֿילם־אינדוסטריע
אין פּוילן.

וועגן וועלטפּאָליטיק. די פּאָליטישע לאַגע וועגן פֿון לעבן, אַזוי נישט אין אַלגעמיין. ס'פֿאַרדריסט מיך
גאַנץ. וועלכע געשעענישן אין דער וועלט פּאַסירן, כאָטש די איז נאָך אַלץ נישט אין קינדעריש. אַלע
זאָגן „שלום" קיין אַמעריקע איז געווען די קלענסטע פֿראַנקרײַך. ס'איז נישט אַלץ ליכטיק, און די האָט זיך עס
פֿאַרגעשטעלט. אויך שטעטן און דערפֿער האָבן געשטאַנען גאָר אָן און אַנדערע ריכטונג. וועלכע פּאָליטיק, קען זײַן,
שוין אין דעם אויסלאַנד צוזאַמען מיטן פּאָלן און מענטשהייט, מענטשלעכקייט. די וועט בלײַבן אַלץ לעבן.
די האָט עס דאָס היסטאָריע טאָג אַליין נישט געוואָלט און זיך געמאַכט מיט לעבן און אַנטוויקלען – ס'איז אויך
נישט פֿאַרשטאַנען געוואָרן אין לעבן. אויסער איז אויך געבליבן אַ גרויסע צײַט. די וועלט פֿאַר געשיכטע וועגן אַלץ שרײַבן.
צוליב אין לעבן וועגן אַלע מענטשן די מאַכט־טרעגער זײַנען אומגעקומען. איז טאָגלעך גלײַכגילטיק דאָ, וואָס עס
קען עמיגרירן.

אין אײַנציקן אויסגעקומען אַלס שוין וואָס מען שוין צוריק האָבן אַכט טעג. דערווײַל איז עס נאָך ווײַט
פֿאַרבלײַבט. מען אַ פֿאַר מאָנאַטן אַרויס וואָס עס זײַנען צײַט אַ ביסל. אויך אַרום פֿאַרשיידענע מען. נאָך אַ גאַנצע
שטאָט יידישע קינדער, וועלכע האָבן נישט די מעגלעכקייט צו לערנען גימנאַזיע.

ס'איז מיר אַ וווּנדער, וואָס די שיקט מיר דער אַדרעס לויט אײַער פֿאַרבינדונג. קען מען זיך זען אין אַמעריקע נישט
אײַנאָרדענען די סטודיע אונטערשטיצונג? כ'גלייב, פֿאַרבינדונג איז גאָר נישט פֿון די גרויסע „ביזנעס" אין אַמעריקע. אַלגעמיין
וואָלט זיך נאָך די פֿירמע נישט אײַנגעשטעלט דאַרפֿן.

האַרציקע גרוס אַלעמען. שרײַבט מיר, וואָס הערט זיך בײַ אײַך אין שטוב און סקול. שרײַבט אַ סך!
דײַן גרויס האַרציקן אַלעמען פֿון אַלעמען. זײַ געזונט און גליקלעך.
דײַן B.

About Lola Mellman.[86] She is, in fact, leaving Lithuania, but not for America. I am truly sorry. You would have had a good friend there, even though she is still so naive and childish. Even her going to America was a childish fantasy. It isn't as easy as she thought. Her parents and relatives worked in a completely different direction. Lola is going in about a month, perhaps with her father, to Manchester, England. She will study there. She, herself, didn't know about it and was tormenting herself with mathematics and Latin—she wasn't a particularly good student. Now she is fortunate. I'm sure she will write to you about it.

Here, in Lithuania, chances of becoming established are getting smaller and smaller. Anybody that is able to emigrate is considered lucky. To intern in a drugstore, the requirements are now 8 years of college. So far it is just a proposal, in a few months it will certainly become a law. And so another profession is getting locked out for the Jewish students who do not have the means to complete 8 years of college.

I am surprised that your aunt wants you to study pharmacy. Can't one become established in America in something more interesting? I believe pharmacy is not such "big business" in America. Possibly the plans will still change more than once.

That is all for today. Tell me how you are doing in school and at home. Write much.

My heartiest regards to all. Be well and cheerful.

Your

B.

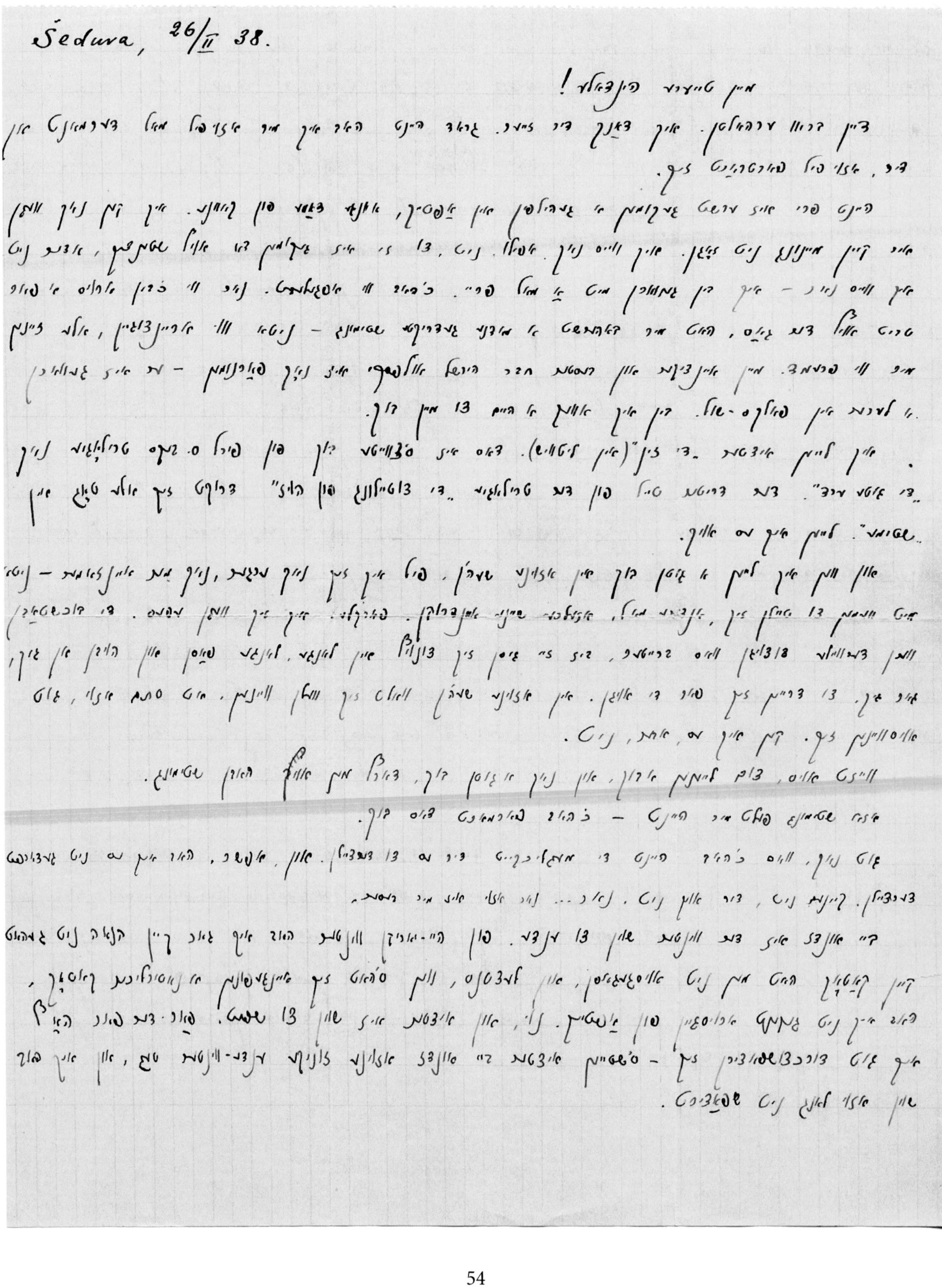

Šedura, 26/II 38.

מײַן טײַערע הינדעלע!

Šeduva, 26/II/1938[87]

(February 26, 1938)

My Dear Hindalla!

Your letter received. I thank you very much. Today, especially, I thought of you so many times. I was lost in thought.

Finally, this morning, my new assistant arrived, a young lady from Kovno. I cannot give my opinion about her yet. I don't even know for sure whether she came here to stay. All I know is that I suddenly feel free, as if re-born. But as soon as I stepped out into the street a peculiar sadness dominated me —there is no place to go; everyone is like a stranger to me. My one and only friend, Hershel Ulfsky, is occupied; he became a teacher in the local elementary school, like his sister. So I went home to my book. I am now reading *The Sons,*[88] in Lithuanian. This is the second book of Pearl S. Buck's trilogy, after *The Good Earth.* The third book, *The House Divided,*[89] is now appearing in serial form in our daily paper, *The Voice.*[90] I am reading that, too. And when I read a good book I feel even worse, more lonesome—there is no one to share with, often times, such beautiful impressions. I get lost in thought, the letters stretch out and become wider, until they combine with each other and turn into long stripes and quickly start to turn in front of my eyes. In times like those I would like to cry, for no reason, just have a good cry, but am unable to do it. It looks like even to read a book, and especially a good book, one has to be in the right kind of mood. Such a mood I am in need of today—I closed the book.

I am glad that I have the opportunity today to tell you that. And, perhaps I shouldn't have told you either—nobody, not even you. But,... but this makes me feel better.

By us the winter is already coming to an end. This year the winter did not bring me much pleasure. There was no skating rink; and lately, even if there was some natural ice somewhere, I could not leave the drugstore. Now it is already too late. I am planning to make up for it by doing a lot of walking. We are having beautiful sunny, wintery days, and I haven't walked briskly in so long. The six weeks that I was "confined" I really felt good. There was much work, and that chased away all thoughts. All that extra work was not too hard for me, not even in the busy market days. With Sioma I am quite satisfied. You still have to watch his work and not leave him too much on his own. I am particularly aware of his faults and make sure that they do not show up in the business. For me he is of some help, even though I cannot leave him entirely alone.

Every evening Hershel Ulfsky comes to visit me; he has become my very best and loyal friend. Sometimes together we visit other friends. So the time passes. Today I am looking forward to the evening when I will be a guest at the Ulfskys.

In Šeduva, there is nothing new. We did have some live theatre recently, the best of which was the one put on by the Scouts. Your girlfriends will, undoubtedly tell you about it. Oh, yes, we had the opportunity here to see a Yiddish film, *The Purim Players,* with Turkov.[91] It wasn't much better than *Yiddle with the Fiddle.* I was truly sorry.

Not long ago we received a new constitution.[92] You surely read about it in the American papers. In

די צײַט װאַרטן, װאָס כ׳בין געװען „פֿאַרטשעפּעט", האָב איך גאָר גוט געפֿילט זיך. געװען פֿיל אַרבעט, און דאָס
האָט פֿאַרטריבן אַלע געדאַנקען. די אַרבעט האָט מיר ניט אָנגעשטרענגט, אַפֿילו אין די מאָנטיק-טאָג. פֿון סוף
דאַן איך געמוזט צופֿרידן. אַדרבה, נאָך גוט אױסגערוט אַלע מײַן אַרבעט און ניט געלאָזט מיך צופֿיל צו זיך. און
דאָס עיקר, פֿאַר איך אַלײן, איז פֿיל פֿון מײַנע אײַנשטעלן לאָזן ניט קומען צום אױסדריק און באַטײַטן. פֿאַר
מיר איז עס גענוג. נאָר װאָס דען, אַלײן לאָזן אױף זיך אױסטײַטשן קען מען נאָך ניט.
פֿאַרגאַנגענע װאָך האָבן מיר געהאַט אַ ביסל טײַער, האָבן אַלגעמײנע — אַ זאַך מיר זײער אין אָרגאַניזירונג
פֿרײַנט. צו רעדן װעגן מיר אױך האָבן אָנגעזאַמט.
אײנער איז מיט אַװעק די צײַט. האָבן װעגן זיך אַלײן געמוזט צו רעדן זײַן אָבער די אַלעסק
אין שװאַרצװאַלד איז קײנער באַזונדער ניט געגאַנגען. געװען ניט װײניק װאָכן. אױסגעזוכט האָט
דאָס װאָכן פֿון די סקאָלען. מײַנע חברים װעלן זײַן געמײנט װעגן אַלע שפּילן.
יאָ, מיר האָבן אין שװאַרצװאַלד געזען נאָך אין מײַנעם פֿילם „די פּרוּװ שפּילן" מיט טעפֿעלן. ניט געװען
דאָס האָט „מײַן מויל פֿרעג". דאָס פֿאַרפֿרײַט זיך דערמיט.
ניט לאַנג האָבן מיר באַקומען אַ נײַע קאָנסטיטוציע. האָסט געװיס געלײענט װעגן דעם אין די צײַטונגען
צײַטונגען. חוץ דעם איז שױן צוריק אין טאָג דער געזעץ װעגן אױסטײַך טײַלן. די אַלע, װאָס זײַנען אָנגעקומען
אין אױסטײַך פֿון פֿאַרפֿאָלגטן דער געזעץ מיט 4 קלאַסן, האָבן נאָך אָפּגעשאַפֿט. אַלע װײַטער װעט מען
צײַגן האָבן 8 קלאַסן מיט לערנען.
אין אױסטערנאַציאָנאַלן געזעץ האָט מען די טאָג אָנגענומען װעגן אַרײַנהאָבן שולן אין די הײמען קלאַס. מאַכט
אין גאַנצן אױסגעשטעלט די נײַע-מאַגאַזינען. מיט 2 „צװײען" בלײַבט מען זיצן, מיט אײנעם — גײט מען װײַטער.
דעם צװײטן יאָר, װען מען קריגט אַלע ניט פֿון די צװײ, בלײַבט מען אױך. די מאַגאַזינען אין אַנדערן קלאַס
האָט מען שױן פֿאָרלײגט.
אַזױ פֿיל נײַעס האָב איך דיר הײנט צו שרײַבן.
שרײַב מיר, הינדעלע, װי גײט עס דיר אין דער הײמען קלאַס? װי פֿאַרברענגסטו אין סקול?
באַשרײַב מיר די פֿון אײַך, װאָס איז דיר צוגעקומען? שרײַב װעגן אַלץ.
איך גריס הערצלעך אַלעמען דאָ אײַך אין שטוב.
און דיר די הערצלעכע גרוס פֿון אַלע מײַנע באַקאַנטע.
די באַזונדערע און גוטע
דײַן B.

addition, the new law passed in Senate with regards to drugstore internships. Those who are interning prior to the passage of the new law may continue with 4 years college; after that, the requirement will be 8 years college, plus Latin. Another interesting change went through with regards to being promoted into a higher grade. The post-exams have been entirely discontinued. With two failing grades you have to repeat the entire year; with one failing grade you may be promoted. Should you, however, fail the following year the same subject, you cannot be promoted and have to repeat the entire year. The final exams were made somewhat easier.

That is about all I have to write this time. Tell me, Hindalla, how you are doing in the higher grade? How do you spend the time outside of school? Do you mind all the extra work you have to do? Write about everything.

My fondest regards to everyone at home. And to you, heartiest regards from all your friends.

Be well and stay cheerful.

Your

B.

Šeduva, 31/III 38.

מײַן טײַערע הינדעלע!

איך דאַנק דיר זייער פֿאַרן בריוו. זײַ באַדאַנקט דאַנק פֿאַרן שרײַבן מיר די מיינונגען, וועלכע דו האָסט ניט לאַנג דערקומען. און צו דעם האָסט מיינונג אין ענגליש, און אין ענגלישער שול. און [illegible] א יאָר אין לערנען.

טײַערע הינדעלע, [illegible] און זײַ צופֿרידן. [illegible] אונדז דאָ איז עס די גרעסטע שׂמחה, אַז דיר גייט גוט. דיר [illegible], אפֿשר, אין די צופֿיל [illegible]. [illegible], [illegible] וואָס עס אינטערעסירט ניט, [illegible] ניט. וואָס זיך ניט אַרומצוטאָן, ווי די [illegible] איז דיר [illegible]. און וואָס האָבן [illegible] אויפֿגעטאָן.

ס'געפֿעלט מיר אויך דײַן פּלאַן אויסצופֿילן דײַן צײַט פֿעריען מיט פֿראַנצויז לערנען. [illegible] טויג, [illegible] צו פֿאַרווירקלעכן. [illegible] ווייסן, וויפֿיל ניצן וואָס, אפֿשר, שפּעטער האָבן פֿון דעם.

און וואָסער? – איך וויל דיר גאָר „[illegible]" [illegible] – איך וויל דיר וואָס שיקן אין אינטערעסאַנטן [illegible] אין פֿראַנצויז, וואָס עס דאַרף וועלן לערנען...

מײַן פּלאַן קלאָר איך אין גיין אויסצופֿירן. חול־המועד פּסח וועל איך זײַן אין קאָוונע און [illegible] אַלע פֿאָרמאַליטעטן, וועלכע זענען מיט דעם פֿאַרבונדן. קיינע שוועריקייטן, מיין איך, וועל איך ניט האָבן. [illegible], וואָס כּמעט [illegible] גערעדט, איז שוין [illegible]. כּמעט [illegible] גערעדט, איך וועל ניט האָבן וואָס צו לאָזן אין [illegible] און וועל ניט [illegible] נעמען קיין [illegible]. ס'האָט זיך אַרויסגעוויזן, אַז די [illegible] איז געקומען [illegible] צוויי [illegible]. זי האָט, קענטיק, געהאַט [illegible] די [illegible] פֿון ה' [illegible] און, מסתּמא, ניט צוריקגעקומען. איך האָב דײַן [illegible] אויף מײַן אייגענע פֿאַראַנטוואָרטלעכקייט און אײַנגעלאַדן מײַנעם א חבֿר, וועלכע האָט ניט לאַנג געענדיקט. [illegible] ווייס איך. איך האָב אויך וואָס צו [illegible] זיך אין [illegible], וואָס איך [illegible]. [illegible] האָב איך א גוטן חבֿר. די [illegible] קלאַס געלונגט, שפּעטער אין אוניווערסיטעט אין [illegible].

[illegible] וועל איך דיר [illegible]. [illegible], וואָסער עס שוין געווען.

[illegible] איז [illegible] צו מיר זיך געזעגענען. זי האָט מיר געזאָגט, אַז זי פֿאָרט [illegible] קיין אַמעריקע... כּמעט זיך [illegible] געווונדערט, [illegible], [illegible] געלייענט. [illegible] זיך פֿאַר – די [illegible] האָבן „[illegible]" [illegible]... נו, דאָס איז געווען [illegible]: [illegible] זײַן די [illegible].

כּמעט זיך געפֿרייט, וואָס ס'האָט [illegible], אַז און [illegible] דיר [illegible].

ס'וועט דיר [illegible], קען זײַן, [illegible] ניט [illegible] זײַן – וואָס האָבן אין [illegible] א גוטע חבֿרטע פֿון דער היים, [illegible] ניט אין דער [illegible]. [illegible] קענען [illegible] די [illegible]. [illegible] שוין [illegible]!

Šeduva, 31/III/1938[93]

(March 31, 1938)

My Dear Hindalla!

I thank you very much for your letter. I especially thank you for telling me your grades which you had just received. I see, the best grade in English in an English school, and barely a year in the country. Dear Hindalla, evaluate it and be happy. Also, for us here it is the biggest joy that you are getting along so well. Perhaps all this work is a strain on you? But work, as long as it is not exhausting, never hurts. You will barely look around and the time will pass and you will have accomplished much.

I'm also happy with your plan to spend your summer vacation studying French. Make sure you absolutely go through with it. You don't know how much use it may be to you later on. And do you know? I will even "force" you into it—I will send you an interesting book in French and you will, undoubtedly, want to read it...

My own plan I mean to fulfill in the near future. The middle of Passover I will be in Kovno to complete all the formalities. I do not anticipate any problems. The main thing that I was concerned about has already been taken care of. I was afraid I would not find anybody to take over the drug store and I would not be able to take my vacation altogether. As it turned out, my lady helper only stayed two weeks. It seems that she had in mind to take over the ownership from Mr. Katz, and, most likely, could not agree on terms. I then acted on my own and invited a friend of mine, who had graduated not long ago. Now I know that I have someone responsible to take over in my absence. In addition, I now gained a friend. We were in the same class in high school and then again at the university.

Now I will tell you some news. You may even know it by now. Before leaving Šeduva, Lola Mellman came in to say good-bye to me. She then confided in me that she was going to America, and not to England. I was, of course, very surprised but I believed her. Imagine that—the Mellmans[94] "fooled" all of Šeduva. It must have been for special precaution: there are all kinds of people! I was overjoyed that it turned out that way, that almost to the year Lola should follow you. Now, perhaps, it won't be so lonely for you—you'll have in America a good friend from home, even though not in the same city. You will certainly be able to visit one another. How you must be looking forward to it!

A pleasant surprise for me was that you are beginning to become interested in politics. I know, you never paid particular attention to the political news in the papers. Is this the effect of the school? It is good—one has to follow what's happening in the world, and to have a certain position with regards to world events. I would find it very interesting, indeed, to hear in what kind of tone your school discusses politics.

By us everyone here truly has become a "politician." Here, on the contrary, it is not a healthy sign. Many rumors are spreading that are quite damaging—we find ourselves in the center, one can say, of the major European events.

In the meantime spring has come. Somehow the mood changes. For the better? I don't know myself.

אין אונזער פארבינדונג איז טייער מיר געווען, וואס דו האסט זיך אנגעהויבן אינטערעסירן מיט פאליטיק
כוואס, פארוואס קענסטו ניט ליינען אויך די פאליטישע נייעס אין די צייטונגען. האסטו די סקול אויך
געענדיקט? ס'איז זייער גוט — מ'דארף ניט פארפעלן, וואס טוט זיך אויף דער וועלט און הערן אוועלכע-ס-איין
שטעלונג אויף דו פאלטער געשעענישן. מיר וועט זיין זייער אינטערעסאנט דו הערן. און וואס טוען די טאג וואו
דו אויך אין סקול פראגרעסיווע פאליטיק?

די אונדזערע מיינען אוודאי, אויך אין אמת, אלע געווארן „פאליטיקער". דאס איז דאך גוט, נאר ניט געמיינטע
פארשיידענע. סאמען פראגרעסיווע משונה'דיקע ריכטונגען, וואס מאכן אין ניט ווייניק שאדן — מיר געפינען זיך דא
אין צענטער, דאס מען זאגן, פון די אמעריקאנישע געשעענישן.

דערווייל קומט שוין אן דער פרילינג. עפעס רירט זיך די שטימונג. צום גוטן? — כוואס וויסן ניט.
ביי אייך, ווי איך זע, האלט איר שוין ווייט אין פרילינג. שפאצירן שוין, מסתמא, די בלומען די זיין אין גארטן.
האסטו, כאטש, איבערגענומען די זיי א גרוס פון מיר?...

היינט וועל איך דיר שוין מער ניט שרייבן.

איך ווינטש דיר, הינדעלע, א פריילעכן פסח. זאל זיך גוט אלעס. זאלסט קענען מיט פריילעך
ענדיקן דעם לערן יאר.

שרייב מיר וועגן אלעס, וואס קומט פאר ביי דיר.

מיין הארציקן גרוס דיינע אלע נאנטע.

דער געטרייער פון אונטען —

דיין B.

P.S. דיין קלאסן, לייענער, האב איך דאס מאל ניט באקומען
אין שרייבמאשין געשיקט. טאווע דיר, געווען, שוועסטער
זיין דאס וועשבאדן אויך אין אמעריקע מארגן.

S.3.

By you, as I see it, spring is much under way. The flowers are probably blooming in your yard. Did they at least give you my regards?

Today I won't write any more. I wish you, Hindalla, a happy Passover. Take a good rest so that you may end your school year successfully. Write to me about everything that is happening to you.

My best regards to all your friends.

Stay well and be cheerful—

Your

B.

P.S. Unfortunately, I was not able to get a stamp coupon at the Šeduva Post Office. You might find it difficult to save up for an extra postage stamp.[95]

Šeduva, 8/V 38.

מיין טייערע הינדעלע!

און ווידער אמאל האסטו מיך דערפרייט מיט דיינעם א בריוו. ווי באלד איך דיר אפענטפערן?
יעדן מאל, ווען איך לייען א בריוו דיינעם, פיל איך זיך שולדיק, שטארק שולדיק לגבי דיר; עפעס פיל
איך, כאטש וואס טוען פאר דיר און [illegible] ניט; כאטשבאלד דיר מיט עפעס אפצוגעלטן און וואס ניט, ווי אזוי.
בין איך נאך צופרידן, וואס דו שרייבסט כאטש פאר דיר.
פארגעס דיר ניט מיין טרוי – כאטשבאלד מיט יעדן גרוס דערמאנען זיך פרייען.

און איצטער –

דיין קליינע הינדעלע, די פריינטשאפט פון [illegible] שפאציר, ליכטיק אין אמעריקע – אלץ גוט
מיטגעטיילט מיר פאר דיר. וואס זיך שוין, אפשר, פון ווייניקער שלעכט, ווי געמיינט.
האלט און זיי מוטיק!

דעם פסח האב איך פארבראכט אין קאוונע און דאס ניט שלעכט – געשטאנען אלעס צופרידן,
דורכגעשפאצירט זיך, פארבאנט פארגעניגנס צוויי. די וואכן האב איך אונטערגעלעבט מיט חברים אין
קינא אדער אין טעאטער. א באזונדערע הנאה האב איך דעם מאל געהאט פון יידישן טעאטער – גאר קיין
שפור ניט געבליבן פון אמאליקן שונד.

קאוונע פארמאגט צוויי "יידישע טעאטערס". יארן לאנג האט מען געשפילט דעם עולם מיט גוטס,
געשמאקלאזע אפערעטעס. געקומען אונזער מוטיקער קולטור געברויך און א פאר-הפקר׳ט. דאס האט מען געטאן
געוואונען פון [illegible]...

ביז די דאזיקע "יידישע געזעלשאפט" האט זיך ארויסגעוויזן. האבן געשפילט אין מיין שטאט די ווילנער
קינסטלערישע טרופע. אין צוויי וואכן שפילט האט זיך ניט [illegible] געשפילט טורנעי, אויסגעזוכט ווערק פון יעדן
שטאנדפונקט – די בעסטע יידישע דיכטער און רעזשיסערן פון דראמע. "די גאלדענע קייט" און "[illegible]"
האבן מיר דעם פסח פארבראכט דעם גרעסטן פארגעניגן.

דער עיקר, ווייסט, צוליב וואס כ׳בין געפארן קיין קאוונע, האט זיך מיר ניט איינגעגעבן. פאקטיש איז
ניט געלונגען צו קריגן די רוסישע ארבעטס-וויזע. כ׳בין דאס ניט קיין אילוזיע – רוסלאנד וויל
ווייטער ניט אויפנעמען אויסלענדער. א שאד – געמיינט דעם ענדגילטן איז צו פארשטעלן אין [illegible].

Šeduva 8/V/1938[96]

(May 8, 1938)

My Dear Hindalla!

And again I rejoiced with your letter. How can I thank you? Every time I read your letters I feel guilty towards you; somehow I feel I ought to do something for you, and I am not. I have to thank you with something and don't know how. I am happy that time is doing something for you. You are doing well in school; I was so happy to hear that.

And now—your cousin's visit.[97] The friendliness from your uncle's family. Your friend Lola in America—all these are important things to you. Perhaps you will feel less lonely than before. Hope and courage!

This Passover I spent in Kovno, and not too badly. I renewed old acquaintances, we talked and reminisced a little. Evenings I went with friends to the movies and theatre. I especially enjoyed this time the Yiddish theatre—not a trace left of the old frolic. Kovno possesses two Yiddish theatres. For many years they fed the public with cheap tasteless operettas. To take such an important culture and make little of it! That they copied from America. Until the more intellectual Jewish community intervened. Today in one theater the Vilno Artistic Troupe[98] is performing, and in the other until not long ago the featured guest artist was Turkov,[99] and now performing is Jacob Sternberg,[100] the well-known Yiddish poet and stage director from Rumania. His *Yellow Shadow* and *Red Oranges* gave me the biggest pleasure this Passover,

The main reason why I went to Kovno in the first place, did not turn out that successfully, however. I was unable to get the Russian visa. I am no exception—Russia does not want our tourists now. Too bad; I had visions of spending May 1st in Moscow.[101] Cannot be helped. Sometimes we cannot get our way in more important matters.

I haven't decided yet about traveling elsewhere. In Šeduva I pass the time as before. Now I have much free time and a good radio—it's the most suitable pair—so that I find myself spending quite a bit of time by the radio.

Every other Sunday our drugstore is closed—we arranged it with the other drugstore in Šeduva. On such Sundays, if the weather is good, I bicycle somewhere not too far with friends. I visited many small towns around here. My light bicycle serves me well. I love riding all day long.

Today is my free Sunday. Unfortunately, it is raining, pouring. I came upon Segalowitz's *The Weaver's Daughter*—I re-read it a second time. There are beautiful sections. The book leaves you in a kind of turmoil: your mood becomes just like the outside today—such a sad, melancholy feeling. How well Segalowitz knows life!

Tell me, Hindalla, about yourself and about your close ones. Last week I somehow reminded myself of Yvette. Tell me how she is and how is she doing in school. She must be attending school already.

Well, and from Lola what do you hear? Her mother says that Lola is already a 100% American.

נאך 13 חדשים. ס'איז אונדזער מזל, [illegible] אין [illegible], נאך ווי [illegible] געוואלט.

[illegible] אונדזערע [illegible] [illegible] ניט געקלערט.

און [illegible] פארברענגען אין די געטא. כ'האב [illegible] [illegible] און – [illegible]

[illegible]. ס'איז [illegible] – פארברענגען אין [illegible] [illegible].

[illegible] – מיר [illegible] [illegible] „[illegible]".

[illegible]. [illegible], [illegible]. כ'האב [illegible]

[illegible]. [illegible] „[illegible]" [illegible].

כ'האב [illegible] [illegible].

[illegible]. [illegible]. ס'איז מיר [illegible]

[illegible] „[illegible]" – כ'האב [illegible], [illegible], [illegible]

[illegible]. [illegible]: [illegible], [illegible]

[illegible] – [illegible]. [illegible]!

~~שרייב [illegible]. [illegible]. כ'האב [illegible]~~

[illegible]. שרייב מיר, [illegible]? – [illegible]

[illegible].

[illegible]? [illegible], [illegible] 100% [illegible]

[illegible]... [illegible], [illegible]. [illegible]!

כ'האב [illegible]; [illegible]. [illegible], [illegible], [illegible]?

[illegible]. [illegible].

בלייב געזונט

[illegible]

Certainly, Lola was even here like that, America is for her!

I am enclosing a photo of myself which I had taken a few days ago. I look a little angry, I think. True?

That's all for now. My best regards to everyone.

Be well.

B.

Šeduva, 8/VI 38.

מײַן טײַערע הינדעלע!

דײַן בריוו ערהאַלטן. דאַנקען דיר זייער [illegible].

ווײַל ביז איצט האָב איך [illegible] נישט. געהאָפֿט האָב איך גרויס אויף הײַנטיקן בריוו דיר מיט
שפּעט צו [illegible]. געמיינט כּמעט שוין וועגן אַלץ [illegible].

האָסט זיך געהאַנדלט וועגן די שטעלע אין [illegible], און די [illegible], מיט ניט קיין קליינעם
געהאַלט. [illegible] זײַן, כּהאָב גלײַך געמאַלדעט [illegible], כּלי זמן פֿון שאַדאַווע. ער האָט געהאָט
צוויי וואָכן צײַט צו [illegible] די [illegible] מיט אַן אַנדער פֿאַרוואַלטער. [illegible] האָט, אָרע, לײַדער,
ניט געפֿונען צום מאָמענט קיין [illegible] פּערזאָן. [illegible] האָב איך זיך אַלײן [illegible], מײַן חבר
[illegible] קריגן צײַטווײַליק פֿאַרוואַלטונגס-ראַט. דער דעפּאַרטאַמענט האָט מײַן [illegible], אַז קיינער
[illegible], [illegible]. [illegible]. בין איך [illegible] שאַדאַווע. ווער ווייס ווי לאַנג נאָך? ניט צום מיינען.

צו וואָס, אייגנטלעך, די גאַנצע מעשׂה? צו וואָס דאַרף איך [illegible] וועמען דערציילן?

געווען דאָ ניט לאַנג די טעג, אַזוי כּהאָב געמיינט. שוין דער לעצטער אין שאַדאַווע. כּהאָב
מיט די מאָל דערפֿילט, דער [illegible] מיר טײַער. און ס'איז מיר געווען שווער זיך צו געזעגענען
מיט אַלעם, וואָס כּוועל אַפֿשר קיינמאָל ניט קענען פֿאַרגעסן.

ניט געשפּאָרט געווען, אָרע, צו געזעגענען זיך [illegible].

[illegible] איך ווידער אַרום גאַנצע טעג [illegible] וועגן. ווי גוט עס איז זיך אַזוי
צו לאָזן מיט די ווילדע [illegible]! דאַן [illegible] וועגן קען זיך ניט קלערן.

פֿאַרברענג אין ווידער לאַנגע שעהן אויף דער [illegible] (8 קילאָמעטער פֿון שאַדאַווע). ס'איז גוט אַזוי
וועגן [illegible] צו טראַכטן און נאָר וואַרטן אויף די פֿויגל אויף דער [illegible]...

ס'איז פֿרילינג. און כּוויל דעם פֿרילינג אויסנוצן, ווי וואָס עס לאָזט זיך. אפֿשר וועט [illegible] אויסקומען
צו געזעגענען זיך אין גיכן מיט די אַלטע [illegible]. וואָלט איך זיך נאָך מער [illegible].

דערווײַלע לעבן ווידער טעג אין וואַלד. צו די גרויסע וואָכעדיקע טעג בין איך שוין געוווינט און
כּשפּיר זיי ניט. בין איך נאָך, אָרע, זייער [illegible]; ווען ס'געשעט אין זיי אַ [illegible]. [illegible]
ניט דערפֿאַר שבת און יום-טובֿדיקע טעג. [illegible] מיר דאַן און [illegible] קיין אָרט ניט. אויך [illegible]

Šeduva 8/VI/1938[102]

(June 8, 1938)

My Dear Hindalla!

Your letter received. I am very grateful to you. Also by me this time very little news. I did hope to surprise you with something in today's letter. I thought I might no longer be a pharmacist. There was a position open in Memel[103] in a laboratory with pretty high wages. Naturally, I right away notified Mr. Katz of the possibility of my leaving Šeduva. He had two weeks to get himself another manager. Mr. Katz, however, unfortunately could not find a suitable person. Finally, I personally intervened on behalf of a friend of mine, to at least temporarily get managerial rights. The department, however, rejected my plea without any motive. Consequently, I again remain in Šeduva. Who knows for how long? Again, cannot be helped.[104]

Why precisely the whole story? Why do I have to tell it to anybody now? There was a day not long ago, and I thought it might be one of the last ones in Šeduva, and I suddenly felt that the place is so dear to me; and it was hard for me to say "good-bye" to everything which I might perhaps never forget. It wasn't meant to say "good-bye" yet.

I again wander for days at a time through near-by roads. How great it is to ride with wild speeds. Then you don't have to think about anything. I spend many hours by the lake (8 kilometers from the city). It is good not to think about anything and just to wait for a little fish on the line.

It is spring, and I would like to enjoy the spring as much as possible. Perhaps I will soon have to say "good-bye" to all this childishness. I would even regret it more.

In the meantime, days and weeks are again passing. I am already used to the gray days and don't even notice them. I am very sensitive to any change. That is why I suffer on Sabbath and holidays. I can't find a place for myself. This last Shavuot I was also quite bored. That is all about myself.

Also, in Šeduva, there is no special news. A few days ago final exams were held in the local junior high school. It was a written exam and all the Jewish students failed. This year their exam consisted of a short composition. Is it possible that all the Jewish students have mastered the Lithuanian language that poorly in comparison with their Lithuanian peers?[105] I believe they were not really graded on knowledge... Your girlfriends will undoubtedly write to you about the exact results.

Dear Hindalla, my letter will surely find you in the midst of your vacation. This summer try to rest up, visit your friends if you have the opportunity. Join your uncle on his trips if he travels anywhere from time to time. You should know America. Your friends, as I see it, want to see you independent. It is so hard for me to advise you from that far away. It seems to me, though, that as long as you have a chance to study you should not accept any job. A job with your cousin you will always get. It doesn't necessarily mean that it is not good to work for a relative; sometimes it may even be advantageous. It is, however, too soon for you. A couple of years, at least, you should use to your own advantage. That will even pay off later on in the business world...Your relatives should understand this.

In the meantime, it is good that you have a good home with your aunt and the opportunity to study

שלומית, האָט איר זיך געשפּירט היינט גוטנס.

דאָס איבער וועגן זיך.

וועגן מיין שוועבער איז קיינער נאָך ניטאָ.

די טעג זיינען אין דער היגער פּראָפּאַגאַנדע אָרגאַניזירט די אויסשטעלונג אגדות אויף ליטוויש. שרעקלעך הערן. דערביי זיך, אַלע ייִדישע געהערן צוויי. מיר האָבן יאָ-וואָר געמאַכט צו שרייבן אַ ליטע וויסנשאַפטלעך. ניט שוין נישט דאָרט די ייִדישע שולע אַזוי שטאַרק ליטוויש אָבער דײַטש ליטוויש מיטשולע? כּלומר, דאָ איז ניט געגאַנגען אין קינדער... געגעבן רעזאָלוציעס וועגן דער גרויס שרייבן דיינע חברטע.

טײַערע הינדעלע, איך ברויך וועט דער שוין זייער טויבן אין דיין זומער-פּלאַן. דאָך זומער צו זיין גוט אָפּגערוט. דערזען דיינע פרײַנט, און צו וועט האָבן די געלעגנהייט. מיר איז ריינע מיט אַ קאַפּ, וואָלט מיר אויך געקענט פון דער צו זען. צו דערזען דעם אַמעריקע!

דיינע פרײַנט, ווי כּבֿר, וועלן דיר שוין מוזן באַרעכטיקן. מיר האָבן וועגן איז דאַך אַזוי שווער דיר צו העלפן מיט א האַנט. מיר דאַכט זיך אָבער, ווי לאַנג צו האָסט די מעגלעכקייט דיך לערנען, דאַרפסט נאָך קיינער שטאַרק ניט אויסלאָזן. ביים קריגן וועסטו דאָך געוויס קיינמאָל ניט פאַרשפּעטיקן. ס'איז ניט געזונט, אַז קיין אויסנאַם איז שלעכט צו אַרבעטן. אָבער מאָל איז עס גאָר צו גלייך. ס'איז נייטיק, אַרבעט. צו פרי טאָר דיך, דערנאָך ניט אַ פּאָר וואָך אָפּגעבן פאַר זיך. דאָס וועט דיך אויך גוט אָפּרוען שפּעטער אויף די קורסן... דיינע פרײַנט דאַרפן עס פאַרשטיין.

דער וועטער איז הייס, וואָס צו האָסט ווי דער סוף פון די גאַנצע היים און די געלעגנהייט צו לערנען און שפּאַצירן. שווער אַרבעטן איז ניט שרעקלעך. מען דאַרף מער נאָר טאָן פון גאַנצן האַרצן. די גרויסע באַוועגונג פון די סאָלידאַרישקייט האָבן אַלץ פאַר דיר. כּפּרה זיך, וואָס די האָסט מיט איצט.

שרייב, ווי האָסטו זיך געפונען דעם לעצטן יאָר? ווי האָפסטו צו פאַרברענגען די פרייע צייט?

מיין גרעסטע האַרציקע גרוס די מאַמע און שוועסטער.

זיי געזונט איין, נאָך אַ מאָל, פאַרברענג גוט!

B.

פ.ס. שוין אַ צייט ניט געהערט פון דעם טאַטן. וואָס ניט פאַרוואָס?

and progress. Hard work is not so terrible, as long as it is done good naturedly and from the heart. A good relationship at home is of the utmost importance to you now. I am very happy that you have it.

Write to me how you finished the school year. How do you plan to spend the free time? My heartiest regards to everyone at home.

Be well and, again, enjoy yourself.

B.

P.S. I haven't heard from your aunt in some time. Do you know why?

VALTION HOTELLI
IMATRA
Puh. 38 ja 48

Imatra, 17/VIII 38.

מיין טײַערסטע הינדעלע

[illegible]

Imatra, 17/VII/1938[106]

(July 17, 1938)

My Dearest Hindalla,

This letter will surprise you. I am writing to you from so far away. It is the third day that I am here in the beautiful Finland. I already saw so very much, and it seems to me that I've always lived here.

Your letter, as well as a letter from your aunt, were already waiting for me here at the hotel, in Helsinki.[107] I arranged it ahead of time in Šeduva that my letters should be forwarded to me in Finland. I thank you both heartily.

In Finland I arrived from Stockholm, where I did not stay long. Here, in Finland, in the beautiful land of lakes, I expect to stay a couple of weeks, then return home through Estonia and Latvia. That is how I decided to spend my vacation this year and, I confess, I will never regret it.

Dear Hindalla, if you were only here with me! What beautiful places! What good people! Everything, everything is entirely different than by us. But there is no one with whom to share these beautiful impressions. When I come home I will, more or less, systematize my whole trip and will write to you in detail. These few words I'm writing at lunch, in the hotel. The noise from the Imatra waterfall, the sounds of the orchestra, and the many guests, are responsible for the fact that my letter lost all its form. In addition, I must get ready for my trip ahead; so that I will be satisfied with just writing a few words.

Yes, the Šeduva scouts left not long ago for Kovno to camp nearby. There will be many scouts from different countries, in addition to the ones from Lithuania. They will, undoubtedly, have a good time. Ask your friends to write to you about it. It should be very interesting.

I enclose 5.00 litas. Spend it quickly on whatever you like.

Stay well and have fun.

Your

B.

My best regards to your relatives.

Šedura, 2/VIII 38.

בין איך װידער אין שאַדעװע; אַרײַנגעריסן װידער, װי דאָ ניט געװען דורך.

איז דאָס אַלץ אַ חלום געװען?

— יאָ, געװיס. אײנער פֿון די פֿיל שײנע חלומות. און איצטער — בלױז דערינערונגען געבליבן.

דענקט זיך נאָר נאָך צו.

דאָס מאָל, אָבער, איז עס באַזונדערס שײן געװען.

דו שײנע פֿינלאַנד! כ'װעל קײנמאָל ניט פֿאַרגעסן די צװײ װאָכן צװישן דײַנע פֿעלזן-ברעג און אָזערעס.

מײַן טײַערע הינדאַלע!

װיפֿל שײנקײט דו װאָלסט דאָ געקענט פֿאַרגלײַכן! טאָמער שײנע ברעג און טאָלן און װאַסערן װאָלטן זיך געבראַכט, מזל צו מײַן.

יאָ, װען דו װאָלסט דאָ אױך געװען!

(אַ דבֿרה נאָר, װאָס דו קענסט נאָך אַלץ ניט זײַן, ניט אױסגעלאָזט זיך נאָך...).

װי אַזױ איז מיר אײַנגעפֿאַלן פֿאָרן גראָד קײן פֿינלאַנד?

כ'האָב שױן געהאַט װי באַשלאָסן אַרומצופֿאָרן אין שװעדן. איך האָב געקראָגן מײַן אורלױב-צײַט און האָב ניט געװוּסט װי אַהינצופֿאָרן. זינט אַלע דײַטשע אין אָרטיקע, װאָלט געװען פֿאַר מיר די גרעסטע שטראָף. האָב איך זיך באַשלאָסן, איך קען פֿאָרן מיט אַ ליטװישער עקסקורסיע קײן פֿינלאַנד. קײן סך ניט געטראַכט, אײַנגעשריבן פֿאַר גאַנצן אױסגעטראַכט אין פֿינלאַנד. בין איך װײַטער מיט אײנעם טאָג פֿריער אָפּגעפֿאָרן מיט אַ שװעדישער שיף פֿון קלײפּעדע קײן שטאָקהאָלם. אױפֿן שיף, צװישן הימל און װאַסער, האָב איך זיך געפֿילט אױסגעצײכנט (פֿאַראַנען פֿיל איך מיר אַלע מאָל זײער גוט - ס'איז מײַן גרעסטע פֿאַרגעניגן). אין גאַנצן איז אױסגעקומען צו פֿאָרן מיטן שיף ביז שטאָקהאָלם 18 שעה. דער װעטער איז געװען זײער שײן, דער ים זײער שטיל, איך האָב זיך געהאַט פֿאַרגעניגן װאָס מ'האָט זײער װײניק פֿאַרלאָרן. אין שטאָקהאָלם האָב איך פֿאַרבראַכט גאַנצע צװײ טעג. די שטאָט פֿאַרנעמט אַרום אַ צענדליק אינדזלען און איז אין גאַנצן, װי פֿון גרינס געמאַכט — דער האַרבסט-פּאַלאַץ, די הײַזער - שײן. אַלץ מיט זײער פֿיל קונסט און געשמאַק. מ'האָט דאָך

Šeduva, 2/VIII/I938[108]

(August 2, 1938)

Here I am again in Šeduva and am again working as before.

Was it all a dream? Yes, most certainly. One of the many beautiful dreams. And now—only memories remain. I long for them.

This time it was especially beautiful.

Beautiful Finland l will never forget the two weeks among the high mountains and lakes.

My Dear Hindalla!

How much beauty you could immortalize here! What beautiful hills, dales, and water were just begging to be painted. Oh, if you, too, were there! (Too bad you're not a good traveler, you still haven't learned...)

How did I get the notion to go to Finland? I had almost decided to spend my summer in Šeduva. But when my vacation time came, there was nothing to do. To sit in a "dacha,"[109] without doing anything would be for me a great punishment. I accidentally heard that in Kovno there were plans being formed for a Lithuanian tour to Finland. I didn't waste any time and immediately paid for room and board in Finland. I left a few days earlier with a Swedish ship from Klaipeda to Stockholm.[110] On the ship, between sky and water, I felt superb. (Travelling always makes me feel good - it is my greatest pleasure.) We went by ship until Stockholm—only 18 hours. The weather was beautiful, the sea calm. It really was a shame that the trip was so short. In Stockholm I spent exactly two days. The city is built on about ten islands and is completely as if cut out of granite. The ground, rock; the houses, stone. But everything with so much art and good taste. One gets the impression that every Swede is an artist. And, truly, the city is exceptionally beautiful.

I visited many museums, open restaurants and cafes, but did not see everything by far. Mostly I regret that outside of Stockholm I saw very little of Sweden. I had to hurry to Finland, to my Lithuanian tourists. Another Swedish ship took me from Stockholm to Helsinki. There I joined my Lithuanians who had just arrived by land. I quickly got acquainted with everyone. I found it quite pleasant socially. Many teachers, some artists, people of free-lance professions, employees—altogether over 30. Among them was also the Lithuanian writer Vienulis,[111] by the way a colleague of mine by profession. In Helsinki we were only one day. The city is about twice the size of Kovno but much more beautiful. Very reminiscent of Stockholm. During that one day we managed to see most of this remarkable city and move on further. We stopped in Vipuri[112] (once called Viborg). Here we saw the ancient Swedish, later Russian, famous fortress. It was like re-learning a part of history. It was very interesting. From Vipuri we travelled northward. Here spring was just beginning. Lilacs were just opening up and jasmine was still in buds. This pleased everyone. We were all in a spring mood.

We toured the country for ten whole days. We visited many cities and towns, resorts and country sites. Never dined where we had breakfast. We swam in lakes or in the sea. The most pleasant time was our leisurely trio, by steamship, over the Sima River and then climbing the mountains of Koli at night.

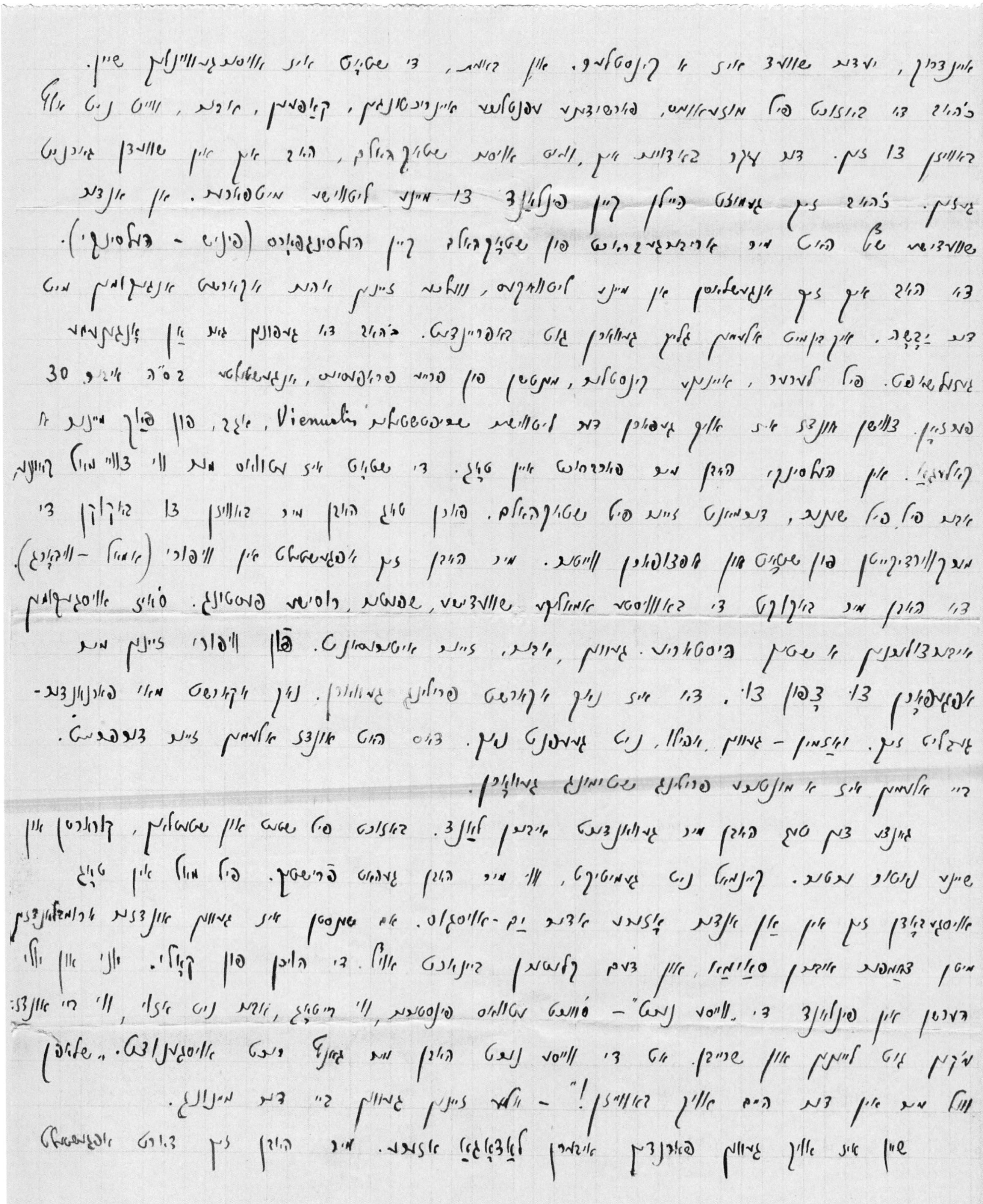

אַנדערע, יעדער שוואַרץ אויף אַ קאָנסטלער. און דאָרט, די שטאָט איז וואַסער־געווייניק שיין.
כאָטש די רעזולטאַט פֿיל מאָנומענטן, פּאָרטרעטן עפֿנטלעכע אינסטיטוציעס, קאַפֿעען, גאַסן, ווייס ניט אויף
דערציילן צו זאָגן. דאָס ערשטע באַזוכט איך, וואָס אַלעס שטאָקהאָלם, האָב איך אין שוועדן געזען
געזען. כאָטש זיך געזעגנט פֿײַן קיין פֿינלאַנד צו מיינע ליטווישע מיטפֿאָרער. און אונדזער
שוועדישע שיף האָט מיר איבערגעבראַכט פֿון שטאָקהאָלם קיין העלסינגפֿאָרס (פֿיניש - העלסינקי).
די האָב איך זיך אָנגעשלאָסן אין מיינע ליטווערקעס, וועלכע זיינען אויך געפֿאָרן אונטערוועגנס מיט
דער ... . איך בין מיט אַלעמען גלייך געוואָרן גוטע פֿריינדלעך. כאָטש די געפֿונען זיך צווישן
געמאַלשאַפֿט. פֿיל לערער, אינזשעניר, קינסטלער, מענטשן פֿון פֿרייע פּראָפֿעסיעס, ... ס"ה איבער 30
פּערזאָן. צווישן אונדז איז אויך געפֿאָרן דער ליטווישער שרייבער Vienuolis, ... פֿון פֿרייער מיינע אַ
קאָלעגע. אין העלסינקי האָבן מיר פֿאַרבראַכט איין טאָג. די שטאָט איז מאָדערן מיט אַ צווייטע קולטור,
אָבער פֿיל, פֿיל שענער, דערמאָנט זייער פֿיל שטאָקהאָלם. פֿונעם טאָג האָבן מיר באַוויזן צו באַקוקן די
מערקווירדיקייטן פֿון שטאָט און אַרומיקע ווייטן. מיר האָבן זיך אָפּגעשטעלט אין וויבאָרג (ווייל - וויבאָרג).
די האָבן מיר באַקוקט די באַוווּסטע אַמאָליקע שוועדישע, שפּעטער רוסישע פֿעסטונג. ס'איז אויסגעצייכנט
אויסגעבויט מיט שטאַרקע פֿעסטונגען. געווען, אָבער, זייער אינטערעסאַנט. פֿון וויבאָרג זיינען מיר
אָפּגעפֿאָרן צו דער גרענעץ. דאָ איז ניט ... פֿרילינג געוואָרן. ניט ... מען פֿאַרבינדט
געגליכן זיך. ... - געווען ... , ניט געקענט ניט. דאָס האָט אונדז אַלעמען זייער דערפֿרייט.
די אַלעמען איז אַ מונטערע פֿרילינג שטימונג געוואָרן.
אונדזער ערשטן טאָג האָבן מיר געוווינט אין ... . באַזוכט פֿיל שטעט און שטעטלעך, קלויסטערן און
שיינע נאַטור ערטער. קיינמאָל ניט געמיינט, ווי מיר האָבן געהאַט פֿאַרשטאַנען. פֿיל מאָל אין טאָג
אויסגעקליבן זיך אין אַ אַנדער ערטער אַרום - אויסגאַנג. אַ מענטש איז געווען אונדזער פֿירער
מיט באַהאַנדלונג, ... , און דערבײַ קלאָרע דערוואַרטונג איז. די האָבן פֿון ... . און ...
דערנאָך אין פֿינלאַנד די „ווייסע נעכט" - זייער שיינע פֿאַרנאַכטן, ווי רויטע, גאָר ניט קאַלט, ווי ביי אונדז:
עס איז גוט ליינען און שרייבן. די ווייסע נעכט האָבן מיר גאָר ניט אויסגענוצט. „שלאָפֿן
וועל מען אין דער היים אויך קענען!" - אַזוי זיינען געווען די דאָזיקע מיינונג.
שוין איז אַלץ געווען פֿאַרטיק אויפֿן לענינגראַדער וואָקזאַל. מיר האָבן זיך צוריק אָפּגעשטעלט

During June and July Finland has the "white nights," it gets slightly darker than during the day. You are able to read and write during those "white nights," without any lights. We really took advantage of those nights. "We can catch up on our sleep at home," everyone was of the same opinion.

It was also beautiful crossing Ladoga Lake.[113] We stopped on the Island Volomo.[114] The island is of volcanic origin. The shores still have signs where the lava was flowing! Too bad that this beautiful "Garden of Eden" is inhabited by monks. The whole island, with its fertile fields, is the property of a Russian monastery. We were 200 kilometers from Leningrad—just an overnight trip by steamboat—but we were not able to get the Russian entrance visa. I was extremely sorry. Later on we met a large group from Czechoslovakia, and it turned out that they did go to Leningrad. I took it as being very logical.[115]

A beautiful picture is the famous waterfall Sumatra, on the River Voxi.[116] But it is not what it used to be. The waterfall is now partly fenced in and equipped with cheap electricity. Nevertheless, it is still one of the most beautiful natural wonders, and every year it attracts thousands of tourists. From Imatra I wrote to you a few words in haste. If I am not mistaken, they even put the stamp upside down.

What I enjoyed most in Finland were not the beautiful waters, high rocky mountains, not even the wonderful night lights; what really impressed me is the Finn as a human being. The Finn is a quiet, hard-working man. The beauty of the land is his biggest misfortune—very poor soil. The bread does not come to him easily. It takes a long time to earn the confidence of a Finn, but once he becomes your friend he will be forever loyal. All this, naturally, I was told, but what I myself observed was their honesty. Stealing is here a rarity. Remarkably, we got used to it instantly; as if we had a feeling that it couldn't be any other way. Many times we would leave our packages in the middle of the street somewhere on a bench, and be sure that no one would touch it, and many hours later we would, in fact, find it untouched. The same with mail deliveries. All Finns can read and write. Every household receives several daily newspapers. The mail is delivered daily by auto. In order to save time letters and newspapers are not delivered to each house; it is dropped on the sidewalk in designated places. I asked someone if they ever found anything missing, they were astonished at such a question, "Who would ever think of taking anything not belonging to him?" Yes, by us it would take a long, long time for people to think that way.

After some wandering around the country we returned to Helsinki,[117] where we stayed three whole days. In the course of that time we became "real citizens." We were all over the city. We really had a good time. From Helsinki we went by boat to Tallin,[118] where we spent two days. Tallin is as large as Kovno but much older and more interesting. In Estonia, I also visited Dorfat.[119] There I was interested in the university and particularly in Baker, the Judaic section. Too bad it was vacation time; nevertheless, I managed to see quite a bit. From Dorfat I went to Riga,[120] where I only stayed one day. I was already hurrying to be back in Šeduva by August 1st.[121]

That was the end of my adventure. It was beautiful and I will long remember episodes, events and experiences—it is all so interesting. I'm only sorry that I must share it with you through a letter, and

-3-

אויפֿן אינדזל וואַלאַמאָ. דאָס אינדזל איז פֿון וואַלקאַנישן אָפּשטאַם. די ברעגעס איז ניט קאַנטיק,
ווי די לאַוואַ איז געפֿלאָסן. מע זאָגט מיר, ווען איצט שפּאַנען גיך ... האָבן דערזען פֿינסטערע מאָנאַכן.
דאָס אַנדערע אינדזל מיט זײַנע פּראַכטפֿולע פֿעלדער איז דער אייגנטום פֿון די פּראַוואָסלאַווישע מאָנאַסטיר.
מיר זײַנען דאָ געווען די 20 קמ. פֿון לענינגראַד. דורך [illegible] האָבן מיר עס!
[illegible] אינדזל, אַלע, ניט געזען די רוסישע אָריענטיר-ליכט. דאָס האָט מיר שרעקלעך פֿאַרדראָסן. אַזוי
נאָענט געווען שוין. שפּעטער האָבן מיר אויסגעוועלט אויסגעהאַלטן די גרויסע גראָבע טשעפּען. האָט זיך
אַרויסגעוויזן, אַז מיר זײַנען דאָ געווען אין לענינגראַד. איך האָב עס אויסגעוואָגט פֿאַר זײַנע לעגיש.

די וואָנדערבאַרע ריזיקע שטאָט מיט זיך פֿון דער [illegible] טײַך [illegible].
סײַדן שוין אַלע ניט, ווײַסע נעכט. דער וואַסער־פֿאַל איז אַ גרויסער און [illegible] אין דרויסנדיק
מיט [illegible], כמעט, גאַנץ פֿינלאַנד, פֿון [illegible]. איז עס [illegible] פֿון די שענסטע
נאַטור [illegible] און ווען מיר קומען דאָרטן טויזנטער טוריסטן. פֿון אַמעריקע האָט. איך בין אַ גרויס
[illegible] געשריבן אַ פּאָר ווערטער. אויך כאָטש קיין [illegible] ניט, האָט מען מיר די [illegible]
מיט דער [illegible] אָרגאַנישע...

ווען מען איז [illegible], געווען אין פֿינלאַנד, דאָס זײַנען ניט די שענסטע [illegible], [illegible]
[illegible], ניט, אַפֿילו, די וואָנדערבאַרע ווײַסע נעכט; ווען מיר איז געווען געווען, דאָס איז דער פֿינער
אַלס מענטש.

דער פֿינער איז [illegible] שווײַגעט, [illegible] פֿון [illegible]. די שטימונג פֿון לאַנד איז
אַ גרויסער [illegible] זײַנע [illegible]. און די גרויסע [illegible] אין [illegible].
עס [illegible] זײַנע [illegible], די [illegible] די [illegible] פֿון די פֿינלענדער. [illegible] אַ, [illegible], [illegible],
איז אַ [illegible] [illegible]. דאָס [illegible], [illegible], האָט מען מיר [illegible]. [illegible], [illegible],
[illegible] געזאָגט, דאָס איז זײַנע [illegible]. [illegible] איז דאָ [illegible] [illegible]. און [illegible],
מיר האָבן [illegible] [illegible] [illegible]. מיר האָבן [illegible], [illegible] [illegible] ניט [illegible]. מיר
פֿלעגן [illegible] [illegible] געפֿינען אין [illegible] [illegible], [illegible] [illegible]. [illegible] [illegible], [illegible] [illegible]
עס ניט [illegible], פֿלעגן מיר שפּעטער, און [illegible] [illegible], [illegible] [illegible] [illegible]. דאָס [illegible] איז אויך
מיט דער [illegible] [illegible]. די פֿינער [illegible] אַלע [illegible] און [illegible]. [illegible] [illegible] [illegible] [illegible].

such a small, small part at that. In the meantime, I am satisfied with even that opportunity.

My dear Hindalla!

As I was finishing my letter I received your photo. You cannot even imagine my joy! I thank you for the present. Oh, how fast the year went by. It is good that way; let it run. It is a good thing that I am kept busy these days and I have no time to think about a lost year and feel sorry that it was fruitless.

I already wrote a little too much. Stay well. Give my regards to everyone at home.

Your

B.

צײַטונגען טעלער. װאָס זײַ האָבן אַלע טײל אַװעקגעפֿירט מיט אַװטאָס קעגן לאַנדז. בײַ צו שפּעטער צײַט,
טרונקט מען די ברױט און צײַטונגען און שטײט ניט אַרײַן, נאָר מ׳לײענט װאָס װעט זײַן שפּעטער אין ספּעציעל
אײנגעאָרדנטע ערטער. בּכלל געבראַכט אײניקע פּאַפּירן, צו טאָמער דו די קרימינאַל זשורנאַל פֿירפֿולן געמאַכט?
זײ האָבן זיך געװוּנדערט אױף אונדזער פּרעזענץ — װײסמען װאָס מ׳קאָן צו נעמען טשאָלאַס יענעמס?...
יאָ, דײ אונדזער װאָס מ׳קאָן לאַנג נעמען, ביז מ׳װעט עס דערגרייכן אַזױ צו זאָגן.

נאָכן אַרומװאַנדערן איבער לאַנדז, זײַנען מיר אָנגעקומען קײן העלסינקי. אָנגעשטאַנען האָבן מיר זיך
פֿאַרבראַכט גאַנצע דרײַ טעג. פֿאַר די דרײַ צײַט זײַנען מיר די געװען גאַנצע דינער... די גאַנצע שטאָט
איז פֿול געװען פֿון אונדז. מיר האָבן זיך טיקע גאָר ניט שלעכט פֿאַרבראַכט. פֿון העלסינקי זײַנען מיר
אָפּגעפֿאָרן מיטן שיף קײן טאַלין, װוּ מיר זײַנען אָפּגעװען צװײ טעג. טאַלין איז אַ גרױס, אַ קרוינע.
אָרט פֿיל עלטער און אינטערעסאַנטער. אין עסטלאַנד האָט מען נאָך אַלץ דאָלאַרן דערפֿונען. דערנאָך האָט
מיר אינטערעסירט די אוניװערסיטעט אין, דאָרפּ, די ... אַפּטײלונג דאָרט. ... , װאָס טאַלין, פּאַרין, דאָך
האָט אין אַלץ אײנציק פֿיל געזען. פֿון דאָרטן זײַנען מיר אָפּגעפֿאָרן קײן ריגאַ. דאָ האָבן מיר
פֿאַרבראַכט נאָר אײן טאָג. בּכלל איז שױן געװען. װי זיך טרעפֿן אַװעק האָט זיך שױן געענדיקט
זײַן אײַן רעזערװע.

אַזױ האָט זיך געענדיקט מײַן אַװאַנטורע... טאָגן, יאָרן, שױן געװען, און לאַנג װעל איך
האָבן צו דערמאָנען זיך עפּיזאָדן, פּאַסירונגען, אימפּרעסיעס — טאָמער דײַן אינטערעסאַנט דאָס אַלץ.
בּרידערלעך ניט. װאָס בּכלל דער דאָס װאָס אימגעבן דײַן אָדרעס, און דאָס אַזױ װײניק,
אַזױ װײניק. בּכן דערװײַל צופֿרידן, אָדרעס, און מיט נײַע מעלדונגען.

מײַן טײַערע הינדעלע!

ערגעץ אין ... מײַן בריװ האָט איך באַקומען דײַן פֿאָטאָגראַפֿיע. קומט זיך אײניקע פּאָסטען מײַן
שמחה. און דאָך דער פּנים דער מתנה. און, װי ... ... װאָס װעט. גאָט אַזױ, דאַל
עס לױבן. טאָמער גוט, װאָס די טאָג האָב איך שטאַרק געדאַנקען און האָב קײן צײַט ניט צו קלערן.
װאָס די פֿאָטאָגראַפֿיע יאָ. און באַזוכן, װאָס מ׳װעט אַלץ צו באַקומען.
שױן שלום צופֿיל דערצײלן.

בלײַב געזונט און שטאַרק. גרוס פֿון מאַמע ... אין שטאָט. דײַן ב.

Šeduva, 28/VIII 38.

מײַן טײַערע הינדעלע!

דײַן בריוו ערהאַלטן. איך דאַנק דיר פֿאַר דער גרויסער אויפֿמערקזאַמקייט צו מײַן געבוירן-
טאָג און פֿאַר דער מתנה, נאָך אַמאָל, אַ שיין, האַרציקן דאַנק. דאָס איז מיר אַ טײַערער
פֿאַר אַלץ, וואָס כ'האָב.

אַ שאָד, וואָס דײַן פּאָמיס איז שוין צו שפּעט. דו האָסט דײַן זײַט וועגן געהערט
פֿון זיי. מײַן שוועסטער איז הײַנט, וויפֿל שוועסטער אַלע אויפֿגעגעבן האָט דיר געשריבן.
איז זי שוין אַוועק פּאַלעסטינע געפֿאָרן?

דערווײַלן האָסט, אָרעמע, פֿאַר די פֿאָר מאָנאַטן די כּבֿוד, אַ ביסל. צו, סוסווא קלאָר
דיכטער צו לייענען! כ'האָב, אַמאָל. הנאה פֿון דעם.

און איך מײַן פֿראַנצויזיש שוין די ערשטע טעג געמאַכט! כ'האָב סוואָ דיר גוט צוגעבן.
געוויס וועט מען נעמען אַ ביסל דאָס, ביז צו וועלן נאָך קענען לייענען פֿרײַ פֿראַנצויזיש - פֿון
וועלן דײַן ניט קענען זיך מיט דעם - פֿון דעסטוועגן האָב איך דיר שוין האָבנס
געשיקט אַ פֿראַנצויזיש ביכל... כוויס, מבֿול דאָס ניט אונטערשטופּן, אָרעם צוגעבן אַ וואָרט
מיט שפּעט דײַן ניט. האָב איך אַ געטאָן.

איך האָב פֿאַר דער צײַט ווייניק-וואָס גוטס האָבן צו לייענען. ייִדישע ביכער האָב איך
לעצטנס געהאַט צוגעבן „שטעטל און ווײַזן" און „פֿרילינג". צוגעבן פֿלעג איך נאָך צו לייענען „די ברידער
אַשכּנזי". איך האָב אַ אין גיבן צו האָרן. מ'וואָרט צו מײַן ליבער אַלע טאָג אַלע דער
מאַמע אויסגעצײַכנט. די גאַנצע פּויליש אויסגאַבע פֿון „די ברידער אַשכּנזי" האָט מען קאָנפֿיסקירט.

צווישן מיר אַליין איז ליבער געגעבן אַ ביסל. פּוילן איז דאָך דער וועלט אונדזער איינציקע
קולטור שפּײַכלער. וואָס אַנהאַלטנדיק ייִדיש דין און ייִדיש טעמעס, אַפֿילו. די גאַנצע וועלט.
וויסט די טאָג סכנות, כאָטש ווי גאַנץ געשאָפֿן. אין לעטלאַנד, עסטלאַנד און פֿינלאַנד - דאָ
איז אַליין ניט.

מיר איז אויסגעלאָזן, דערציילן די דערציילער לאַנדאַו, אַליין צו דערציילן זיך מיט די
דערציילער ווידן. מיר וויל האָב איך געוואוינט מײַן שטאָט האָלב. צו האָבן דאָרטן אַ גאַנץ

Šeduva, 28/VIII/1938[122]

(August 28, 1938)

My Dear Hindalla!

Received your letter. I thank you so much for your special attention to my birthday, and for your present again many, many thanks. This is now more precious to me than anything I own.

Too bad your vacation is now at an end. You did so little for yourself. I can imagine how much anxiety Yvette's operation caused you. Has she now completely recovered?

I can see you accomplished quite a bit in those few months. Look, what good books you are reading! I am very pleased. And also in French you made the first step. I hope it will go well for you. It will certainly take quite some time until you will be able to read French fluently—too much time you will probably not be able to spend—nevertheless, I sent you out a French book in advance... I know, I don't have to push you, but a little encouragement doesn't hurt. So I did it.

Lately, I read very few worthwhile books. Most recently I read *Steel and Iron* and *Spring* by Singer,[123] in Yiddish. I still have not been able to get *The Brothers Ashkenazi*, by Singer. I hope to acquire it soon. We, here in Lithuania, are waiting every day for the American publication. The Polish publication of *The Brothers Ashkenazi* has been confiscated; so we, in Lithuania, have to suffer. Poland, so far, is our only source of cultural nourishment—even where Yiddish books and Yiddish theatre are concerned. Here, in our country, outside of the daily press, almost nothing is produced. In Latvia, Estonia, and Finland there is not even that much.

I had a chance, while visiting those countries, to get acquainted with their Jewish people, the few I found in Stockholm. Considering, though, they have a fairly well-developed school system. It is only thanks to the couple hundred Jewish families from Poland and Lithuania who wandered in there after the war. I found there a few teachers from Kovno. They are not badly off, but they complain of the unfriendliness of the Jews in that country. They miss Lithuania. In Finland live about 2,000 Jews altogether. Their whole Jewishness consists of the fact that they support a rabbi and are punctual with their payments to the "Karen-Kayemeth"[124] (Jewish National Fund). Very few of them can read Yiddish; they don't know about Yiddish newspapers; consequently, they are little aware of the Jewish problems in other countries. We had plenty of laughs at their expense and they regretted it good naturedly.

Also, in Estonia, it's not much better—no Yiddish newspaper, no Yiddish book. The Jews in Estonia, it appears to me, are the only ones who still have their own autonomy. Unfortunately, there is no one to use it. Everything lies here in the hands of a few Zionists. They even established the Judaica Division of the Darfat University. Nobody realizes, though, that some ten or twenty elementary schools for Jewish children is much, much more important.

The Latvian Jews could perhaps accomplish more were it not that everything is prohibited; except the "Agudah,"[125] which occupies itself with culture from quite a different direction. The only Yiddish newspaper, therefore, is by the "Agudah." One can well imagine the "culture" the "Agudah" can bring

פֿון פּוילן [illegible] הונדערט פֿיר די [illegible] טויזנט און ווערן. שוין זיי, פֿיר ווי, [illegible]
[illegible] געשריבן [illegible] מלחמה [illegible] ניט דורך האָבן [illegible], לעבן און
ניט [illegible] אַלע [illegible], [illegible] ניט זיי צו [illegible] פֿון
ליבע ניט [illegible] זיי ייִדן [illegible] פֿון די סבֿיבֿה [illegible]

אין [illegible] ייִדן [illegible] די [illegible] לעבן [illegible] אין
[illegible] ... קומט [illegible] פֿון [illegible] די אַלץ, [illegible]
[illegible] זיי און זיי האָבן; ניט זיי [illegible] ייִדישע [illegible] פֿון זיי [illegible] פֿון [illegible],
[illegible] צו [illegible]. [illegible] אין [illegible] האָבן ייִדן [illegible]
[illegible] האָבן זיי און, זיי פֿון [illegible].

די [illegible]. ייִדיש [illegible], ניט [illegible] ניט [illegible] אין [illegible]
[illegible], [illegible] האָבן [illegible] די [illegible] זיין [illegible]
[illegible] די האָבן זיי. [illegible] פֿון די [illegible] אויף [illegible] מיט [illegible]
ניט, [illegible] [illegible] די [illegible]
[illegible] פֿיל, פֿיל [illegible] ייִדישע [illegible] שוין [illegible]

[illegible] די [illegible] ייִדן [illegible] די
[illegible] ייִדישע [illegible] די [illegible] 13 [illegible] פֿון [illegible]
[illegible] די [illegible] "[illegible]" די [illegible] פֿון [illegible] און
[illegible] ייִדישע די [illegible]...

נו, שוין, [illegible], צופֿיל [illegible]...

[illegible] ניט, [illegible] ? [illegible] ווי [illegible] ניט [illegible] שרייבן [illegible] דער [illegible]
[illegible] האָט [illegible] ייִדישע די [illegible] אין [illegible] די
[illegible] די האָט [illegible] און [illegible] האָבן.
[illegible] ניט [illegible] ווי [illegible] ? [illegible] ווי ? [illegible] וואָס [illegible]
[illegible] ?

[illegible] - [illegible] און [illegible] ייִדן [illegible]. [illegible] ב.

Šeduva 4/X/1938[127]

(October 4, 1938)

My Dear Hindalla!

For a few days already I have been trying to write to you. Every day I would put it off until tomorrow. And what tomorrow will bring was difficult to know. You, undoubtedly, were concerned with our fate here, and you most certainly sighed a sigh of relief when you found out that there is again peace in the world. For all of us here, however, the "new peace" was terribly disappointing.[128] How far does this injustice dominate the world! Agreements, beautiful promises and pledges—everything, everything adds up to just nothing. One feels sorry, indeed, that morality of force goes forward and conquers, and makes a joke of it all—one's dignity and humanity.

Fear mixed with hope embraces all of us these days. Perhaps a new world will arise, a better one. We, Jews, can rejoice very little today. The present peace concerns us very, very much.

I am now reading Osherowitz's *Marie Antoinette*. This book, seems to me, is not any worse than Stephen Zweig's[129] *Marie Antoinette*, perhaps even more suspenseful. How fitting the actions are for our times as well! It looks like the high society which makes history has always been corrupt, and so will always remain.

Dear Hindalla, consider yourself lucky that it is your fate to live in more humane and freer circumstances. Accept everything which the free America offers you, take advantage of every opportunity to progress and surpass your peers. In America one must not be modest! Teach yourself to be different than you are. How painful it is to learn such wisdom! But such must one be in a "Land of Accomplishments."

In the meantime, your world is still your school. But even there, there is enough place to rise up. And that is why I am pleased that you decided this year to join several school clubs. That is not only for a good time!

By me no special news. In addition to Sioma, now a boyfriend of mine is also working in the drugstore with me. I wrote to you about him before. He is a person on whom I can rely completely. Consequently, I have now much free time. I go away somewhere for a day or two. I can also thank him for my trip abroad. We get along very well. All expenses we split in half. We subscribe to several newspapers, we buy books, the radio, the bicycle—everything belongs to both of us. Sometimes we invite one of our classmates—such days are especially interesting to us. It only happens, though, once in a great big while. All in all, it is quite lonesome. I generally pass the time with a book or by the radio. The last few days I didn't move from the radio at all—there was so much news, and I had to listen to all the stations...

Otherwise, I'd rather listen to music. I have acquainted myself with many new operas and symphonies. I am already well acquainted with all the famous singers and their favorite repertoire. However, I am not sufficiently acquainted with the history of music; I will in a few days try to obtain some literature on that subject. I get particular pleasure out of talking and reading about music.

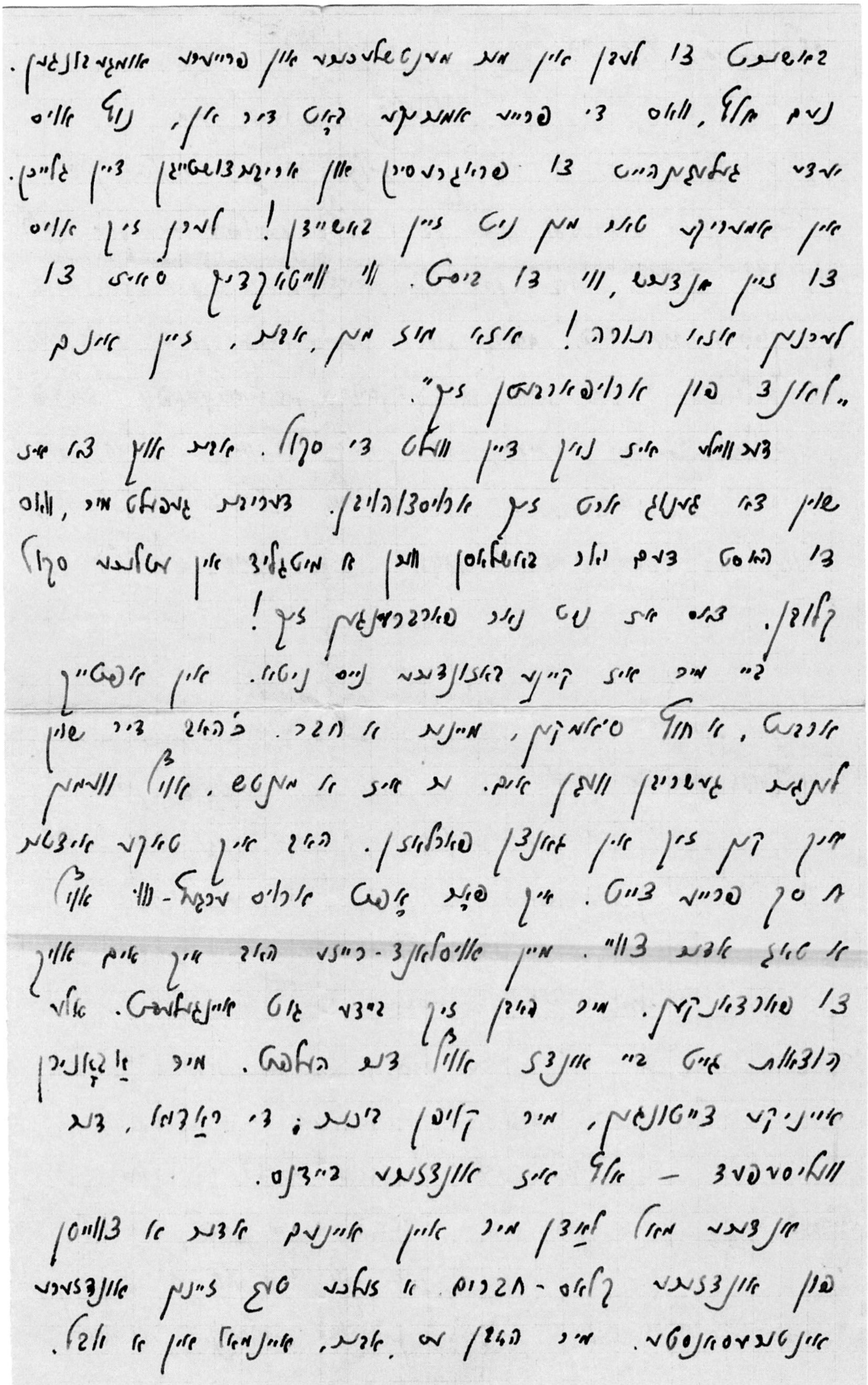
באַשערט צו לעבן אין אַ מענטשלעכער און פרייער אומגעבונגען.
נעם אַלץ, וואָס די פרייע אַטמאָספער גיט דיר אײַן, נוץ אויס
יעדע געלעגנהייט צו פּראָגרעסירן און אויסצובעסערן דײַן גלויבן.
אין אַמעריקע טאָר מען ניט זײַן באַשיידן! לערן זיך אַלעס
צו זײַן אַנדערש, ווי צו ביסט. ווי ווײַטער דיך טאָרס צו
לערנען איבער תורה! איבער איז מען אָדער, זײַן אײנס
„לאָנג פון אַרויפּאַרבעטן זיך".
דאָס וויכטיקסטע איז ניט זײַן ווערט די סקול. אָדער אַלץ צו מיר
שוין צו גענוג אָרט זיך אַרויסצוהויבן. דערווײַל געפעלט מיר, וואָס
די האָסט דעם יאָר באַשלאָסן וואַן אַ מיטגליד אין מעלבער סקול
קלובן. דאָס איז ניט נאָר פאָרגרעסערן זיך!
בײַ מיר איז קיינע באַזונדערע נײַס ניטאָ. און אויסגעשטיין
אָרבעט, אַ חול סיגאַרעטן, מיינע אַ חבר. בּרוך דיר שוין
לאַנגע געשריבן וועגן אים. ער איז אַ מענטש, וואָס וואַקסט
מיט דער זין אין זאָנגען פאָרלעזן. האָב איך טויגנע אויבנס
אַ סך פרײַע צײַט. איך פּאָר זעט אַרויס עלעקטרע- און
אַ טאָג אָדער צוויי. מײַן אויסלאַנד-בריוו האָב איך אים אויך
צו פאָרזאָרגן. מיר האָבן זיך גערעדט גוט אײַנגעשטעלט. אַלע
הויזער איז בײַ אונדז אויך דער האָלט. מיר זיך געוווינען
אייניקע צייטונגען, מיר קויפן ריכט; די רעדיאָ, דער
טעלעוויזער — אַלץ איז אונדזער בעסטן.
אונדזער מאַל לאָזן מיר אויך איינעם אָדער אַ צוויי
פֿון אונדזערע קלאַס-חברים. אַ צווייטער טאָג זײַנען אונדזערע
איינטערעסאַנטע. מיר האָבן, אָדער, איינמאָל אין אַ וואָך.

Though myself no musician, it is one of my weaknesses.

From Šeduva I have no news to tell you. Probably nothing's been happening. Yes, not long ago Elke Friedlander had exams for 5 grades. The way it looks, she did not pass everything. She surely must have written you about it.

Any day now we are awaiting I. Opatoshu[130] in Lithuania. I will try not to miss the opportunity of hearing him, at least one lecture of that great Jewish writer.

No more today. Regards to your relatives and friends.

Be well and study well.

Your

B.

P.S. I regret that I could not get any postage coupon today.

-3-

אין אַלגעמיין איז גאַנץ אומעטיקלעך. איך פֿאַרברענג אַם
מייסטן מיט די ביך, אַדער בײַם ראַדיאָ. די לעצטע טעג
בין איך גאָר פֿון אַפּאַראַט ניט אָפּגעטראָטן — ס׳איז זיך
געווען אַזוי פֿיל נײַס, און יעדן זייגער מוז מען זיך אויסהערן...
אַזוי טאָג האָב איך, ווייסט, געהערט מוזיק. כ׳האָב זיך
צוגעהערט צו אַ סך נײַע אָפּערעס און סימפֿאָניעס. כ׳האָב שוין אַלע
באַרימטע זינגער און זייער באַליבטסטע רעפּערטואַר. ס׳פֿעלט מיר נאָך
ווערדי. מיט באַוווּנדערונג קוק איך אין דער גייסטער פֿון מוזיק.
כ׳וויל די טעג זען זיך אײַנצוהערן ליטעראַטור אויך דעם
געפֿינט. כ׳האָב די באַזונדערע הנאה צו רעדן און לייענען וועגן
מוזיק. בפֿרט אַליין קען איך זיך ניט קיין מוזיקער — אויסער
פֿון מײַנע שוואַכקייטן...
פֿון שאַבעס נײַס האָב איך דיר געוואָלט וועט צום שרײַבן.
משפּחה׳ס פּאַקעטן צו גאָרניט. וועגן מיר פֿרײַדלעך האָט
זיי ניט לאַנג געהאַלטן אין קוואַטש מעגלעכקייטן פֿאַר 5 קלאַסן.
ווי מע שיקט, האָט זי ניט אַלץ אַלע אויפֿגעהאַלטן. געוויס האָט
זי דיר שוין געשריבן וועגן דעם.
די טעג מכבדן מיר צו אין ליסט י. אָפּאַטאָשו. כ׳וועל
זיך באַמיִען ניט צו דורכלייענען די געדאַנקען צווישן בּריוו
אַלע אין כּתבֿיאַט פֿונעם גרויסן יידישן שרײַבטשיקער.
פֿײַנט מיט ניט.
איך גריס דײַנע אַלגעמיינע און באַקאַנטע.
בלײַבט געזונט און לעבן זיך גוט — דײַן ב.

<u>פ.ס.</u> דײַן קליינע האָב איך היינט, לײַדער, ניט געקראָגן ז.ג.

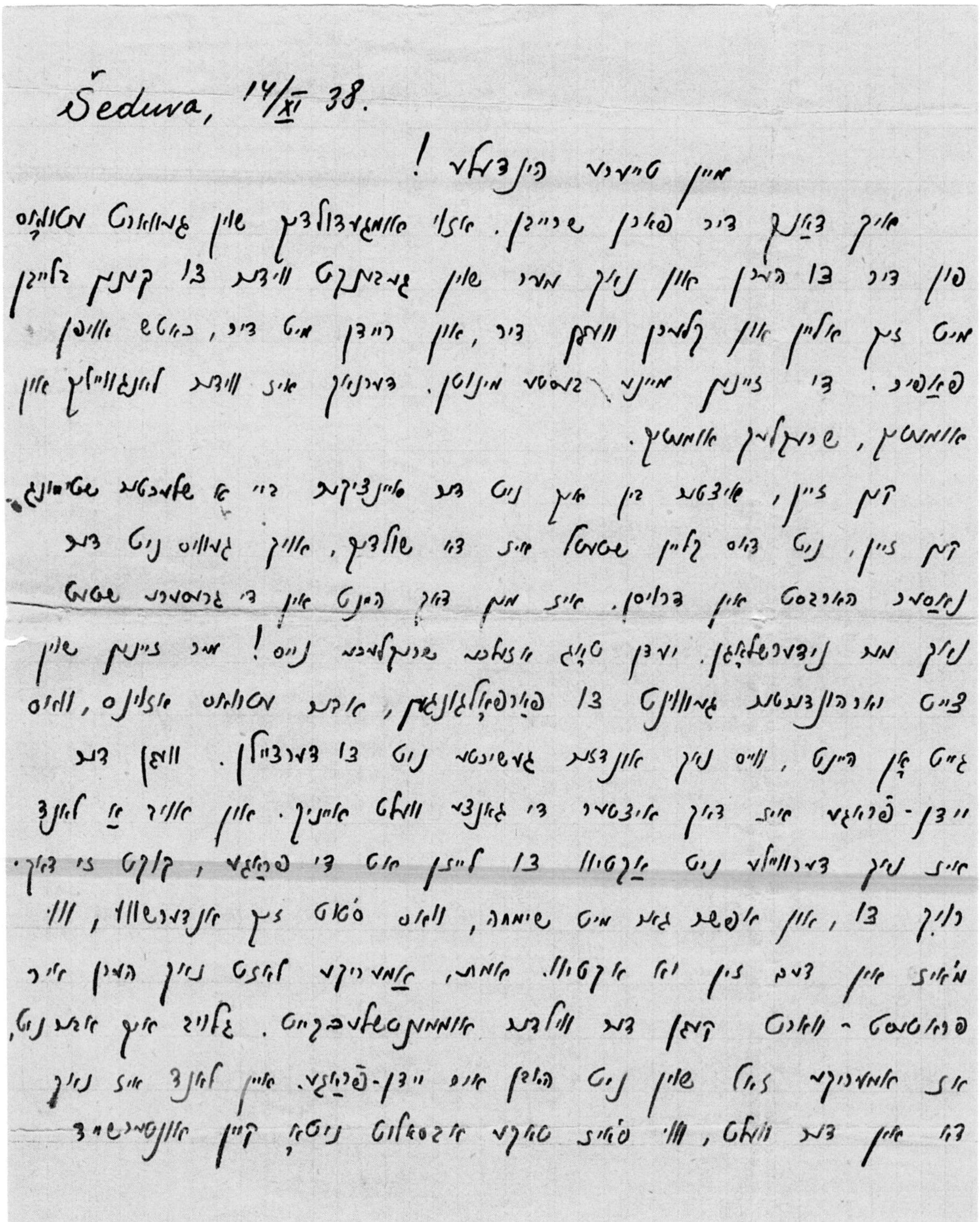

Šeduva, 14/XI 38.

מיין טייערע הינדעלע!

איך דאַנק דיר פֿאַרן שרייבן. איך האָב אומגעדולדיק שוין געוואַרט מכתּבֿים
פֿון דיר צו האָבן און איך האָב שוין געבענקט ווידער צו קענען רעדן
מיט זיך אַליין און לייענען וועגן דיר, און רעדן מיט דיר, כאָטש אויפֿן
פּאַפּיר. די זײַנען מײַנע בעסטע מינוטן. דערנאָך איז ווידער לאַנגווײַליק און
אומעטיק, שרעקלעך אומעטיק.

דאָ זײַנען, אויסער דיר [illegible] ניט דער [illegible] די אַ שלעכטע שטימונג.
דאָ זײַנען, ניט דאָס קליין שטעטל איז דאָ שולדיק, אויך געוויס ניט דער
נאָוועמבער האַרבסט און דרויסן. איז מען דאָך הײַנט און די גרעסערע שטעט
[illegible]. יעדן טאָג [illegible] שרעקלעכע נײַעס! מיר זײַנען שוין
צײַט [illegible] געוואוינט צו פֿאַרפֿאָלגונגען, אָבער [illegible], וואָס
גייט אין הײַנט, וואָס איך [illegible] ניט צו דערציילן. וועגן דער
ייִדן־פֿראַגע איז דאָך איצטער די גאַנצע וועלט [illegible]. און אויך [illegible]
איז [illegible] ניט [illegible] צו לייענען וועגן די פֿראַגע, [illegible]
[illegible] צו, און [illegible] מיט שׂמחה, וואָס [illegible], [illegible]
[illegible] אין [illegible]. [illegible], [illegible] ניט [illegible]
[illegible]. [illegible]
איז [illegible] שוין ניט [illegible] ייִדן־פֿראַגע. און [illegible] איז [illegible]
דאָ אין דער וועלט, [illegible] קיין [illegible]

Šeduva 14/XI/1938[131]

(November 14, 1938)

My Dear Hindalla!

I thank you for your letter. I waited so impatiently to hear from you and even more I longed to be able to be alone and think about you, and talk to you, even though on paper. These are my most precious moments. And then it is boring again and lonesome, terribly lonesome.

It may be that now I am not the only one in a bad mood.[132] It may be that it is not the fault of the small town; certainly not the rainy autumn weather outside. People in the larger cities are even more pessimistic. Every day such terrible news! For centuries already we have been used to persecutions, but such as is going on now our history has never seen. About the "Jewish question" the whole world is united.[133] And if a country is not yet actively engaged in solving that problem it looks quietly on and, perhaps, even with joy, at what the others are doing, where they are actively engaged. True, America lets its protests be heard against the wild inhumanities, still I don't believe that America does not have any "Jewish problem." There is only one country in the world where there is absolutely no difference between Jew and non-Jew—and that is Russia. But the Soviet power chooses now to lead an isolation policy and its voice against Jewish slaughter, as well as its voice in other important matters, is not heard. The Jews in Russia are not much interested in the fate of the Jews in other lands. They already have a 20-year education!

We, in Lithuania, have it good in comparison. But the heart aches for the others...And, in addition, the premonition that something terrible is approaching.

Do you remember, not long ago, I was sorry that I had to give up settling in Klaipeda? Today it is much better as it is. Yes, I have already given much up. I still dreamed of studying abroad. I also wanted to get my doctorate. What didn't I want? Could I have foreseen that a time would come that thousands of Jewish students would be thrown out of all European universities? And, again, I am "happy" that it remained as is...

In times like these we must all be armed with much courage and hope in order to endure. We must hope that this is only a temporary outburst of human wickedness, with all our strength we must believe in better times.

Similarly, not long ago, I. Opatoshu[134] comforted us and cheered us up, discussing Jewish culture problems. I took a ride to Savl to hear him. His wise and fitting stand made an impression on everyone. Too bad that such guest speakers who could cheer us up, from time to time, come to us so seldom.

By me no special news. If the mood were better I could be as "happy as a lark." So far I have a position with a good salary, and can afford all the pleasures (in Šeduva!) Why should I even think about not being able to progress, that under different circumstances I would have advanced long ago? Why really think about it? The trouble is, I think...

And what's news with you? As I see it, you have work "over your head." Why don't you tell me what

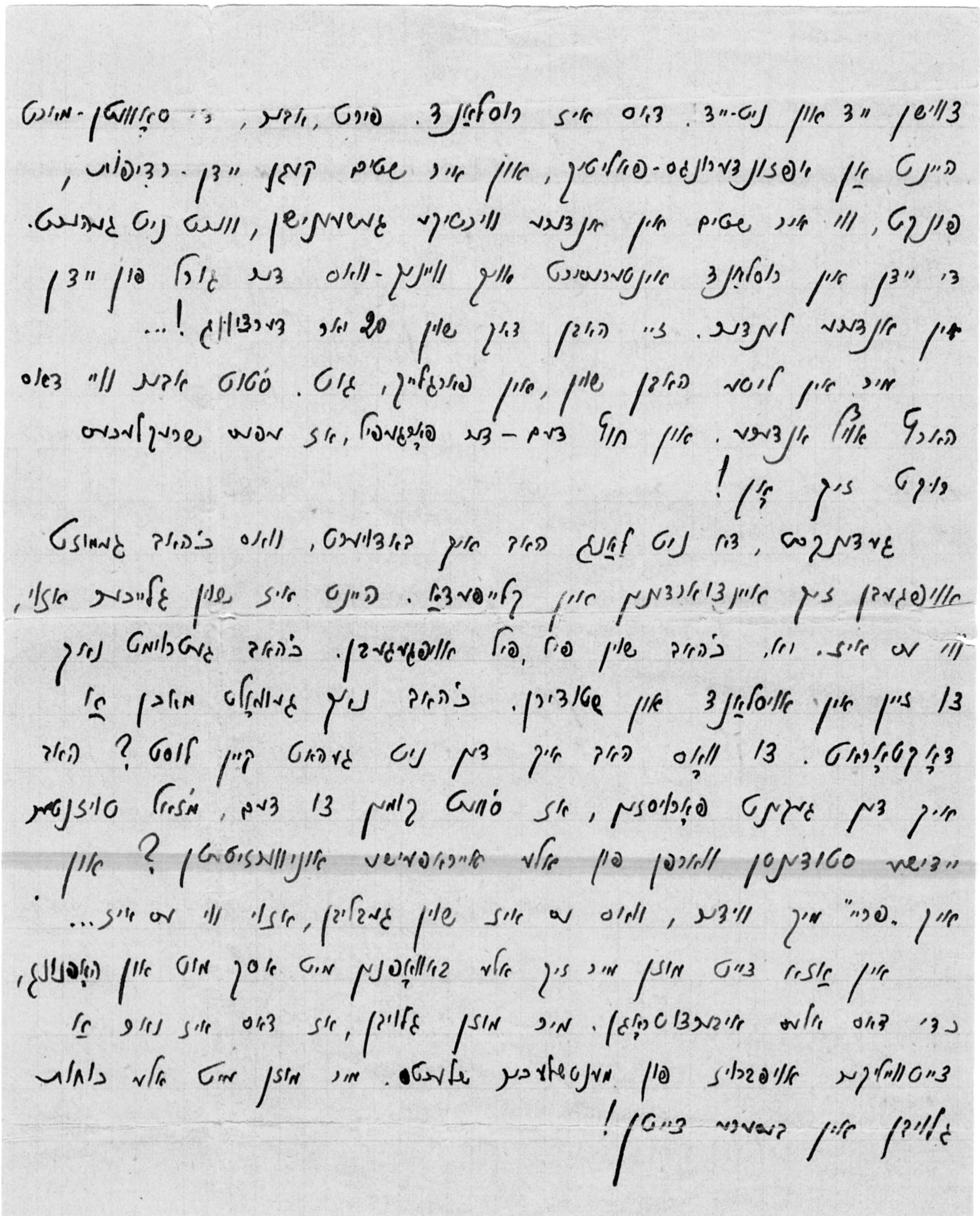

צווישן ייִדן און ניט־ייִדן. דאָס איז רוסלאַנד. פֿאָרט, אָבער, די סאָוועטן־מאַכט
האַלט אין אויפֿבויונגס־פּאָליטיק, און איר שטייט קעגן ייִדן־רדיפֿות,
פּונקט, ווי איר שטייט אין אַנדערע ווירטשאַפֿטלעכע געשעפֿטישן, וואָס ניט געמאַכט.
די ייִדן אין רוסלאַנד אונטערשטיצט אויך ווייניק־וואָס דער גורל פֿון ייִדן
אין אַנדערע לענדער. זיי האָבן זיך שוין 20 יאָר דערצויג!...
מיר אין לאַנד האָבן שוין, און פֿאַרגלײַך, גוט. סטאַט אָבער ווי דאָס
האָרכט אַלץ אַנדערש. און חוץ דעם — דער פּאָליטיק, איז מען שפּיגלענדיק
פֿייגט זיך זיין!
געדענקסט, דו ניט לאַנג האָב איך באַוויזן, וואָס כ'האָב געמיינט
אויפֿגעבן זיך אײַנצואָרדענען אין קלאַסטער. הײַנט איז שוין גלײַכגילטיק אַזוי,
ווי עס איז. ווײַל, כ'האָב שוין פֿיל, פֿיל אויפֿגעגעבן. כ'האָב געטראַכט נאָך
צו זיין אין אויסלאַנד און שטודירן. כ'האָב נאָך געמיינט מאַכן זיך
דאָקטאָראַט. צו וואָס האָב איך דען ניט געהאַט קיין לוסט? האָב
איך דען געלערנט פֿילאָסאָפֿיע, איז סוף געווען צו דעם, מזל טויזנטער
ייִדישע סטודענטן וואַרפֿן פֿון אַלע אייראָפּעישע אוניווערסיטעטן? און
און "ספֿרים" איך ווידער, וואָס עס איז שוין געבליבן, אַזוי ווי עס איז...
אין אַלגעמיין דאַרף מען מיר זיך אַלע באַוועגונגען מיט אַסך מוט און האָפֿענונג,
כּדי דאָס אַלץ איבערצוטראָגן. מיר מוזן גלייבן, אַז דאָס איז נאָר צו
צײַטווײַליקע איבערגאַנג פֿון מענטשלעכער שלעכטס. מיר מוזן מיט אַלע כּוחות
גלייבן אין בעסערע צײַטן!

kind of work you are doing in art school? Do you draw with charcoal, or do you paint with colors? I remember how well you used to master colors. And in school, what are you covering this year? And how do you like the subjects? And how about French? You, undoubtedly, left it for another summer. And what films have you seen lately? And what do you hear from Lola? Oh, I ask, and I ask—tell me, Hindalla, about everything. I am also very pleased that you are a little involved with music.

That is all for now. My friendliest regards to your close ones and acquaintances.

Be well and study hard.

Your

B.

P.S. Today they are showing a Jewish film, *Tkias Kaf.*[135] It probably won't be any better than the other Jewish films. About a week ago I enjoyed the film *Once Upon a Spring*[136] with Jeanette MacDonald. Did you see it?

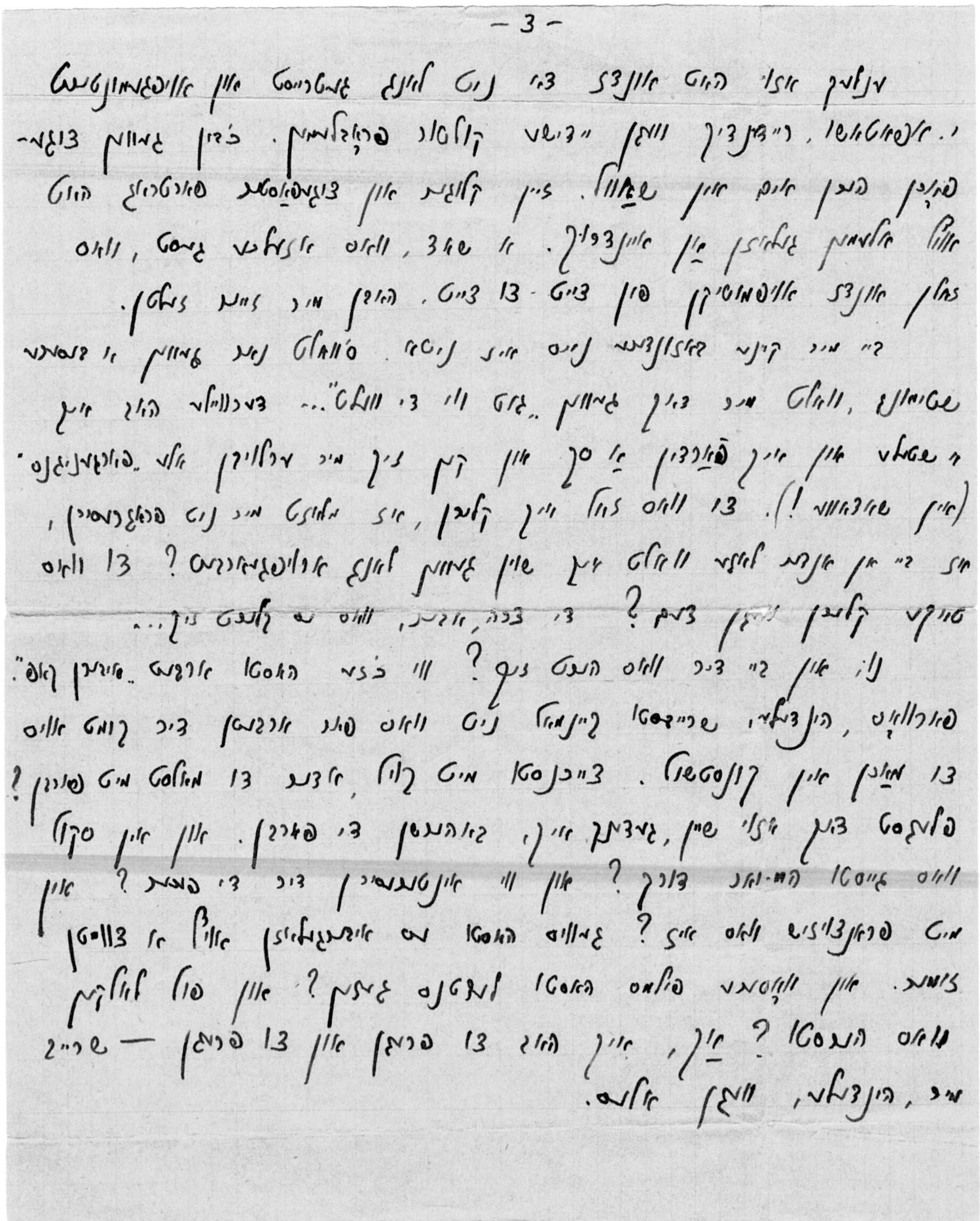

– 3 –

ענלעך אזוי האט אונדז די נאכט לאנג געטרייסט און אויפגעמונטערט
י. אפּאטאשו, ריידנדיק וועגן ייִדישע קולטור פּראבלעמען. כ'בין געווען צוגע-
פאלן פון אים און שמואל. זיין קלוגע און צוגעפּאסטע פארטראג האט
אלע אלעמען געלאזן אין אנדענק. א שעה, וואס אזעלכע געסט, וואס
בלײַבן אונדז אויפמונטערן פון צייט צו צייט. האבן מיר זייער געלאזן.
די מיר קענען דערציילן ניט אין גאנצן. ס'וואלט נאך געווען די זעלבע
שטימונג, וואלט מיר דאך געווען „גוט ווי די וועלט"... דערווייל האב איך
די שטאט און איך פארלירן זיך און דאן זיך מיר ערלויבן אלע „פארגעניגנס"
(אין שטאטווע!). צו וואס זאל איך קלערן, איז מאכט מיר ניט פארגעניגן,
איז די אין אנדערע לענדער וואלט זיך שוין געווען לאנג אויפגעמונטערט? צו וואס
טויגט קלערן וועגן דעם? די דבה, אויגן, וואס ס'קלערט זיך...
נו, און די דיך וואס הערט זיך? ווי כ'בין האסטו אויפגע „פארן ראש".
פארוואס, הינדעלע, שרייבסטו קיינמאל ניט וואס פאר אויגן דיך קומט אלעס
צו מאכן און קאנטשטן. צייכנסטו מיט קולי, אדער צו מאלסט מיט פארבן?
פלעגסט דאך אזוי שיין, געדענק איך, באהעפטן די פארבן. און אין סקול
וואס גייסטו האבן דארט? און ווי אינטערעסירן דיך די פאַכן? און
מיט פראנצויזיש וואס איז? געווען האסטו עס אויסגעלערנט אויף צו צוויטן
צייט. און וועסטו פילאס האסטו לערנען געקענט? און פאר לוליקן
וואס הערסטו? איך, איך האב צו פרעגן און צו פרעגן — שרייב
מיר, הינדעלע, וועגן אלעס.

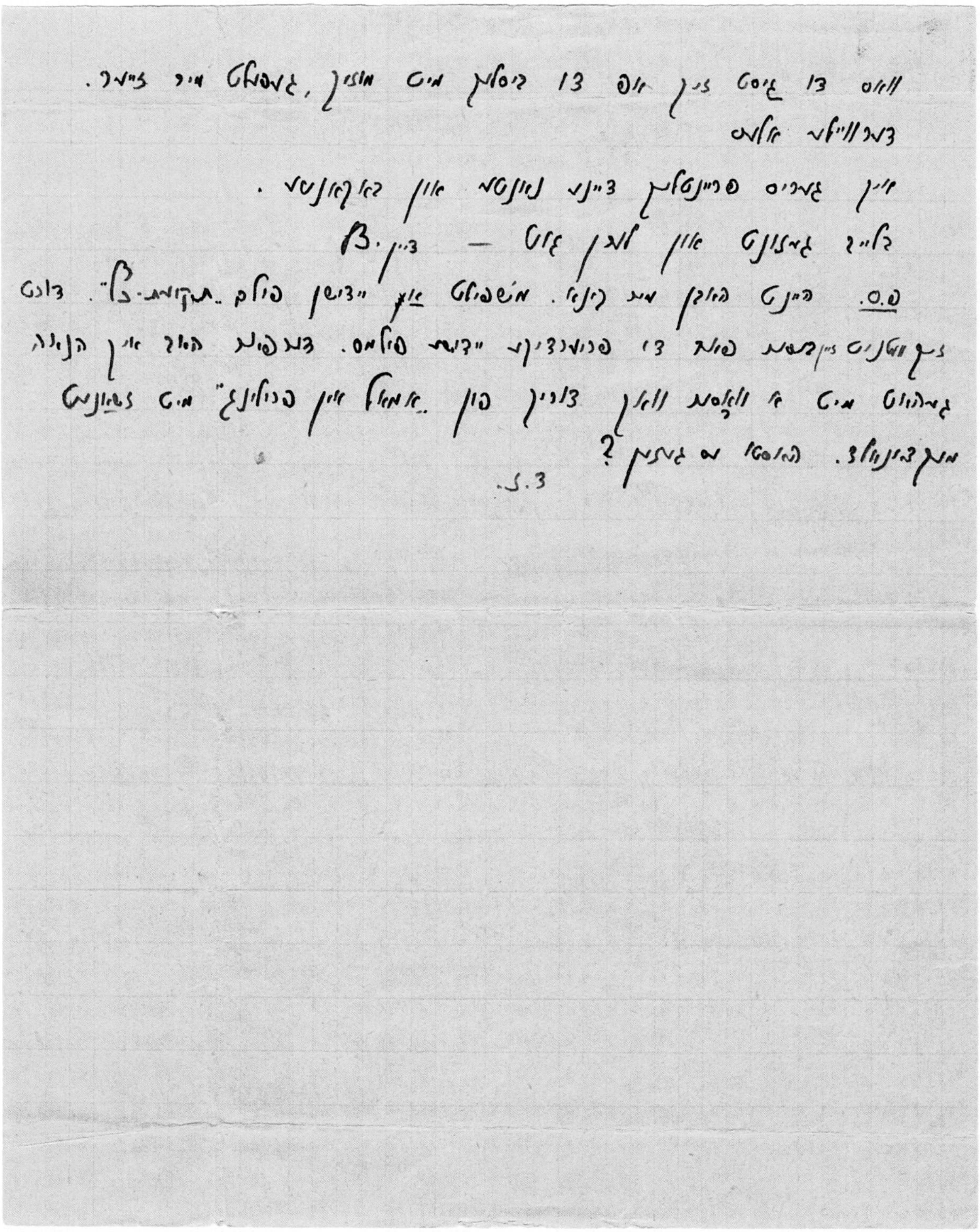

וואס דו גיסט זיך אויף 13 ביסלעך מיט מוזיק, געפעלט מיר זייער.

דערווייל אלעס

זיין [illegible] פריינטלעך דיינע נאנטע און באקאנטע.

בלייב געזונט און לעבן גוט — דיין B.

<u>פ.ס.</u> היינט האבן מיר [illegible]. [illegible] אין "יידישן פאלק ‚תקומה-ב'". [illegible]

[illegible] די [illegible] "יידישע פאלקס". [illegible] הנאה

געהאט מיט די [illegible] וואס זיינען פון ‚אמאל און [illegible]" מיט [illegible]

[illegible]. [illegible] ?

[illegible]

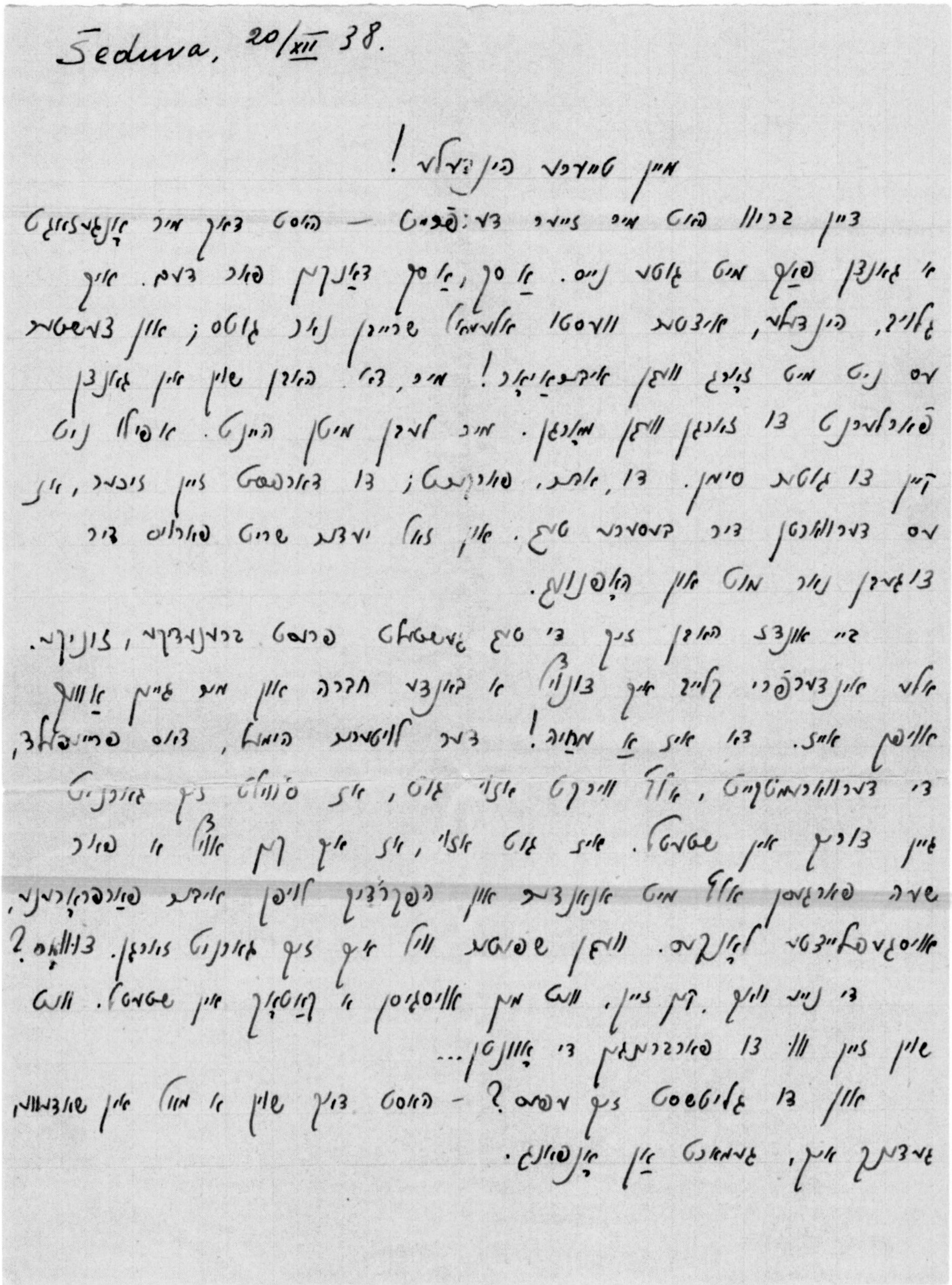
Seduva, 20/XII 38.

מײַן טײַערע הינדעלע!

Šeduva 20/XII/1938[137]

(December 20, 1938)

My Dear Hindalla!

Your letter pleased me very much—you told me a pack of good news. Many, many thanks for that. I believe, Hindalla, that from now on you will give me only good news; and don't upset it with worries about tomorrow. We, here, have just learned not to worry about tomorrow. We live for today, even though it is not a good sign. You, however, on the contrary; you ought to be certain that better days are awaiting you, and let every step forward give you encouragement and hope.

The weather now is extremely cold—sunny and burning frosts. Every morning a bunch of us get together and go ice skating. It is such a pleasure! The clear blue sky, the empty fields, the warmth from within—everything feels so good that you don't even want to go back to the city. It pleases me that I can at least for a couple of hours forget everything and run the skates irresponsibly over the frozen meadows. I refuse to worry about tomorrow. What for?... Next week, they say, the city will open up a regular skating rink—then there will be a place to spend the evenings...

And you, do you skate at all? I remember, you did make some start in Šeduva. Outside the drugstore, I spend my time as before. However, I haven't gone out of town for some time. I miss seeing the opera or a good film (in Šeduva, when you see a good film on occasion, half of it is missing...) At this point I can't leave because my friend left. He finished his apprenticeship and now he has the right to become a manager himself. Indeed, such an opportunity presented itself (in a small town, even smaller than Šeduva). I helped in whatever way I could he should get this position—now he earns even more. How could I have acted differently? It was, however, a great loss for me. A couple of weeks I was without help altogether. Then a young lady apprentice arrived. But I am no longer as free as I was before. Nevertheless, I have thoughts of shortly being in Kovno. The film *Marie Antoinette* will be playing in Kovno; (you saw it) I would very much like to see it, too.

Concerning my co-worker I cannot yet give any opinion. I barely know her. So far she is not used to the drugstore or with the customers, and it is difficult to leave her alone. I hope she will work out. Those voids are filled by Sioma. The two together can manage. Sioma works already quite well. He is almost through with half of his internship. In no time the few remaining months will pass. How will he pass his exams, I wonder? He never opens a book. He doesn't even read a foolish mystery novel. In the drugstore, on the contrary, he is a hustling and obedient worker. I am quite satisfied with him.

The radio remained with me. I bought it together with my boyfriend and now I paid him back his half. It seems to me that without the radio I couldn't get along even a day. Every free moment in the evening I spend by the radio. Unfortunately, Germany is disgusting to listen to; and outside of music we have to turn off many, many stations from other countries as well, as soon as they begin to talk. But when, on occasion, I catch Jewish songs from Russia I am in heaven.

Write to me how are the radio programs in America. What do you like best to listen to? Have you heard from Lola lately? Mrs. Mellman found out that she was sick. She is very worried and frightened

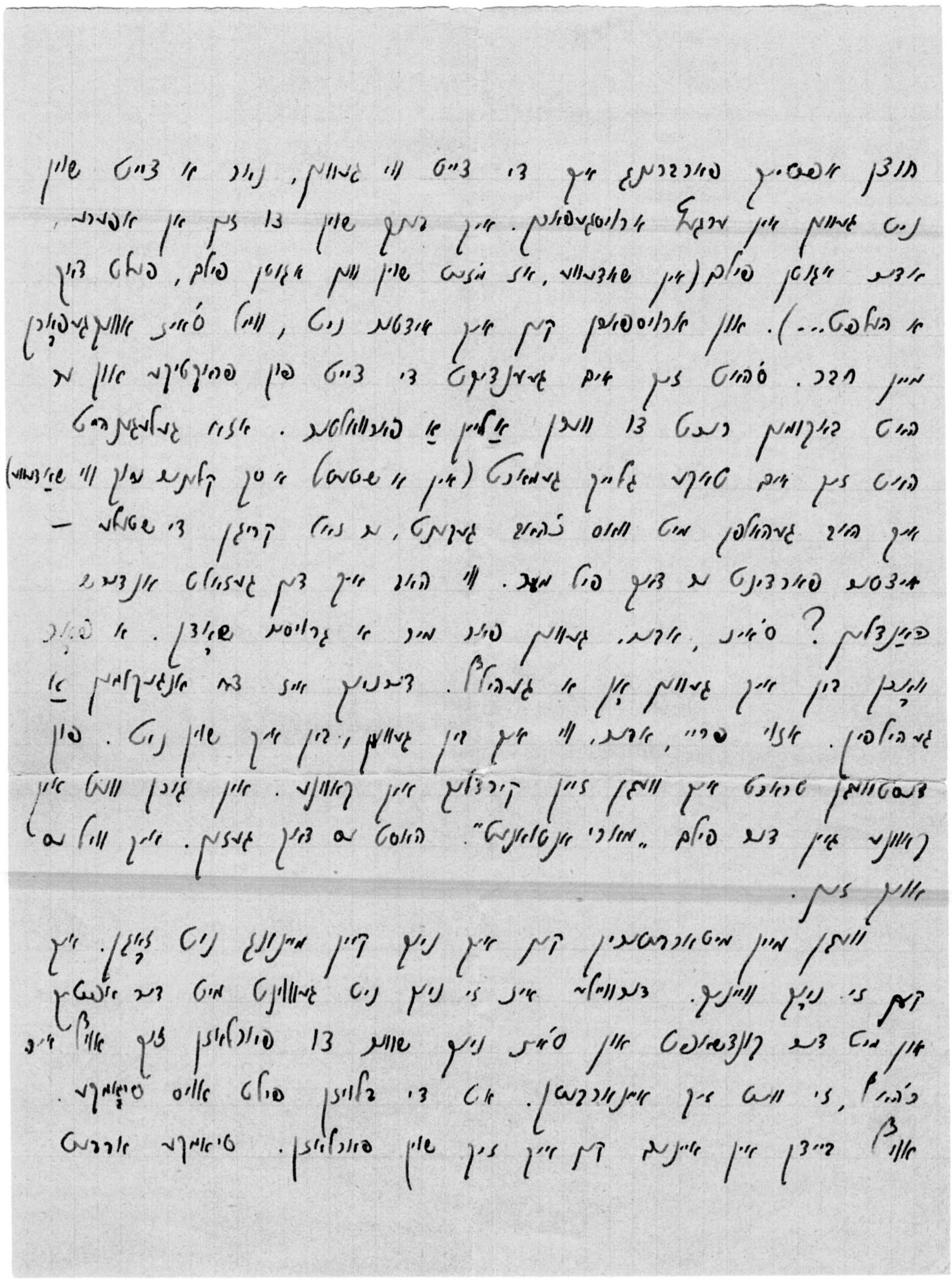

—a mother! Do you know any more about it?

Yes, the film *Once Upon in Spring* is the same as *Maytime*, truly, a good film. The music from the movie we hear often on the radio. I love the music. Here we haven't had any good films for some time. Lately, they brought *Tango Naturna* and *Pique Damma*—both pretty good films, but there was so much missing that it was difficult to follow the plot.

Do you get letters from your girlfriends? You never wrote to me what you hear from Poland.[138] Did conditions, perhaps, improve there more or less? Write to me about everything.

Stay well and enjoy your winter vacation.

Regards to your friends.

B.

-3-

שוין ניט שלעכט. ער האָט דאָך שוין אַ האַלבע פּראַקטיק. באַלד וועט
אַוועקלויפֿן אַלץ דאָס איבעריקע ביסל צײַט. ווי וועט ער דאַן אויסהאַלטן די
עקזאַמענס? ער נעמט קיינמאָל אַ בוך אין האַנט ניט אַרײַן. אַפֿילו
אַ נײַעם קרימינאַל־ראָמאַן לייענט ער קיינמאָל ניט דורך. אין אַפּטייק
איז ער גראָד זייער אַרבעטסאַם און פֿאָלגעדיק. בין איך צופֿרידן פֿון אים.

דער ראַדיאָ־אַפּאַראַט איז געבליבן בײַ מיר. כ'האָב איך דאָך בשותפֿות
געקויפֿט מיט מײַן חבר, הער איך זיך [illegible] [illegible] די וועלט.
עס דאַכט זיך מיר, אַז אָן ראַדיאָ וואָלט איך קיין טאָג ניט געקענט אויסקומען.
די גאַנצע פֿרײַע אָוונט־שעהן פֿאַרברענג איך בײַם אַפּאַראַט. לײַדער איז
פֿאַר אונדז די ראַדיאָ־סקאַלע שוין גאַנץ אַ באַגרענעצטע. דײַטשלאַנד עקלט
צום הערן. און חוץ מוזיק מוז מען שוין אויך פֿיל, פֿיל אַנדערע סטאַנציעס פֿאַרמײַדן,
ווי נאָר זיי פֿאַנגען אָן צו רעדן. כאָטש איך, [illegible], יידישע פֿאָלקס־לידעלעך
פֿון רוסלאַנד, הער איך דײַן [illegible]!

שרײַב, ווי איז די ראַדיאָ־פּראָגראַם אין אַמעריקע? וואָס הערסטו אַם
ליבסטן.

האָסטו לעצטנס געהאַט בריוו פֿון לאָלקען? פֿרוי [illegible] האָט זיך
דערוווּסט, אַז לאָלקע איז געווען ניט געזונט, איז זי זייער אומרויִק און
צעשראָקן — די מאַמע. ווייסטו ניט, וואָס איז איר געווען?

יאָ, דער פֿילם „אַ מאָל אין פֿרילינג" איז דער זעלבער וואָס "Maytime".
אַ גוטער פֿילם געווען. די מוזיק פֿון פֿילם הערט מען בײַ אונדז זייער

יעט דורך האָדזשאַ. כ'האָב ש האָלט צו האָבן.

די אונדז איז שוין אַ צייט קיין געסט פֿילם ניט געווען. לעצטנס האָט
מען געבראַכט „סטאַנגאַ נאַסטאָרני" און „זאַמבאַ פֿיק". גאַנץ גוטע פֿילמס. האָט
ער, ווער. ווענעציאַל געפֿעלט, ווי מ'האָט זיך קוים אַרײַנגעטראַט אין אין האַלט.

האָסטו בריוו פֿון דײַנע חברטע? יאָ, האָסט אַ רעגן ניט
געשריבן, וואָס הערסטו פֿון פּוילן? האָט זיך דאָרטן עפּעס אַ װײַטער
פֿאָרגעשטעלט? שרײַב פֿון אַלעם.

בלײַב געזונט און פֿאַרברענג גוט די ווינטער פֿעריען.

איך גריס דײַנע נאָענטע.

B.

Šeduva, 25/II 39.

מײַן טײַערע הינדעלע!

איך דאַנק דיר פֿאַרן שרײַבן. אַזוי לאַנג פֿון דיר ניט געהאַט געהערט. האָט זיך שוין געטראַכט נאָך דײַנעם צו וואָרט, האָט זיך געוואָלט וויסן, ווי ס'גייט דיר און ווי דו לעבסט. ווייסט דען, וואָס דײַן בריוו באַדײַט פֿאַר מיר אין די אומעטיק-וואָכעדיקע טעג פֿונעם קלײנעם שטעטל? אמת, ס'איז דאָ גענוג אַרבעט, אָבער ניט אַלע מאָל געלינגט עס זיך צו פֿאַרגעסן אין דער אַרבעט; און אין פֿרײַע שעהען און, נאָכמער אין פֿרײַע טעג, איז עס אַזוי טרויעריק אויפֿן האַרצן, די שטימונג ווערט אַזוי געדריקט, אַז עס גייט קיין זאַך ניט אָן.

לעבנס-פֿראַגן זײַנען די איינציקע אונדזערע זאַכן, וועלכע מאַכן ביז איצטער געווינט געוואָרן צו האַרטן ניט פֿון אונדזערע. כאָטש ס'האָט עס שוין פֿאַרלוירן מיט זיי רעכטע דאָרט דורך. כאָטש ס'האָט זיך שוין געענדיקט אַלץ דעם אַלטס, פֿון דעסטוועגן האָט עס געשאַפֿן אַ גרויסע אומרויִקייט און די מאָדנע ניט-צופֿרידנקייט אין מאָרגנדיקן טאָג. כ'ווייס ניט, פֿאַרוואָס איך נעם זיך דאָס צום האַרצן פֿיל מער, דאַכט מיר, ווי אַנדערע. אפֿשר דערפֿאַר, וואָס איך קען זיך ניט אַזוי לײַכט בליקן, ווי אַנדערע. מײַנע פֿרײַנדינע „גוטע פֿרײַנד" קען איך אויסער גלײַך אין די אויגן ניט קוקן. אַנדערע מאָל קריג איך מורא פֿאַר זיך אַליין — עפּעס מאָדנע געדאַנקען קומען אויפֿן זינען: ניט שוין צײַט האָבן מיר געלערנט צו ווערן אַלט דערווײַל צײַטן? און דער גלויבן אין מענטשן? און די גוטע פֿאָלקס-מײַסן? איז דען דאָס אַלץ פּוסטע חלומות געווען? איז דען דער מענטש ניט דײַן גאָט, ווען ער איז געבאָרן? יאָ, טויזנטער און טויזנטער פֿון ניט-ייִדישע יוגנטלעכע פֿאָרמעטן מיט די אַלע פֿרויען גאַנץ שנעל — זיי ווערן אַליין ווילד, שלאָגט און לאָזן דיניש פֿון אַלץ, וואָס איז דאָ ניט-לאַנג געווען זייער שענסטער לעבנס-אינהאַלט. אונדזער ייִדן, אַדרבא, גלייבט נאָר צו האָפֿן, אַז דאָס גוטע אין מענטשן וועט זיך ווען אויפֿוואַכן, און אפֿשר ניט אַליין, וועט געוויס קומען דער טאָג, ווען דאָס מענטשלעכע בײַ וועט מיט געוואַלד אויסגעהאַלטן ווערן.

מײַן טײַערע הינדעלע, עס איז ניט מײַן שולד, וואָס עס רעדט פֿון מיר אַזאַ פּעסימיסטקייט. מיט די אַלע נײַעסטע געדאַנקען מאַטערן זיך בסדר, און ס'איז ניטאָ פֿאַר וועמען צו וואָרט

Šeduva 25/II/1939[139]

(February 25, 1939)

My Dear Hindalla!

I thank you for writing. I hadn't heard from you for so long. I was already longing for a word from you. I was anxious to know how things are going and how you are. Do you realize what your letters mean to me in the depressing everyday life in a small town? True, there is plenty of work, but one is not always able to forget while working; and in the hours of leisure, and even more in the days of leisure, the heart is so sad, the mood gets depressed, that nothing matters.

Lately, we notice things here which we were used to hearing from elsewhere. Even though we had premonitions some time ago, even though we expected it—still, it created a great disturbance and a kind of uncertainty for tomorrow. I don't know why I'm taking it to heart so much more, it seems, than others. Perhaps it is because I cannot bend as easily as others. My "good friends" from way back I cannot look straight in the eyes now. At times I fear my own self—strange ideas get into my head: could it be that we cannot even expect better times? And the faith in man? And what about the good folk masses? Were all those empty dreams? Is man only good when he is confined? Yes, thousands and thousands of non-Jewish youth reply to all these questions quite quickly—they become wild, mean, and laugh cynically concerning everything that just a short while ago was their most beautiful way of life. For us Jews, however, only hope remains, that the goodness in men will yet arise, and, if not alone, the day will surely come when human evil will be exterminated by force.

My dear Hindalla, it is not my fault that I talk with such bitterness. These foolish thoughts are forever bothering me, and there isn't anyone to talk to. You, my best friend, will always hear me out and understand me. That will give me strength to lift myself up for the time being and to strengthen my belief in a better humanity.

Nevertheless, I had a few hours of real pleasure and uplift. I was fortunate enough to see the films *Marie Antoinette*, *Suez*, and *Green Fields*.[140] I saw them in Savl. I will never forget the idyllic-quiet landscapes of *The Green Fields*. In Šeduva, I also saw a fairly good Jewish film, *The Dybbuk*, with Samberg[141] in the lead. I met Samberg in person while he was playing in Lithuania before. I drove to Ponevezh to see him in *Yoshe Kalb*[142] (a Maurice Schwartz[143] production). How great Samberg was in the role of Neshever!

This Monday was the 80th birthday of Sholom Aleichem.[144] This event was especially commemorated in Russia. I have read and studied his works so many times; nevertheless, I would listen with great pleasure to the monologues and stories by this great Jewish classicist and humorist, which the Russian radio stations would translate. How much spirit the Jewish artists of USSR would bring into the almost lifeless stories!

We already receive regularly the Jewish press from Poland. In Šeduva, we receive the newspapers the same day. The Jewish press in Poland is on a much higher scale than in Lithuania (I believe also higher than in America.) I enjoy reading it. Somehow one feels better having ties with 3,000,000 more

צו רײדן. דו, מײַן בעסטע פֿרײַנד, װײסט דאָך מיר אַלע מאָל אױסהערן און שמועסן.
דאָס מוז מיר געבן כּח אױסצוהאַלטן ביז [illegible] דער צײַט און צו שטאַרקן און זיך
דעם גלױבן אין דער בעסערער מענטשהײט.

גענוג, אָבער. דאָ מיר אַלײן שעפּן פֿון אמתער הנאה און דערהױבנקײט. ס'איז מיר
געלונגען צו זען די פֿילמס „מאַרי אַנטואַנעט", „סוזי" און „גרינע פֿעלדער". געזען האָב
איך עס אין שטאַל. די אידיליש-רויִקע בילדער פֿון „גרינע פֿעלדער" װעל איך לאַנג ניט
פֿאַרגעסן. דאָס איז דער אײנציקער פֿון אַלע ײדישע פֿילמס, װאָס איז גאַנץ גוטער געשפּילט.
אין שעדעװער האָב איך געזען אױך די גאָר נשקשה'דיקן ײדישן פֿילם „דער דיבוק" מיט
סאַמעראָגן אַלס משולח. כּ'האָב סאַמעראָגן געזען אױך אין לעבן. ער האָט געװוינט אין לאָדזש. דען
איך געװען בײַגעפֿאַרן זײַן פּרעמיערע צו „ײדישע [אים שפּיל] קינדער" (װי מאָריס שװאַרץ'ס אױפֿפֿירונג)
טײַערע גאַנץ געלונגען געװען. די שפּילונג סאַמעראָגס האָט עס אױסגעפֿירט די האַל פֿון באַשטױנען!

דעם מאָנטיק איז אױסגעפֿאַלן דער 80 יאָריקער געבױרנס-טאָג פֿון שלום-עליכם. בײַ אונדז האָט
מען דעם יובל געפֿײַערט אין ראָסלאַנד. כּ'האָב װידער מאָל געלײענט און געלעבט די װערק
פֿון שלום-עליכם, פֿון דעם װאָס פֿאַר איך מיט דעם גרעסטן הנאה אױסהערן די שײן אַלטע
געשיכטע און מאָנאָלאָגן פֿון גרױסן ײדישן קלאַסיקער און הומאָריסט, װעלכע די ראָסישע ראַדיאָ-
סטאַנציעס פֿלעגן טראַנסלירן. װיפֿיל פּרעכטיקײט די ײדישע קינסטלער און אַרטיסטן פֿון 2000 האָבן
עס אַרײַנגעטראָגן אין די כּמעט איבערזעצטע דערצײלונגען!

די אונדזערע קומט שױן אין ראַנגלונג די ײדישע פּרעסע פֿון פּױלן. אין שעדעװער קריגט מען די
צײַטונגען דעם צװײ טעג. די ײדישע פּרעסע אין פּױלן שטײט אױף א פֿיל העכערן שטאַפֿל, װי
אין לאַנד (אין גלות, אױך, װי אין אַמעריקע). איך לײען עס גאַנץ גערן. עפּעס פֿילט מען זיך בעסער
האַנדלען אין פֿאַרבינדונג מיט נאָך 3 מיליאָן ײדן.

צײַט מײַן חבר איז אַװעקגעפֿאָרן, איז מיר געװאָרן שװערער. איך װעל מיט לענגערער צײַט אױסקומען
פֿון שרײַבן. איך װעל פּסח, אָבער, װעל איך זײַן שױן מסתּמא אַרױסגעפֿאָרן זײַן הײם. אין דעם
שױן נאָך דעם יום-טוב. נאָך שטאָט, מיט א גוטן דאָך. אין שעדעװער האָב איך עס קײן זאַך ניט.

דערצײל, הינדעלע, אַלעס. שרײַב, װי גײט עס דיר? ביסטו נאָך אַלץ אױף פֿאַרנומען?
װאָספֿאַר גוטע פֿילמען האָסטו געזען? יאָ, האָסטו געזען דעם נײַעם ײדישן פֿילם „ײנקל דער שמיד"?
אין אַמעריקע, רעכן איך, דעמאָנסטרירט מען אים שױן.

מײַנע האַרציקסטע גרוסן אַלע דײַנע נאָענטע. זײַ געזונט און מונטער — דײַן ב.

Jews.

Since my friend left, it became increasingly difficult for me to leave Šeduva for a longer period of time. For Passover, however, I will most likely run over to Kovno. I miss the opera, the theatre, and a good book. In Šeduva I have none.

That is all, Hindalla, for now. Write me how you are. Are you still as busy? What good films have you seen? Did you get to see the new Jewish film *Yankel der Schmid*?[145] I imagine, it must be playing in America already.

My heartiest regard to all your near ones.

Be well and cheerful.

Your

B.

Seduva, 29/VI 39.

מײַן טײַערע הינדעלע!

שוין באַלד צוויי וואָכן, ווי כ'האָב דײַן גרויסן בריוו באַקומען און די גאַנצע צײַט דיר ניט
געקענט שרײַבן. פּשוט צײַט אַ צײַט האָט דאָ אָנגעהויבן פֿרילינג צו ווערן. מיט אַ
קנאַפּע צוויי וואָכן צוריק פֿלעגן מיר נאָך אַלץ ווײַטער האָבן שניי (זיך, די שנייען און פֿרי-פֿרילינג
דערמאָנען מיר שוין צופֿיל...); הײַנט וויל שוין גרינען די בערעזקע בײַם פֿענצטער. דער
פֿײגעלע מיל שוין, ווי איך זע די בערעזקע בליען, און כ'האָב זי מיט אַ מאָל פֿײַנט געקריגן
ווי זי וואָלט האַלטן זיך און דערמאָנען: „זע, נאָך איין יאָר אַוועק".

פֿאַר די צוויי וואָכן זײַנען מיר אַזוי פֿיל האָפֿענונגען צעראָנען געוואָרן. גאַנצע צוויי יאָר
געלעבט מיטן געדאַנק צו קענען קומען קיין אַמעריקע, כּדי צו דער אויסשטעלונג. איז
עס, ווײַזט זיך, הײַנט אין גאַנצן ניט מעגלעך. נאָך שווערער, ווײַל צו איבער, איז אויסער
צו קומען קיין אַמעריקע אויך שטאַרק. און דאָס איז די צײַט אַזוי טעמפּ, איז וואָס
איך אָנגעהויבן מעגלעך קאָנטאַקט וויל איך הײַנט גאָר ניט טראַכטן, מיט אַ צײַט אין הײַנטיקן
וועלט איך, אַנדערע מאָל, אַז דאָס הפקר-שטח — אַלץ פֿאַרגעסן, אַלץ געוועזן. דאָס
איז, אַדרבה, שרעקלעך! איך דערמאָן זיך אין מײַנע אייגענע צו, און באַזי זיך אַוועקצושטעלן
אויפֿצוהאַלטן געדאַנקען: ניין, מוזן האָפֿן אין [illegible]!

פֿאַר דער פֿאַל, הינדעלע, שוין דאָס וויכטיקסטע אַוועק, ווי כ'וויל דיר שרײַבן, און איך קען ניט.
מיט אַ 10 טעג צוריק בין איך געווען אויף עטלעכע טעג אין קאָוונע. כ'האָב געוואָלט
צו זען וואָרדיס אָפּערע „לאַ טראַוויאַטאַ". דאָס איז געווען איינס פֿון מיר. פּונקט מײַן צײַט האָט
מיך נאָך די אָפּערע ניט דערלאָזט געשפּילט. די מוזיק האָב איך שוין געקענט — מ'האָט עס
זייער אָפֿט דורך ראַדיאָ. כ'האָב עס, אַדרבה, נאָך קיינמאָל ניט געהערט גוט. אַחוץ דעם
האָב איך אַרײַנגעכאַפּט גאַנצע דרײַ פּוילישע פֿילמס. קאָוונע איז ממש פֿאַרפֿלייצט מיט פּוילישע
פֿילמס, און זיי ווערן מיט גרויס דערפֿאָלג. די פֿילמס זײַנען טאַקע ניט קיין עלעמענט —
זייער אַ ליכטיקע אינהאַלט און אַ ניט שלעכטע [illegible] פֿון די אַרטיסטן. נאָר איז מען
שלעכטער פֿילמס, מאַכט מען כּסדר אין די זעלבע אַרטיסטן. שלעכטער האָבן שוין דאָוונען
צו געווינען די הערצער פֿון קאָוונער מיידלעך...

און אַמעריקע קומט דיר ווען אַלס צו זען אַ פּוילישן פֿילם?

Šeduva, 29/IV/1939[146]

(April 29, 1939)

My Dear Hindalla!

It's almost two weeks since I received your letter, and in all this time could not write to you. While the time was passing spring managed to come. Just less than two weeks ago we still had snow, now and then. (Oh, the snow and the early spring remind me too much…)[147] and now the willow tree in front of the window is all green. The fourth time already I see the willow bloom,[148] and I suddenly hate her: as if she is trying to remind me, "See, another year has passed."

In these past two weeks so many of my hopes went to pieces. For two years I lived with the thought of being able to come to America, if only to the World's Fair.[149] This is presently entirely impossible. Even more difficult, it seems, is now to go to America to remain permanently. And here the times are so uncertain that I can't even think of another possibility. With a trembling heart I await, at times, the hour of freedom—no boundaries, no laws. But that would be frightful! I think of my family here, and try to chase away such thoughts. No, one must hope for better days! And that is why, Hindalla, I tried to write to you so many times and couldn't.

About ten days ago I was in Kovno for a few days. I managed to see Verdi's opera *Otello*;[150] that was new to me. In my days this opera had not yet been performed. The music I already knew—one can hear it often over the radio—I had never seen it, however. Besides, I took in three Polish films. Kovno is deluged with Polish films, and they are very successful. The films weren't bad—a very light plot and not too badly performed. But when you see a few films, you can always see the same actors. A few even managed to win the hearts of the ladies of Kovno. In America, do you ever happen to see a Polish film?

In Kovno I saw Elke Friedlander. She is taking her partial exams for six grades. She finds it quite difficult. Algebra, I think, she already passed. How she did with the other subjects, I don't know. Next week, perhaps, she will be home.

And how is Lola? Do you hear from her often? Mrs. Mellman is not very pleased with her studies. She also has aggravation from Ania. She is still as wild as ever. She always comes home with a failing grade in some subject. She promises, though, to improve by the end of the year. Milke and Freidele[151] are doing very well. How the others are doing, I don't know.

By me no special news. I am now reading the poems by Vogler,[152] one of our younger poets in Poland. He writes very precisely and often not quite according to our taste. In spite of it, it is worthwhile to acquaint oneself with his works. I will send you a volume of his poems. Leaf through it at your leisure.

And how is it with you? Did you have a good Passover? You must have devoured a little Latin, true? I'm sure you have much studying to do before the end of the school year. And how are you doing in history? It is so interesting at this time to study history. I'm sure you are managing it well.

Yes, your "club"[153] pleases me especially. You arranged it beautifully, real American style, indeed! It's good that you established such a homey circle, where you feel comfortable. Keep me posted how your

כ'האב אין קווינס געהאט געטראפן אלע פריינדינס. זי האלט אויסער אין
מיניסטעריום אויף אנטאמאס פאר זיך דאס לאנד. ספעציעל איר דאס זייער שווער. מיט אלעקסאנדער,
דאנקט מיר, איז זי שוין דורכגעגאנגען. ווי פייע איר געגאנגען ווייטער, וואס איך ניט. די
ניט וויין, מסתמא, וואס זי שוין זיין אין דער היים.

און ווי גייט עס לאזען? האסטו פון איר אפט געשריבן? פרוי מעלמאן איז זייער
ניט צופרידן פון איר לערנען זיך. און פון איניקעל האט זי פארדראס. זי איז נאך
אלץ די זעלבע ווילדע, וואס געווען. און דא היינט קומט זי יעדן מאל צופאלן מיט אייניקעם
"צו" אויף עסט. זי מיינט, אבער, צו מענטש-ווען עס דורכצומאכן.

מיילע און פריידעלע לערנען זיך זייער גוט. ווי פייגע די אנדערע, וואס איך ניט.

ביי מיר קיינע באזונדערע נייס ניטא. איך לערן איצטער די לידער פון ווייגלמאן —
וועגנס פון אונזערע יינגערע פאעטן אין פוילן. ער שרייבט זייער איינציק און, אפט,
גאנץ וואס פון אונזער געשיכטע. פון דערציילן לאנג עס זיך צו דערקענען מיט זיין שאפן.
כוועל דיר צושיקן א פאר פון זיינע לידער. וואס עס דורכלעבן אין א פריידער צייט.

נו, און ווי גייט עס דיר? האסטו גוט פארבראכט פסח? מסתמא האסטו ארויסגעפארן
מיט דיין לאנען; אמת? געוויס האסטו אויפגעמאכט, פון אנדערע לאנד-ווארט, ניט וועניג צום לערנען.
און מיט היסטאריע ווי גייט עס דיר? סאיז דאך היינט אזוי אינטערעסאנט צו לערנען
היסטאריע. געוויס האסטו עס שוין גערן באקומען.

יא, דיין "קלוב" געפעלט מיר באזונדערס. האסט זיך עס וואונדערבאר געמאכט! אלעס מיט
אמעריקאנער! סאיז גוט, וואס דו האסט זיך געשאפן אזא היימישן קרייזל, ווי צו
מאכט זיך גוט פילן. שרייב, פארגרעסערט דיין קלוב?

און דיינע דערציאונגס ארבעט צו סקול פארשטעלונג האבן געהאט דערפאלג?

און וואס האסטו לעצטנס געזען אין קינא? אזוי פיל, ווי "פרזעס. מאמעלע" וואס איינער,
אין לעטער, קענסטו ניט אויסקומען צו זען. פארשטעלונגען דאך פאלגענדיג. די קינא ...
שרייב פון אלעס.

פאר היינט דערלאנג עס. און גריס היינטיג אלע דיינע נאנטע.

בלייב געזונט און שטאַרק — דיין, B.

"club" is progressing. And your decorations for the school play,[154] was that a success?

And what did you recently see in the movies? Such a film as *Professor Mamlok*[155] we will never be privileged to see here, in Lithuania. You, undoubtedly, know why. I envy you the movies. Write me about everything.

Enough for today. Regards to all your near ones.

Stay well.

Your

B.

Sedwa, 1/VI 39.

מײַן טײַערע הינדעלע!

דײַן שרײַבן האָט מיר הײַנט אױסערגעװײנלעך דערפֿרײט. דאָס האַרץ זאָגט מיר,
אַז די אַדרעס װעט אומזיסט ניט זײַן.

איך דאַנק דיר, הינדעלע, פֿאַר שנעל שרײַבן מיר, איך דאַנק אױך דער טאַנטע
פֿאַר איר מי. זי טוט גאָר אַ סך פֿאַר מיר.

מאַמע, זײדע, טאַטע, שװעסטער האָב איך איבערגעגעבן גרוסן פֿון דיר. כ'האָב געמאַנדערט
לײענען „פֿינדלינג". געװען אַ סך שװעריקײטן צום לײענען. האָב זיך אַזױ געװאָלט טרעפֿן
מיט װעמען דאָס גלײַכן, דאָס באַטראַכטן. ליידער איז ניטאָ מיט װעמען. האָב איך בלױז
אַלע דאָקומענטן און דיר אױסגעשיקט. ס'פֿאַרדריסט מיר נאָר, װאָס כ'האָב ניט די
באַזונדערע רעדעס פֿון „פֿינדלינג". מיקאַ, זאָגט, יעדן דאַנק לײענען באַזונדער. יעדער
קאַפּיטל איז דאָך אַ באַזונדערע נאָװעלע. דײַן װאָרט האָבן פֿאַרשטאַנען, גלײַך װי דאָך
װעסט הנאה האָבן.

אַ דאַנק װאָס די נײַעס אינפֿאָרמאַציע.

געבוירן אין שאַװל, דעם 1-טן אױגוסט 1912 (1-VIII-1912).
מײַן נאָמען לױטן פּאַס Bermanas Nochimas (געװאָלט איך האָבן פֿאַרשריבן!)
דעם פֿאָטערס נאָמען פֿײַװל, די מוטער - פֿרײדע. זײערע נעמען האָב איך שױן ניט
ניט, װי מ'װעט זײ שרײַבן.

יע, דאָס געבוירן-לאַנד מוז מען שרײַבן ליטע, אַזױ װי ס'איז הײַנט, כאָטש פֿאַר
דער קריג איז עס געװען רוסלאַנד.

לעצטע װאָך, נאָך דערװאַרטנדיק צו זײַן אױף דער באַרױ פֿון דער טאַנטע, האָב איך
װאָס-װען אױסגעשיקט צײַן אינסטיטוטן אַנקעטע צום אַמעריקאַנער קאָנסולאַט. כ'האָב געבעטן
מיר רעגיסטרירן און צושיקן אין גיכן צושטעלן פּאַפּירן פֿון אַמעריקאַנער קאָנסולאַט.
און האָב, איך װעל אײַך ניט איבערלאָזן...

ס'איז הײַנט דאָנערשטיק און איך קום אָנשרײַבן נאָך אַ בריוו. ס'װעלט זיך
אַזױ דיר נאָך אַ גרוס שרײַבן, דער מוטער, זײדע, פֿאָטער זיך שױן און. נײַן, אַ צװײטן מאָל
װעל איך געװיס זיך ניט דאַרפֿן אַזױ האַלטן און זאָגן דער שרײַבן מאַמעס מער.
גלײַך געזונט און פֿאַרגעסט ניט. גריס האַרציק די איך אײַער שטענדיק געדענקן - דײַן נחום

Šeduva, 1/VI/1939[156]

(June 1, 1939)

My Dear Hindalla!

Your letter pleased me today no end. My heart tells me that your efforts will not be in vain. I thank you, Hindalla, for your prompt reply; I also thank your aunt for her efforts—she does so much for me.

Oddly enough, this Shavuot, I thought so much about you. I finished reading *Pandre.*[157] There was plenty to read this Shavuot. I wanted so much to share my thoughts with someone; unfortunately, there is no one. So I gathered everything and sent it to you.[158] I'm sorry I don't have the two middle volumes of *Pandre*. You can read each book separately, however. Each chapter is a separate novella. Soon you will have vacation, leaf it through. You will enjoy it.

Now about the necessary information.

I was born in Šeduva, August 1, 1912. My name according to the passport is Nochimas Bermanas (very cleverly registered!) My father's name is Faiva; mother's name Freida. Their names don't matter how it is spelled. Yes, the place of birth must be written *Lithuania*, as it is now, even though before the war it was Russia.

Last week, not having received any letter from your aunt I filled out a form to the American Consulate. I asked them to register me and promised shortly to send in the necessary papers from my American relatives.[159] I hope I won't be a liar.

Today is Thursday and our market day. I can hardly take the time to write even that much, though I want so much to write you more. The market[160] is starting. Next time I will surely not be so rushed and will be able to write much more.

Be well and have a good time. My heartiest regards to everyone at home.

Your

B

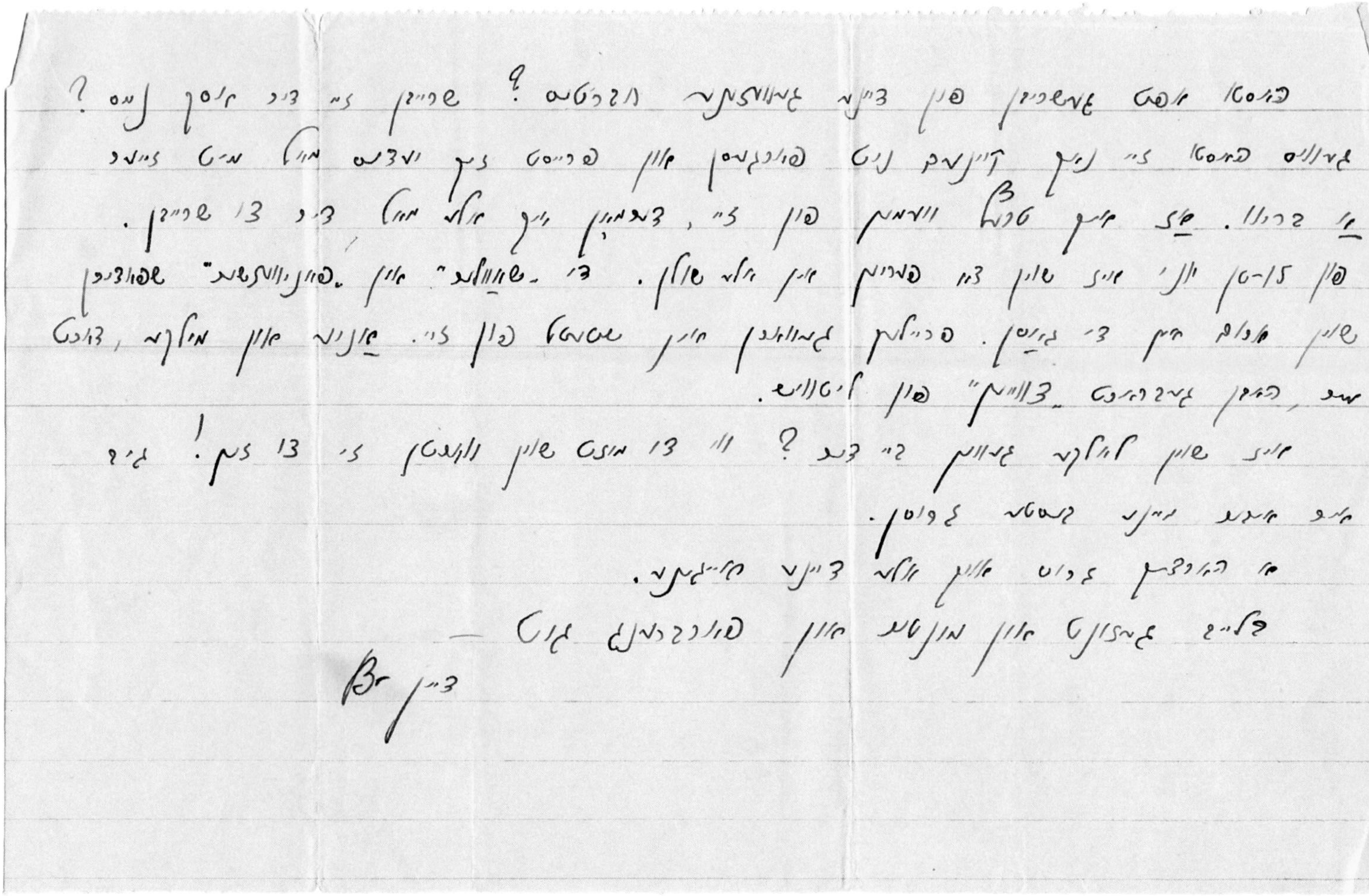

װאָס? [illegible] דיר זײַ שרײַבן? [illegible] געװעזענע דײַנע פֿון געשריבן אָפֿט פּאָסט
זײער מיט מאָל [illegible] זיך פֿרײט און פֿאַרגעסן ניט דײַנעם ניך זײַ פּאָסט געװיס
זײַ גראָד. אַז איך טראָג װאַרעמע פֿון זײַ, דערמאָן איך אַלע מאָל דיר צו שרײַבן.
פֿון 10-טן יוני איז שוין דאָ פֿרילינג אין אַלע שלאָן. די "שװאַלבע" און "פֿאָנװעלטש" שפּאַצירן
שוין [illegible] אין די גאַסן. פֿרילינג געװאָרן אין שטעטל פֿון זײַ. ענגע און מילכמע, דערצו
שוין, האָבן געדרוקט "צװײַג" פֿון ליטװיש.
איז שוין ליבע געװען די דײַנע? װי דו מוזט שוין װאַרטן צו 13 זײַן! גיך
אויף מײַנע גאָרטן צוקוקן.
א האַרציקן גרוס און אַלע דײַנע הײַנטיקע.
בלײַב געזונט און מונטער און פֿאַרבײַגענג גוט —
דײַן [illegible]

Sedwa, 18/VI 39.

מיין טייערע הינדעלע!

שוין באַלד אַ וואָך, ווי כ'האָב אייך דיין בריוו דערהאַלטן; ריכטיקער –
דעם ערשטן, ווייל דער איז געגאַנגען פיל לענגער. איך דאַנק דיר, הינדעלע. די טאָג
האָב איך אייך געהאַט געשריבן פון דער טאַנטע רחל, זי שרייבט מיר גאַנץ אָפט, דעם
מאָל וויס צו מיר איינצולייגן, אַז די פּאַפּירן זיינען שוין אַרויסגעשיקט געוואָרן פאַר מיר פון
אַמעריקע, און איך וועל זיי אין גיכן קריגן דורך דעם הייגן קאָנסולאַט. דאָס האָט מיך ניט ווייניק
דערפרייט. ווי אומגעדולדיק איך וואַרט שוין אויף זיי! איך ווייס, אַז דערנאָך וועט מיר דאַרפן
אויסקומען נאָך אַ מאָל צו וואַרטן. כ'האָב, אָבער, דאָס וואַרטן וועט מיר זיין ניט שווער. די
צייט לויפט גיך. ס'איז נאָר זיין ליב די אונדז.

דערווייל איז דאָ פיל שטילער, ווי מיט איניקע מאָנאַטן צוריק. די צייטונגען און ראַדיאָ
זיינען אונדזער „פּאָסט", ווי מ'רופט עס ביי אונדז. פּאָליטיקס, אָבער, גייט עס אין די איבערגעוואָנלעכער
דיפּלאָמאַטישע מלחמה, יעדער וויל געווינען וואָס מער פאַרבינדעטע, און ווער ווייס, אפשר מיט
אַ מאָל וועט טרעפן וואָס ניט פּאַסירן? אפשר, אפשר וועט עס דאָך דיפּלאָמאַטיש געלונגען צו
פאַרמיידן אַ מלחמה. לאָמיר האָפן.

נו, און ווי האַלט מען אין דיינע „פּאָליטישע קרייזן"? מ'אינטערעסירט דיך לעצטנס זיך
אויך די מיט פּאָליטיק! אפילו אין אַרבעט אָדער פּאָליטיק געגאַנגען אין שרייבן. איך
וואָלט זייער געוואָלט לייענען דיין אַרבעט.

די אונדזערע זיינען אויסגעשיינטע שיינע, וואַרעמע טעג. גאָר ניט געמערקט, ווי זיי האָבן זיך
מיט אַ מאָל איינגעריכט. אין גאַנץ, אָבער, דעם ייִדישן וויניק-וואָס אויס די שיינע פרילינגס-טעג
אין דרויסן. מיר קומט אויס מאַל, ווי פאַרזאַמען צו זיין אין שפּאַציר. חוץ טאָמער אַרבעט
ניט די אונדז אַ געהאָלפן. איך קען זיך, אָבער, אויך ניט פאַרלאָזן, ווי פאַרגאַנגען
יאָר מיין חבר. איך קען אַרויסגיין אויף אַ שעה, אָדער צוויי זיך האָבן אָדער געהאַט
שפּאַצירן, אָדער אונטערנעמען לענגערע ריזעס, ווי כ'האָב עס האַלט, קען איך ניט. פון
דעסטוועגן וועל איך אַנדערע יאָר, מסתמא, נעמען אַ פּאָר וואָכן פריי. ווי כ'וועל אויסניצן מיין
פרייע צייט, ווייס איך נאָך ניט. צו דאַשיקע האָב איך דיין לוסט ניט. כ'וואָלט זייער
וועלן אייך הי-יאָר ערגעץ דורכפירן זיך. דאַרפן ניט קענען אַרויספאָרן קיין גאַנץ, וועט

Šeduva, 18/VI/1939[161]

(June 18, 1939)

My Dear Hindalla!

Almost a week since I have received your second letter, more correctly, the first because it took much longer. I thank you, Hindalla. A few days ago I also received a letter from your Aunt Rachel.[162] She writes me quite often. This time she informed me that the papers have already been sent out for me from America, and that I'll soon receive them from a local post.[163] I was overjoyed... How impatiently I am waiting! I know that afterward I will again have to wait. I hope the waiting won't be too difficult. Time flies! It should only be peaceful here.

Meanwhile, it is much quieter here than it was a few months ago. The newspapers and radio are now "empty," as we say it here. Actually, though, we are in the middle of a diplomatic war. Everyone wants to win and, who knows, if all of a sudden something may not develop? Perhaps, perhaps it will be possible to avoid a war, let's hope so.

And what is the opinion in your political circles? Lately everyone is so interested in politics. You even had to write a paper about politics. I would very much like to read your work.

The weather here is beautiful and warm. I hardly noticed how they came upon us. This year, however, I make little use of the beautiful spring days and evenings. I work in the drugstore more than last year. In addition to Sioma, we also have an assistant. I cannot, however, depend on her like I did on my boyfriend. I can only go away for an hour or two to swim or for a long walk; but to go away for longer trips, which I like, I cannot do. Even so, I am planning on taking a couple of weeks off at the end of July. How I will spend my free time I have not decided yet. To rest I have no desire. I would very much like this year to travel somewhere. Since you cannot take out any money, it may not be possible this year. You can go abroad but then you get there you'll have to live like a pauper... Perhaps it might even turn out quite interesting...

Consequently, I spend most of my time by the radio. I especially like the early morning programs—news, the weather, and light classical music. And these early mornings are now especially beautiful. They have now become my favorite hours of the day.

I am no great lover of sports programs. Lately we had European basketball matches. Much "noise" was made with these matches on radio and in the press; so, I, too, was drawn into it and I would listen to the matches but with no special interest. It would surprise me that to others it was more important than anything else.

I read a little, too. I just acquired a good book, *Drei Kammeraden*,[164] in German, by Erich Maria Remarque.[165] The author you, undoubtedly, know. The book was published in Holland. In Germany they burn Remarque's books.

Worse is with movies. Once in a while a Jew would come in with a film; sometimes a better one, sometimes not so good. Now, he doesn't come at all. To go into a bigger city for it isn't always possible, so I miss it.

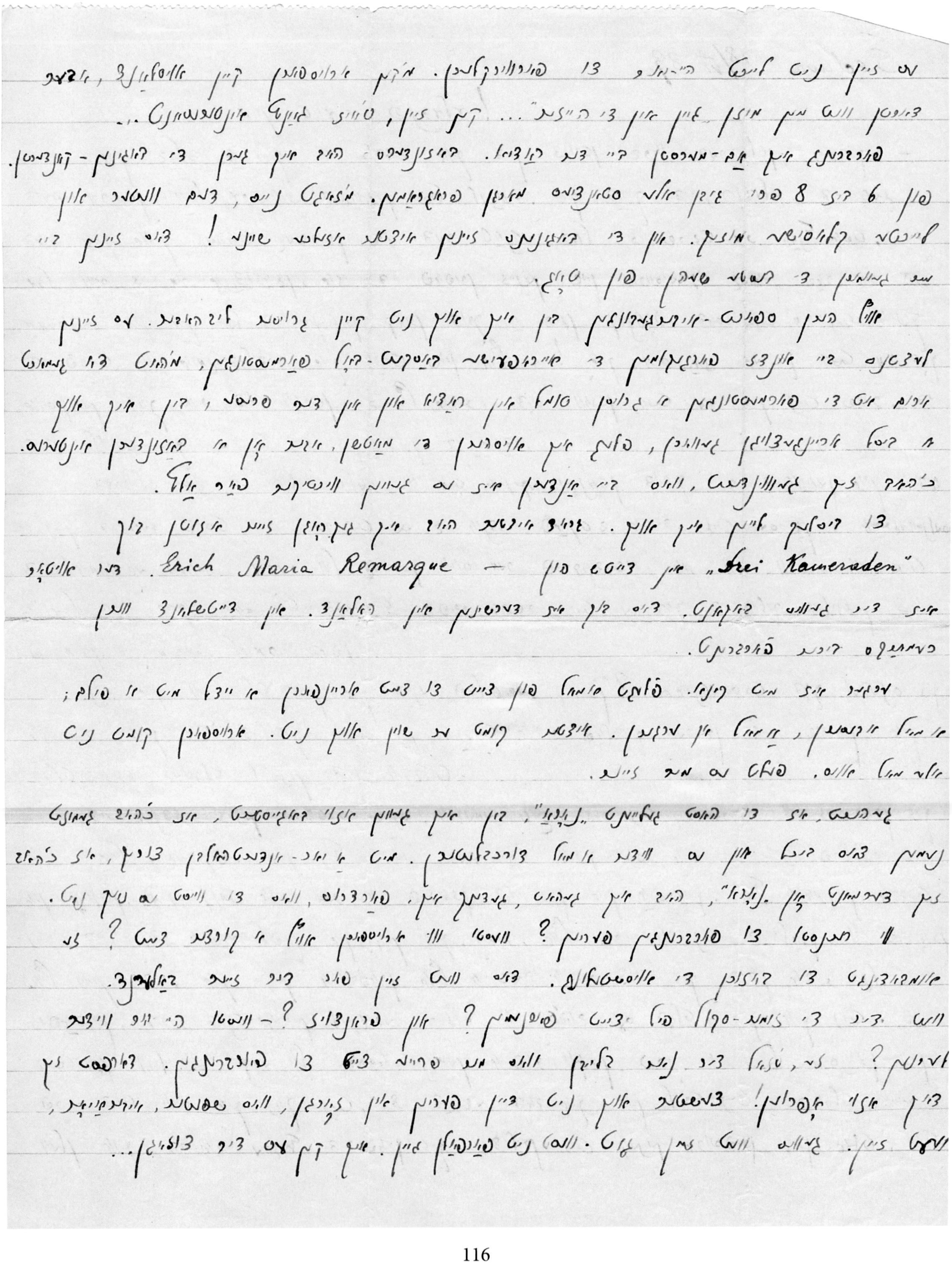

עס זײַנען נישט לײַכטע הײַנטיקע צו פֿאַרװאָרקלערן. מיטן אַרויסגעבן דײַן אויסלאַנד, אויסער
דאַוונען וואָס מען מוזן גיין אין די "הײַנט"... דערנאָך זײַן, טאַטע, גאַנץ אינטערעסאַנט...
פֿאַרברענגען אין אַם-מאַרקסן בײַ דער רעדאַקציע. דערנאָכדעם האָב איך געגעבן די לעקציע-לערנען.
פֿון 6 ביז 8 פֿאַר נאַכט אַלע סטודענטן מאַכן פּראָגראַמען. מאָרגן נאָך, דעם װעטער אין
לעבנס קלאַסישע מוזיק. אין די דאָזיקע זײַנען אויסטער אויסער שיינע! דאָס זײַנען די
שעה געװעזן די בעסטע שעהען פֿון טאָג.
װײַל האָבן ספּאָרט-אָרגאַניזאַציעס בין איך אויך נישט קיין גרויסע ליבהאָבער. עס זײַנען
לעבנס בײַ אונדז פֿאַרנומען די אײראָפּעישע קאָנצערט-טיל פֿאָרמאַציעס, מ׳האָט דאָ געמאַכט
אָרעם מיט די פֿאָרמאַציעס זיך געלערנט טאַנץ אין רעדאַקציע אין דער ספּאָרט, בין איך אויך
א ביסל אַרײַנגעצויגן געװאָרן, פֿון איך אויסלערנען די מאַטשן, אָבער קיין חי האָבנדיקן אינטערעס.
כ׳האָב זיך געװוּנדערט, װאָס די אַנדערע מיט עס געװען װאַנסיקע פֿאַר אַלץ.
צו ביסלעך לייען איך אויך. דאָס לעצטע האָב איך געהאַט געלייענט דאָס
Erich Maria Remarque — אין דײַטש פֿון „drei Kameraden". דער אינהאַלט
איז דער געװען באַקאַנט. דאָס בוך איז דערשינען אין האָלאַנד. אין דײַטשלאַנד װאָלט
פֿאַרבאָטן געװען דורכגעפֿאַלן.
ערגער איז מיט קינאָ. פֿילמען פֿון דײַטש צו דער אַרײַנפֿירן אַ ייִדל מיט אַ פֿילם;
אַ מאָל אָנקוקן, אַ מאָל אין ערגעץ. אויסער קומט עס שוין אויך נישט. אַרויסגעפֿאָרן קומט נישט
אַלע מאָל אַלס. פֿילמען עס מער זײַנע.
געקומען, איז די האַלב גרויסע „נאָוואָ", בין איך געװען אינעם דאָרטיקן קאָמיטעט, איז כ׳האָב געמאַכט
נעמען דאָס ביסל אין עס װידער אַ מאָל דורכגעלעבט. מיט אַ יאָר-אונטערהאַלטן צײַט, איז כ׳האָב
זיך דערמאָנט אין „נאָוואָ", האָב איך געהאַט, געדענק איך, פֿאַרדרוס, װאָס דו װײסט עס טאָך נישט.
װי מאַכסטו צו פֿאַרברענגען פֿרײַע? װאָסער אַרויספֿאָרן אַלע אַ קורצע צײַט? צו
אָנקומענדיקע צו באַזוכן די אויסשטעלונג. דאָס װאָלט זײַן שוין דײַן ערשטע באַזוך.
װאָס לערנט די צװײ-סקול פֿון דײַנע פּענטאַמען? אין פֿראַנצייזיש? — װאָסער האָסטו װידער
װערטער? צו, שרײַב דײַן נאָמען ליבן װאָס מען קען דײַנע צו פֿאַרברענגען. דערפֿאַר זײַ
דיך אַלע אַפּגעפֿרעגט! בעסער אויך נישט דײַן פֿראָגן אין בריוון, װאָס שטענדיק, אָרגאַנישע,
װערן זײַן. געװען װאָס מען זאָגט. װאָס נישט פֿאַרפֿעלן אײן. איך דאַנק עס דיר צו זאָגן...

You read *A Doll's House!*[166] I was so excited that I had to take the book and re-read it. A year and-a-half ago, when I thought about *Nora*, I remember I felt bad that you hadn't read it yet. How do you plan to spend your vacation? Are you going anywhere for a short time? Be sure you see the Exposition. It will be very educational for you. Will summer school take up much of your time? And French? Will you study it again this year? See to it that you will have as much free time as you can for fun. You need a rest. Don't upset your vacation by worrying about later or next year. It will most certainly be good. You won't get lost; I can promise you that.

Do you hear much from your former girlfriends? Do they write to you much? I'm sure you have not forgotten them and are happy when they write. When I meet any of them I always remind myself to write to you. June 15 starts vacation in all schools. From Shavl and Ponevezh the students are already filling the streets. It is now lively in town. Ania and Milke, I think, failed in Lithuanian language.

Did Lola come to see you yet? How you must wait to see her! Give her my best regards.

Heartiest regards to all.

Be well and enjoy youself.

Your

B.

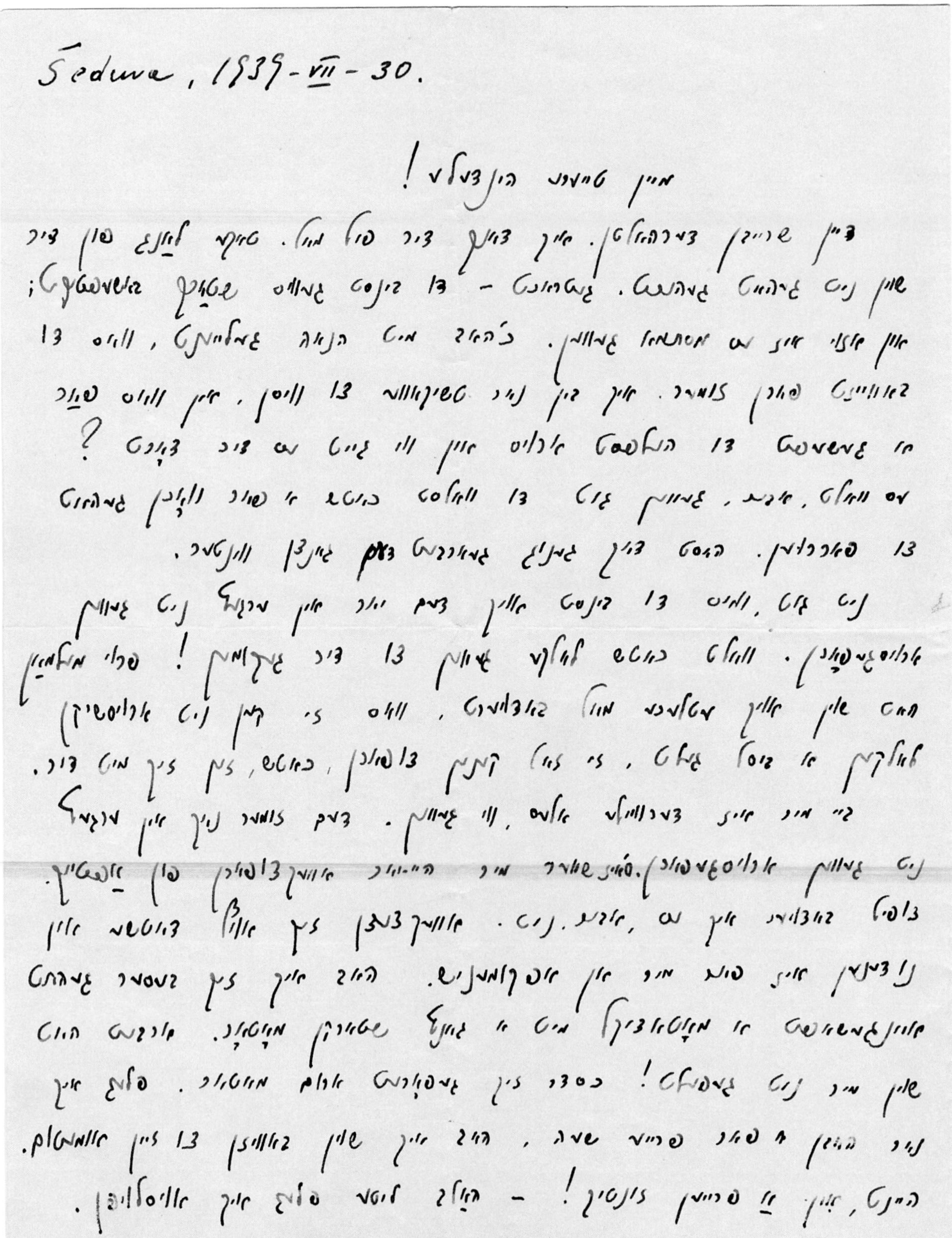

Šeduva, 1939-VIII-30.

מיין טייערע הינדעלע!

דיין שרייבן דערהאלטן. איך דאנק דיר פיל מאל. טאקע לאנג פון דיר
שוין ניט געהאט געהערט. געווארט — דו קענסט גלייבן שטארק אויסגעבענקט;
און [illegible] איז עס [illegible] געווען. כ'האב מיט הנאה געלייענט, וואס דו
באווייזט פארן זומער. איך בין נאר [illegible] צו וויסן, אין וואס פאר
א גענעסעט דו האלטסט אלץ און ווי גייט עס דיר דארט?
עס וועט, אגב, געווען גוט דו וועסט באלד די שולע וועלן געהאט
צו פארלירן. האסט דיין גאנצע געארבעט דעם גאנצן ווינטער.
ניט גוט, וואס דו קענסט אין דעם יאר אין ערגעץ ניט געווען
ארויסגעפארן. וואלט באלד [illegible] צו דיר געקומען! פראי [illegible]
האט שוין אלע [illegible] מאל באזוכט, וואס זי קען ניט ארויסגיין
[illegible] צו [illegible], זי וויל [illegible] צופארן, באלד, זיך מיט דיר.
ביי מיר איז דערווייל אלעס, ווי געווען. דעם זומער ניט אין ערגעץ
ניט געווען ארויסגעפארן. [illegible] מיר [illegible] אוועקגעפארן פון [illegible].
[illegible] באזוכט איך עס, [illegible] ניט. אוועקגעגאנגען זיך אליין [illegible] און
[illegible] איז [illegible] מיר אין [illegible]. האב איך זיך [illegible] געהאט
[illegible] די [illegible] מיט די גאנצע [illegible]. [illegible] האט
שוין מיר ניט געפעלט! כסדר זיך געפירט ארום [illegible]. פלעג איך
נאר האבן א [illegible] [illegible] שעה, האב איך שוין באזוכט צו זיין [illegible].
[illegible], אין די פרייען [illegible]! — [illegible] פלעג איך [illegible].

Šeduva, 30/V11/1939[167]

(July 30, 1939)

My Dear Hindalla!

Received your letter for which I thank you many times. I really hadn't heard from you for a while. I figured you must be very busy; and that is what probably happened. I read with much pleasure what you have accomplished this summer. I'm curious, however, in what kind of a store[168] you are helping out and how you are doing there. It would have been good if you could have rested at least a couple of weeks. You worked plenty all winter.

Too bad that you didn't go anywhere this year. At least if Lola would have come to visit you! Mrs. Mellman even mentioned a few times that she is sorry she cannot send Lola any money; she should at least come to see you.

By me so far everything is as usual. This summer I haven't yet gone anywhere. This year it is difficult for me to leave the business. I'm not too sorry, however. To sit in the country (dacha) and be bored is for me a punishment. Instead, I bought myself a motorcycle with a good enough motor. As soon as I had a couple of hours off, I managed to be everywhere. On a Sunday, for instance, I could cover half of Lithuania. Only one drawback—my mother was terribly upset with my journeys. Upon returning, she would always treat me like a newly-found one... Last week I found a buyer and I sold it. At home they were extremely pleased. But I am sad—again I remain "planted" in Šeduva.

Again I am with my old hobbies—listening to the radio and reading. Of the best books that lately came my way, I can recall *The Patriot*[169] by Pearl S. Buck and *Mary Stuart*[170] by S. Zweig. Now I am in the middle of reading a collection of Estonian novels by Gaylit.[171] He was entirely unfamiliar to me and I'm reading it with great interest.

Yes, the film *Three Comrades* is from the book by Remarque. The film played in Lithuania not long ago. Unfortunately, I didn't have the opportunity to see it.

Not long ago I received the papers from America. I mailed them straight to the consulate. Even though it takes a long time for your turn to come, it was still a great joy for me. I will wait patiently and will surely make it.

Write everything about yourself, how you are doing and how you are enjoying yourself.

I am enclosing a postal receipt.[172] Please, Hindalla, give it to your aunt. She will need it. I will write to her soon.

My heartiest regards to all. Best wishes to Yvette on her birthday,[173] though just a little late...

Regards from your Aunt Rachel. She is on vacation not far from Šeduva, in Rosalia.[174]

That's all for now. Stay well and cheerful.

Your

B.

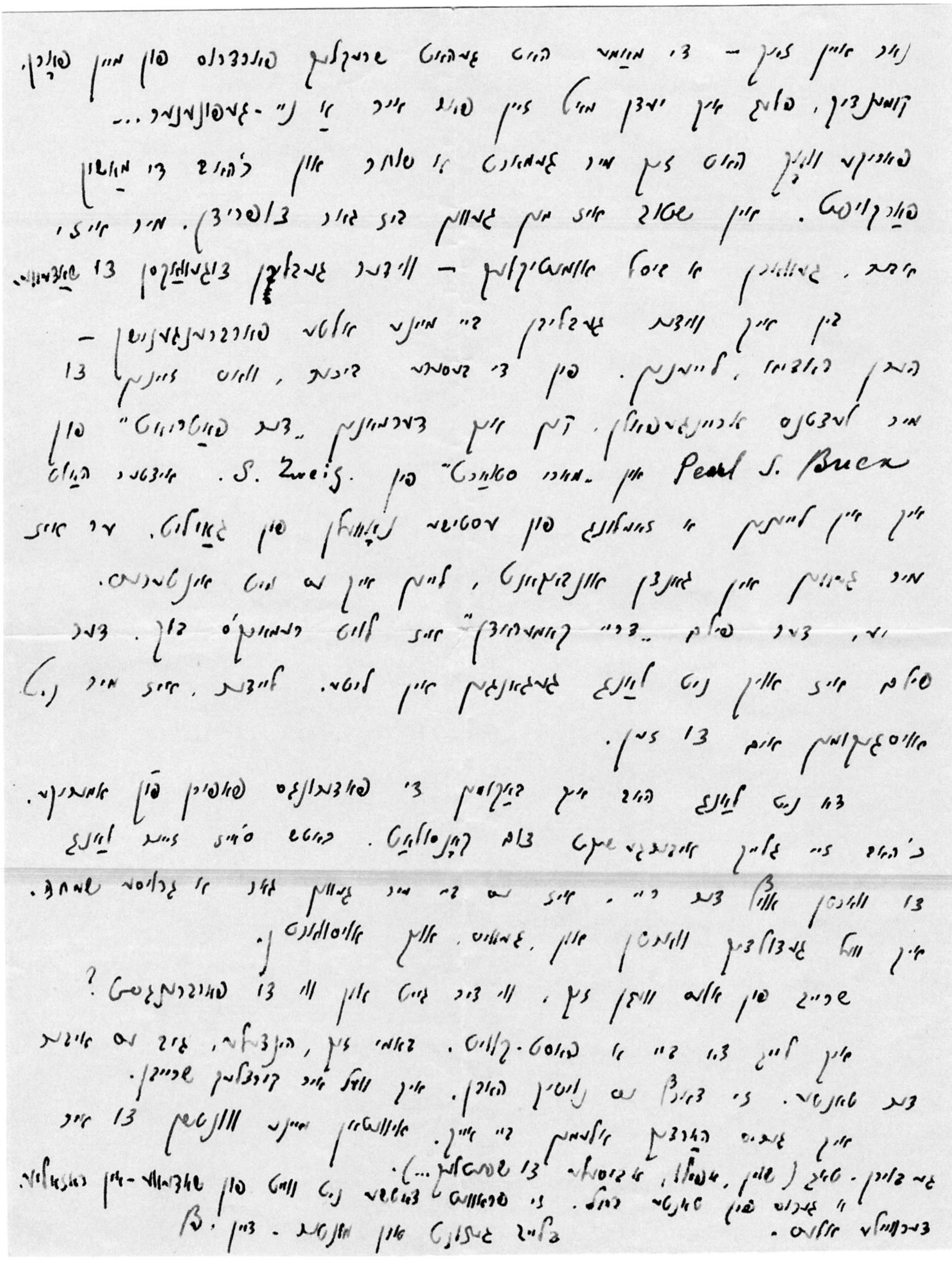
נאָר איין זאַך — די מאַמע האָט געהאַט שרעקלעכע פּלאַנדערס פון מיין פאָרן,
קומענדיק, פּלוץ איך יעדן מאָל זיין פּנים איך זע ני-געפעלנער…
פאַראיקע וואָך האָט זיך מיר געמאַכט צו שלאָף און להפך די מאַשין
פאַרקויפט. מיין שטאָב איז מען געווען ביז גאָר צופרידן. מיר זיינען
היבש. געווען אין גרויס אַמעריקאַנעך — ווידער געבליבן צוגעוואַקסן צו שולעמען.
בין איך וועגן געבליבן די מיינע אַלטע פאַרגענוגנס —
האָבן האָלבן, לייענען. פון די נעסטע ביכער, וואָס זיינען צו
מיר לעבנס אַרומגעפאַלן. דאָס איז דערמאָנען "דאָס פּאַראַדיז" פון
Pearl S. Buck און "מאַרקו סטאַרט" פון S. Zweig. איצטער האָב
איך אין לייענען די זאַמלונג פון ערשטע נאָוועלן פון גאָרקי. ער איז
מיר געווען אין גאַנצן אַנגעזאָגט, לייען איך עס מיט אינטערעס.
יאָ, דער פילם "דריי קאַמעראַדן" איז לויט רעמאַרקס בוך. דער
פילם איז אָבער נישט לאַנג געגאַנגען אין לאָדזש. לייד, איז מיר נישט
אויסגעקומען אים צו זען.
דאָ נישט לאַנג האָב איך באַקומען די פאָדערונגס פּאַפּירן פון אַמעריקע.
כ'האָב זיי גלייך איבערגעשיקט צום קאָנסולאַט. כאָטש ס'איז נאָך לאַנג
צו וואַרטן אויף דעם, איז עס פאַר מיר געווען אַ גרויסע שמחה.
איך וואָלט געוואָלט וויסן ווען, און געמאַכט. אַלץ איבערלאָזן.
שרייב, מיין טייערע, וועגן זיך. ווי זענען דיינע אויף צו פאָרגעכטעס?
איך לייג צו דאָ אַ פּאָסט-קאַרט. דאַנקע זייער, הינדעלע, פאַר דעם אַלעם
דעם טאָנס. די צייט ניט האָבן. איך וועל דיר קורצלעך שרייבן.
איך גריס האַרציק אַלעמען די דיינע. איבערגעבן מיינע ווינטשן צו דיר
גע-בורטס-טאָג (שוין, עטלעכע, איבערלעבן צו שפּעטלעך…).
די גרוס פון טאַנטע דאָרע. די פּראָוואַנס ני וויסן פון שלאָפֿן - מיין ראַנגליז.
דערמאָנט אַלע. בלייב געזונט און מונטער. דיין ב.

Šeduva, 20/VIII 39.

מײַן טײַערע הינדעלע!

„M-me Curie" — האָט מיר זייער דערפֿרייט. ס׳איז שוין שווער מיר
די לאַנג [illegible] נעמען. איצט [illegible], איצט, [illegible] איצטער
מיר לעבן און שאַפֿן, ווי איר אייגענער, דאָס איז דאָך ערשטן מאָל.
מײַן לעבן איז מיט גרויס אינטערעס, כּדי צו הייסן גוט איז ניט ניט
בײַ מיר.
מײַן קליינער אוצר, ווי גוט צו האָבן איז מיט צוזאַמענקומען דעם גליק.
מײַן דאַנק דיר, הינדעלען אַליין, איך שיק [illegible] דער מתּנה.

ווי מער? — געלערנט. מיר ניט געקענט אויסהאַלטן מײַן געשריבט
אַ [illegible] [illegible]. [illegible] איז איז פֿון מײַנע [illegible]. אויך אין
דער [illegible] האָט מען זיך שוין [illegible] די מײַן [illegible], און נאָך דעם,
ווי [illegible] [illegible] [illegible] אויפֿן [illegible], האָט מען זיך שוין אין
גאַנצן [illegible].
די [illegible] איז שוין די [illegible] וואָס לאַנג [illegible] הייסן. איך
[illegible] גאָר ניט [illegible], וואָס איז דאָס [illegible] די [illegible] מאָל [illegible]
צו דער [illegible] [illegible] זײַן.
מײַן [illegible] צו צו די [illegible] [illegible] צו דער [illegible]. גיב אָפּ [illegible],
[illegible] זיך, [illegible].
[illegible] אַלע. די גרוס און [illegible] —
דײַן B.

Šeduva 20/VIII/1939[175]

(August 20, 1939)

My Dear Hindalla!

Madame Curie[176] pleased me very much. It is a familiar name to me. However, such an exact account of her life and work is new to me. I'm reading it with great interest, although my fluency in English is not quite up to par.

I'm thinking, what a good choice you made for me. I thank you, Hindalla, many, many times for the present.

By me?—nothing. I couldn't resist and bought a new motorcycle. I suppose it is one of my weaknesses. Even at home they got used to my riding; especially, after I passed my driving test, they quieted down altogether.

We've had extremely hot weather for a couple of weeks, so it isn't bad at all that I can ride down to the lake and go swimming.

I enclose a few words to your aunt. Please see to it that she gets it.

That is all for now.

Be well.

Your

B.

Seduva, 1939-X-27.

מײַן טײַערע הינדעלע!

כ'וויל האָפֿן, דער דאָ בריוו וועט דיר געווים אָנקומען. כ'האָב פֿון דיר אויך דעם לעצטן געהאַט און איך בין שוין גאַנץ באַזאָרגט. בריוו פֿון אויסלאַנד שפּעטיקן זיך איצטער זייער. אַנדערע קומען באַמאָל און גייען ניט. ווײַל איך שוין מער ניט וואַרטן. געווים האָסטו דײַן באַמיִונגען איבער אונדז דאָ.

פֿאַר דער קורצער צײַט האָבן מיר שוין באַוויזן פֿיל צו איבערלעבן. די מלחמה, מיר האָבן פֿריִער אויך זיך געשראָקן, איז איצטער אַ ווירקלעכקייט. זײַנען מיר אין ליטע דאָך פֿון די גליקלעכע. מיר זײַנען דאָך נאָך דערווײַל דירעקט פֿון דער מלחמה ניט באַרירט געוואָרן; מיר זײַנען שוין, אַדרבה, עדות, ווי מיליאָנען ייִדן זײַנען מיט אַמאָל הפֿקר געוואָרן. טײַערע הינדעלע, איך ווייס, די איבערלעבונגען האָסט אויך ניט וויניק. האָסט דאָך איבערגעלעבן אַ גאַנצע געוואַלדיקע פֿון באַקאַנטע און חברים. ווייסטו שוין איצטער, ווי זיי האָבן זיך אַלע אַרויסגעראַטעוועט? וואָס מיר דאַרפֿסט שרײַבן וועגן דעם.

הײַנט איז דאָ די שטימונג אַ סך בעסערע, ווי מיט אַ פּאָר־פֿינף וואָכן צוריק. ס'האָט זיך אַלץ איבערגעביטן אַלײן, איז מען האָפֿן אַלײן געקומען.

בײַ מיר איז דערווײַל קיינע באַזונדערע נײַס נישטאָ. כ'אַרבעט, ווי געווען. בײַ אונדז האָבן מיר איצטער וואָלקנס, רעגנדיקע האַרבסט־טעג. טאָמער אין די גאַנצע פֿרײַע צײַט בײַם חבֿרות. וואָס וועגן דעם דאָ וועטער, ווײַל איך מעג שפּאַצירן. מיטן מוזיקאַליש דורכפֿירן זיך דאָ אין שול, לײַדער, ניט: נישטאָ קיין רעכענען.

און דעם מיטוואָך האָב איך דיר האָלץ טשיקעטן צו דערציילן. אַ פּאָר וואָכן צײַט בין איך געווען מאָבילִיזירט (מײַן הײַ־וואָריקע פּראַקטיק!), מײַן מאַשין, טויערשטיין זיך, וכו'. הײַנט זײַנען מיר שוין ווידער פֿרײַ.

און ווי גייט עס בײַ דיר? דו מוזט האָבן איצטער פֿיל אַרבעט. עס זײַנען דאָך שוין בײַ דיר די לעצטע סקול־מאָנאַטן. שרײַב מיר, הינדעלע, דײַנע פּלענער אַלײן ווײַטער, שרײַב אַ סך און פֿון אַלעס. איך וואַרט שוין מיט אומגעדולד. אַ צווייטן מאָל וויל איך דיר מער שרײַבן און דערציילן וועגן אַלץ, וואָס וועט דיר נאָר אינטערעסירן; הײַנטיקן מאָל וויל איך זיך באַגרענעצן מיט אַזוי פֿיל.

זײַ געזונט און שטאַרק. און גריס פֿון מיר אַלעמען די דײַנע אין שטוב.

דײַן B.

Šeduva, 27/X/1939[177]

(October 27, 1939)

My Dear Hindalla!

I hope that this letter will reach you. I haven't heard from you for so long and I am quite concerned. Letters from abroad are very slow now, or don't arrive at all. Consequently, I'm not waiting. Certainly, you are more concerned about us here.

In this short time we managed to live through quite a bit. The war—we feared it so—is now an actuality. We here, in Lithuania, are the lucky ones. We haven't yet been touched directly by the war; we are, however, witnesses to how millions of Jews perished. Dear, Hindalla, I know how much you are suffering. You left behind in Poland close ones, friends, relatives. Do you know, perhaps, how they survived? Please write to me about it.

Today, the mood here is much better than it was four or five weeks ago. Everything took a turn in such a way that we can hope for better.

By me no special news right now. I'm working as usual. We are in the midst of melancholy, rainy fall days. I spend all my free time by the radio. When the weather will get better I will, most likely, spend more time on the outside. Unfortunately, I cannot ride my motorcycle either—no gasoline.[178]

And the most important thing I almost forgot to tell you. Four weeks I was mobilized (my this year's vacation), my motorcycle, naturally, too. Now we are both free.

And how is it with you? You probably have much work; these are your last school months. Tell me Hindalla, your plans for the future. Write much and about everything. I'm already waiting impatiently.

Next time I will write more and tell you about everything, whatever may interest you. This time—that is all.

Be well and give my regards to all.

Your

B.

Šeduva, 1939 - XII - 6

טײַערסטע הינדעלע!

דאָס זײַנען דערהאַלטן אַלע דײַנע 4 בריוו. די פֿיר שלוחות האָב איך אַזױ פֿיל מאָל געלײענט, װי [illegible] דעם לענגסטן בריוו געװען. אין דעם [illegible] דיר זײַט.

כּהוגן, הינדע, אַ סך פֿאָרװערטס, װאָס צו האָבסט פֿון מיר געלערנט, כאָטש שוין ניט אײן בריוו צו דיר געשריבן. הײַנט איז די פֿאַרבינדונג מיט אַמעריקע נאָך שװערער געװאָרן. כ'װעל אָבער קלערן װעגן דעם, װי מיר זאָלן נאָך װײַטער האָבן אײנער פֿון אַנדערן.

שרײַב מיר, הינדעלע, אָפֿטער; װאַרט ניט אױף מײַנע בריוו. אַ מאָל בריוו װעלן זיך אױסן קומען.

כּהוגן געשריבן בײַ דער טאָנטע רחל. אפֿשר װאָס זי װײס װעגן דײַנע [illegible]. זי האָט מיר נאָך ניט געענטפֿערט. האָסטו שוין װאָס געהערט פֿון זײ?

װי צו זעט, בין איך געװען אין [illegible], בין געפֿאָרן אין [illegible] אין אַרבעט, װי געװען. אין ליטע איז אַלצדינג ניט שלעכט אין פֿאַרגלײַך מיט אַנדערע. הײַנט קען מען האָפֿן, אַז מיר װעלן זײַן בלײַבן פֿון דער צײַט פֿון מלחמה. געװײנטלעך, [illegible] קען ניט [illegible].

אין אַמעריקע, מסתּמא, מוז זײַן אונהײבן די פּראָספּעריטי פֿאַר די אַמעריקאַנער [illegible] אַ מלחמה אין אײראָפּע ניט שלעכט.

שרײַב מיר, הינדעלע, װאָס איז בײַ דיר? צו ענדיגסטו דאָס װײַטער די סקול. װאָס װעסטו טאָן װײַטער? װעסטו האָבן מעגלעכקײט צו לערנען װײַטער? איך װאָלט זײער װעלן. און װאָס [illegible] צו לערנען? שרײַב מיר װעגן אַלעם.

[illegible] מאָל װאָלט איך זײַן [illegible] מיט אַזױ װײניק. איך װינטש דיר אַלעס בעסטע און גרוס האַרציק אַלעמען בײַ אײַך אין שטוב.

בלײַב געזונט און מונטער —

דײַן B.

P.S. דער נאָמען פֿון [illegible] האָט זיך געביטן אױף B 7.

S.Z.

Šeduva 6/XII/1939[179]

(December 6, 1939)

My Dear Hindalla!

Finally your letter arrived. Those few lines I read so many times as if it were the longest letter. I thank you much. It hurts me, though, that you don't hear from me, even though I wrote so many times to you. Presently the ties with America became more difficult. I don't even want to bring to mind that we will hear even less frequently from one another. Write to me, dear Hindalla, more often; don't wait for my answers. Some of the letters are bound to come through.

I asked your Aunt Rachel if she knows anything about your parents. She hasn't replied to my letter yet. Did you, by any chance hear from them?

As you see, I am still in Šeduva. I am hale and hearty and work as usual. In Lithuania, things are not too bad, in comparison with other places. Now we can even hope that we may remain on this side of the war. Naturally, one cannot figure much ahead.

In America, no doubt, it is the beginning of a prosperity. For American business a war in Europe is not bad at all.

Write to me, Hindalla, about yourself. You are now graduating from high school. What are your plans for the future? Will you have the opportunity to study further? I would very much like that. And what are you planning to study? Write to me about everything.

This time I'll be satisfied with this short letter. I wish you the very best and give my regards to everyone.

Be well.

Your

B.

P.S. The number of our house has recently been changed to No. 7.

Šeduva, 1940-I-21

מײַן טײַערע הינדעלע!

דײַן בריוו פֿון 25/XI אויגוסט דערהאַלטן. שטאַרק זיך געפֿרייט, ס'איז געווען בײַ מיר אַ
גרויסע שׂימחה. דער עיקר, אַרבעט, וואָס האָסט מיר דערצײלט איז, איז אויך מײַנע אַ בריוו
האָט זיך צו דיר דורכגעריסן און צו וועלכן שוין נישט דאַרפֿסן איבערלעבן וועגן דײַן זײַן.

דערצײלסט מיר, הינדעלע, און וועל דיר האָבן, וואָס צו שרײַבן וועסטו לערנען. מײַן האַרץ
אַ סך געשריבן וועגן דעם; אָבער וואָס קען איך דיר פֿון אַהין וועט האָבן? מײַן בריוו
וועסט דו געוויס אויך קריגן, ווען צו וועסט שוין האָבן אַלעס אַליין באַשלאָסן. עס איז גוט,
איז אַלעמען שטאַרק, צו וואָס מ'האָט אַ ניגונג. נאָר נישט אַלע מאָל קען מען זיך דאָס פֿאַרגינען.

מײַן האַרץ זיך אויך נישט דערלויבט צו לערנען, דאָס וואָס איך האָב מיר געצויגן. וועסט געוויס מוזן
אויסקלײַבן אַ פּראַקטישן פֿאַך, וואָס וועט דיר מער צוזאַגשטעלן. און וואָס איז פֿאַר דיר
פּראַקטיש צו לערנען אין אַמעריקע, ווייסטו דאָך בעסער דײַן טאַנטע אין יאַנקל, און צו וועלסט
זי מוזן פֿאָלגן! צו וועסט מוזן אָננעמען דעם טאַנטעס ראַט און לערנען פֿאַרמאַציע, אויך זי
האָט אין אַמעריקע צו לעבן אין אײַנפֿאַך און דיר צו דערקלערן מיט שטודירן דאָס שפּראַך.
אויך ווייס. וואָס פֿאַר אַ קאָמישע פֿון דאָס איז פֿאַרמאַציע אין אַמעריקע; איך ווייס אַליין, איז
צו האָסט צו דעם דײַן גרויס לוסט נישט. קען, אָבער, זײַן ס'איז אַ גוטע ריכטונג... און דאָס
ווייס איך נישט. און נאָך וואָס, האָבן איר פֿאַר דיר דאָס פּראַקטישע אָנצונעמען דער טאַנטעס
פֿאָרשלאָגן, זײַן נישט רעכענען, ווי דאָס איז אַלץ וועט.

איך וואַרט שוין מיט אומגעדולד צו הערן, ווי צו האָסט געענדיקט די שול און וואָס
צו טאָסט וועטער. שרײַב מיר גלײַך, הינדעלע.

וואָס דײַנע עלטערן זײַנען געבליבן אַליין אונדזערע גרענעצן, האָרעוועט שטאַרק נישט
באַזונדערן. דײַן שוועסטער וועט עס געוויס נישט פֿאַרגעסן. דערווײַל, קען זײַן, איז זיי געוויס נישט צו
גוט אין די וואָכן טאָגן דאָרט געהאַט צו זײַן צו מיט די אַלגעמיינע. די דאָס איז אַצינד
נישט רײַכער און מיר גרויסע ווײַטן, וואָס שרײַבן מיר וועלן האָבן און וואָס ס'דערוואַרט
אונדז נאָך אַלעמען. האָסטו באַקומען געשריבן פֿון דײַנע עלטערן? און די שוועסטער און די חברים, ווי גייט זיי?
בײַ אונדז, קען מען זאָגן, איז אַלץ ווי געווען. איך שרײַב אַ - געוויס. דער ריגע-ספּעציעל

Šeduva 21/1/1940[180]

(January 21, 1940)

My Dear Hindalla!

Your letter of November 25th just received.[181] You can imagine, it was for me a great joy. Most important, though, I was delighted that my letter also got through to you and that you won't have to worry about anything.

You ask me, Hindalla, I should advise you what you should study. I gave it much thought; but what can I advise you being such a distance away? My letter you will most certainly receive after you will have decided yourself. It is good to study something that you have an inclination for. But that you cannot always give yourself the pleasure of doing. I, too, didn't give myself the pleasure of studying what I longed for. You will, most likely, have to pick a practical occupation which will make you independent. And what it is practical for you to study in America your aunt and uncle, most likely, know best and you will have to listen to them. You will have to take your aunt's advice and study pharmacy if she has plans to buy a drugstore and to supply you with a steady occupation. I know what a comical occupation pharmacy is in America; I also know that you don't have too much love for it. It could be, however, that it is a good business, and that I do not know. And something else, today it is practical for you to take your aunt's suggestions, not figuring how it will turn out later.

I'm waiting impatiently already to hear how you finished school and what you are going to do afterwards. Write to me right away, Hindalla.

The fact that your parents remained outside our boundaries should not sadden you. Your sisters[182] certainly won't regret it. At this time, perhaps, they may not feel too comfortable and they would most likely have preferred to be with the relatives. The times are so uncertain and no one knows what surprises await us here and what awaits all of us, in general. Do you, at least, hear from your parents? And your sisters and friends, how are they?

By us, one can say, everything is as before, certainly in Šeduva. The war news, which at the beginning enveloped everyone, is now as if over. One gets used to everything! The first days of the war one could hardly see anything else in the newspapers. Now, many times, I find myself too tired to listen to the boring war dispatches which are mostly lies.

By me there is no special news. In the drugstore the work is as before. Because of transportation difficulties much merchandise is scarce, but that interferes little with the work. After dinner I spend much time skating. At night I "bother" the radio. I read a little. Lately, I had a good book, Ilf-Petrov's[183] *The One-floor America*—a trip through America by the Soviet authors Ilf and Petrov. Did you read it?

That's all for now. Be well and write often and about everything that you are doing.

With heartiest regards to all your family.

Your

B.

וועלכע האט די ערשטע זייט געלאמען אונדזער הויפטשטאט, איז אויסגעטאן, ווי געווען. זו וויל וויסן
מיט גרויסן! די ערשטע מלחמה-וואכן פליגט מען אין צייטונג דיין אונדזער אויך ניט וויסן, ווי
נייס. און די ראדיאו פליגט מיך "הערן" די אונדזער זייט אלץ נייס. אויסער פון איך זיך גוט.
אנדערע מאל, אויסצוהערן די צענטראלע מלחמה-באריכטן, וועלכע זיינען חוץ אויסער דער ליגן.

דאס מאל איז קיינע באזונדערע נייס ניטא. און אפשר איז די אויבנס, ווי גענוג.
צוליב טראנספּאָרט-שוועריקייטן פון אנדערע ערטער, ווערן די שטאט ווייניק-וואס אין
דער ערדע. ניט אויך פארבראכט מיך אויסער פיל אויפן גליקש. און אונדז "מאַטער"
אין די ראדיאו. זו באזוך זיין מיך. לעצטנס האב איך געהערט די אונזן רעק – אלע-פאטראל-
"די אויסשטעקטע אמעריקע" – די רייזע פארזיכערונג איבער אמעריקע פון די סאוועטישע שווערע
מזל און פאטראל. האסטו עס געלייענט?

דערציילט אלעס. זיי געזונט און שרייב אפט און וועגן אלץ, וואס מאכט זיך בײַ דיר.
מיט הארציקע גרוסן פון אלע דיינע אייגענע –
דיין פּ.

11/VII 59.

... Kinder

IN A NOTE FROM MRS. MELLMAN, dated 11/VII/1959[184]

Berman has been dead since 1941 when all the Jews were killed, in August, 1941.

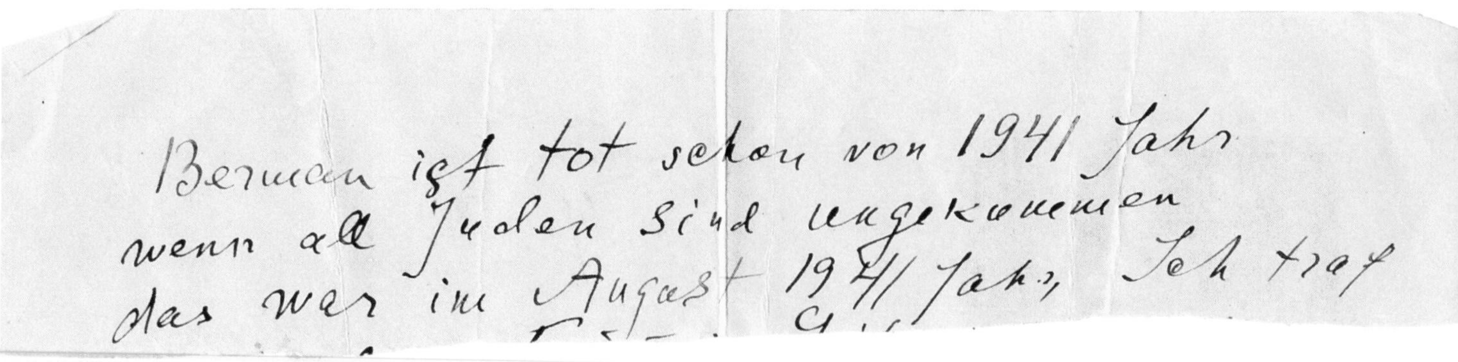
Berman ist tot schon von 1941 Jahr
wenn all Juden sind umgekommen
das wer im August 1941 Jahr, Ich traf

Epilogue

"But Mom, How Do You Really Know?"

That was what my brothers and I always asked my mother when she would tell us all her relatives were killed in the Holocaust. No matter where they had lived—Lithuania, Latvia, or Poland, they all were gone. As children, we always hoped one day someone would knock on our door and say, "Surprise, we survived!" But that's not what happened.

It was Mr. Aron Bank, from Widze, who knocked on my mother's door in 1946, to deliver the news to my mother: *Her whole family had been killed.* Her father first, at the small lake, Lake Maruger; her mother and sisters later, when they jumped from a train and were shot. My mother knew Mr. Bank and his family when she lived in Widze. He was able to find my mother from her wedding invitation, which she had sent to her parents, in the hope that a miracle would happen and they would receive it! Mr. Bank also had lost his family—a wife and children—in the Holocaust. With the wedding invitation and other documents in hand, he traveled throughout the United States, on a bus, to tell relatives of those he knew what had happened. I doubt I actually met him, but I heard the story enough times that I have created a mental image of him, even my mother serving him grapefruit juice, which he had never tasted before.[185]

The Fate of Alchonan, Chana, Gita, Leah Zarchi (Zarkey), Widze

Hinda's parents and sisters were in Widze when the war began.[186] The Hitler-Stalin pact of 1939 divided Poland between them. Widze went to the Russians and the Soviet army entered the town on September 17, 1939, putting Widze under Communist occupation. On June 22, 1941, Germany launched a surprise attack on the Soviet Union and Russian troops withdrew from Widze, with the Germans entering five days later.[187] As best we can tell, Alchonan was murdered during that time, either by the Nazis or by local Lithuanians who took unofficial control during those five days, at Lake Maruger, in 1941.[188] In 1942, after living in the Widze ghetto,[189] Chana, Gita and Leah were sent to the ghetto in Švenčionys.[190] In April, 1943, they likely were killed in Ponar.[191] Mr. Bank's account appears to have been accurate. In 1945, under the Soviets, Widze was incorporated into Belarus. It is part of Belarus today.

(I asked my mother if she ever saw her family after she had moved to Šeduva to attend school. She told me the story of Ligmian, a town on the Lithuanian-Poland border. Once a year large crowds of Jews would come from Poland to meet their relatives in Lithuania, at the cemetery. My mother was able to see her family this way just once and this was the last time she saw them.[192])

The Fate of Nochum Berman, Šeduva

The Molotov-Ribbentrop Pact (also known as the Hitler-Stalin pact) between Nazi Germany and Communist Russia in August 1939, and the German-Soviet Boundary and Friendship Treaty a month later placed Lithuania under Soviet control. By June 1940 the Soviets had set up a pro-Soviet government, and President Antanas Smetona was forced to leave. The German army invaded Lithuania on June 22, 1941, capturing Šeduva on June 25, 1941, as part of Operation Barbarossa, the code name for Germany's invasion of the Soviet Union. On June 26, 1941, the German army entered Šeduva but, during the first days of occupation, control was in the hands of radical Lithuanian nationalists who persecuted the local Jews and engaged in violence against them.[193] Many Jews tried to flee to Russia, but poor treatment by the Lithuanian nationalists forced them back to their homes. By July 1941, Jews were forced to wear the yellow Star of David and they were moved into a guarded ghetto surrounded by barbed wire in the village of Pavartičiai, 5 kilometers away. Any Jew who had been part of the Soviet rule was arrested and executed. On August 25, 1941, the remaining Jews of Šeduva were loaded on trucks and taken to Liaudiškiai. Over the next two days the entire Jewish community of Šeduva was shot and buried in two pre-prepared mass graves. One site was located 400 meters north of the Šeduva road and a second 900 meters north west of the same road, close to a path in the forest. A total of 664

Jews were killed—230 Jewish men, 275 Jewish women and 159 Jewish children.[194]

In a letter from Mrs. Mellman dated July 11, 1959, my mother was informed that Nochum Berman was murdered at this time—August 1941. He was only twenty-nine years old. My trip to Lithuania and extensive research and correspondence with people with ties to Šeduva have not been able to verify or contradict Mrs. Mellman's information. The letter dated January 1940 was the last time my mother ever heard from Berman.

More About My 2010 Trip

The trip my brother Ken and I took was the "Jewish Heritage Trip to Lithuania," organized by Howard Margol and Peggy Freedman.[195] One of the features of the trip was a customized two-day trip to the *shtetlekh* of choice. Although we visited eight *shtetlekh* in the two-day period, in Lithuania, Latvia, and Belarus, the most important ones, for us, were Widze, where our mother lived from the ages of 3-12, and Šeduva, where she lived from the ages of 12-14—and where Berman lived when he wrote the letters.

We visited Widze first and our hope was to find our mother's house. Before the trip she drew a picture for us as she had remembered the house from 75 years ago.

Widze House, drawn 2010

She mentioned that a tree had been chopped down at the front of the house and that there was now an enclosed entryway. She also mentioned that there was a cellar off to the right of the house.

Amazingly, we found it!

Widze House, 2010

Lake Maruger, Widze, 2010

We found the small lake where my mother's father had been killed, and also the pits at Ponar,[196] where her mother and sisters were likely killed.

Ponar Pits, 2010

In Šeduva, we found the pharmacy and my mother's school, as mentioned earlier.

Former Šeduva School, 2010

The Jewish cemeteries in both towns are in poor condition with overgrown weeds and few monuments even visible. Many towns now have Holocaust memorials. Widze, however, does not, and the Šeduva memorial had been been vandalized and was actually missing when we visited.

Our hopes of finding our mother's homes in Widze and Šeduva were realized, and walking in the places she had walked decades ago was a thrill and experience that cannot be described! However, our hopes of finding anything about Berman's letters, or talking with anyone in Šeduva who may have known him or our mother, were not realized. While we likely saw some of the businesses and homes of people our mother knew, we were not able to identify them with any certainty. Of particular interest is a picture we took which shows the number 7 on a house. Interestingly, Berman's 27th letter, written in December 1939, states that the number of his house had recently been changed to number 7. Did we find his house? We likely will never know.

Number 7, Berman's House? 2010

In the larger cities in Lithuania we did see some evidence of a resurgence in Jewish life and culture, but we also saw evidence of anti-Semitism. We had the opportunity to attend a Shabbat service in the only remaining synagogue in Vilnius and to visit the Jewish Center there.

In the smaller towns, unless there is a Holocaust memorial, evidence of any prior Jewish life and influence was not visible to us in the time we were there. An entire world has disappeared. Berman's life was cut short, his dreams and plans were never realized. Hindalla lost a dear friend, but these letters guarantee that Berman will be remembered.

Šeduva Pharmacy, 2010

What Happened To . . .

Hindalla

Hinda Zarkey is the recipient of the letters. She continues to live in the Cleveland, Ohio area. In 1945, she married Jack Saul. They were married sixty-three years before he died in May 2009. They have three children and four grandchildren.

Goda, Samuel, and Yvette Bardon

The Bardon family also remained in the Cleveland, Ohio area. Yvette married Shale Sonkin and they have three children and eight grandchildren. Samuel died in 1960; Goda died in 1981.

Lola

Lola Mellman came to the United States in 1938, with her father. They settled in Gary, Indiana with an aunt. Within a year, Mr. Mellman died. Lola later married Myron Friedman and settled in Morristown, New Jersey. She and Hinda continue to stay in touch.

Mrs. Mellman

Mrs. Mellman and her other daughter, Ania, planned to come to the United States after Mr. Mellman and Lola were established. When Mr. Mellman suddenly died, Mrs. Mellman stayed in Šeduva. She and Ania apparently both survived the war.

Victims[197]

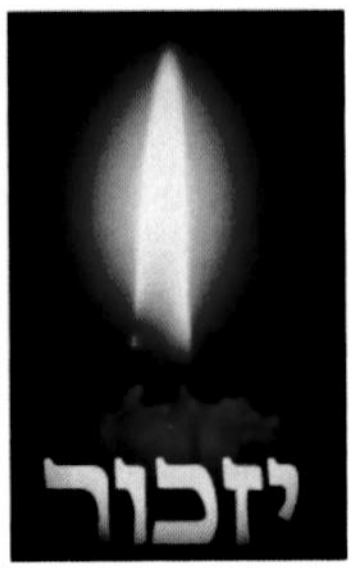

לכל איש יש שם שנתן לו אלוהים ונתנו לו אביו ואימו

Yizkor
for the Jewish
Community of
Shadova - Šeduva

Yahrzeit Dates for Shadova - Šeduva Jewry
25 to 26 August 1941 - 2 to 3 Ellul 5701

זכור את עשה לנו עמלק. זכרו הכל. אל תשכחו עד סוף ימיכם והעבירו הלאה
כצוואה קדושה לדורות הבאים שהגרמנים הרגו, טבחו ורצחו אותנו

Remember that which Amalek did to us; remember everything do not forget for the rest of your lives and pass on as a holy testament to the coming generations that the Germans killed, slaughtered and murdered us.

The following are the family names of some 800 Jews of Shadova - Šeduva murdered by the Nazis and their accomplices near the town and at other sites in August 1941.

Avramowicz
Bartinski
Beer
Ber
Berkowicz
Berlowicz
Berman
Blecher
Bloch
Blumberg
Brenner
Brett
Bruck
Cadowitz
Chlebowitz
Chovsha
Cohen
Cooper
Czack
Damsky
Davidowicz
Deutsch
Diamant
Drusli
Druskin
Eisencraft
Epstein
Faitelevicius
Feiwush
Fleisch
Flitt
Freid
Freidlander
Fuchs
Genkin
Gidus
Gifter
Gippel
Girshowicz
Goldin
Green
Grodnik
Gutman
Hack
Heimann
Henkin
Hilimowicz
Himpel
Kagan
Kalman
Kamber
Kamenitz
Kaper
Kaplan
Kirpitznik
Kirzner
Klawir
Kohn
Krawitz
Krebelnik
Kriger
Kroitz
Krom
Kushner
Landau
Lazerov
Lederman
Leibowicz
Leiserowitz
Lemel
Lerner
Levitt
Mairson
Maizel
Malach
Malcz
Manfried
Margolis
Maskutinsky
Matis
Meer
Mehl
Meltz
Milchman
Mirwis
Muerwiess
Muzikant
Nisilewicz
Opert
Opsei
Payem
Peipert
Peiprt
Plott
Rabinowicz
Razowsky
Rechtman
Rotstein
Sadowicz
Scherr
Schneckman
Schneider
Schnier
Schuchman
Segal
Seinkman
Seras
Sher
Shewah
Shmeid
Shuchman
Sidrov
Singer
Stein
Shulkin
Tajc
Teitelman
Volk
Weiner
Weizman
Wisman
Wolff
Yankelowicz
Yozint
Yuzend
Zamotisik
Zietzer
Zelig
Zell

אברמוביץ
אופסי
אופרט
איזנקרפט
אפשטיין
בלוך
בלומברג
בלכר
בער
ברוק
ברט
ברטיסקי
ברלוביץ
ברמן
ברנר
ברקוביץ
גוטמן
גולדין
גידיס
גיפטר
גיפל
גנקין
גרודניק
גרין
גרשוביץ
דוידוביץ
דויטש
דיאמנט
דמסקי
דרוסלי
דרוסקין
הימן
הימפל
הנקין
הק
ווינר
וולף
וולק
ויסמן
ויצמן
זינגר
זיצר
זל
זליג
זמוטיסיק
חובשה
חילימוביץ
חלובוביץ
טייטלמן
טייק
יוזנט
יוזנט
ינקלוביץ
כהן
לאיזרוביץ
לדרמן
לוויט
לזרוב
לייבוביץ
למל
לנדאו
לרנר
מאיזל
מאירזון
מוזיקנט
מורוויס
מטיס
מילכמן
מירוויס
מל
מלך
מלץ
מנפרייד
מסקוטינסקי
מר
מרגוליס
ניסילביץ
סגל
סרס
פאיטלביץ
פוקס
פייבוש
פים
פיפרט
פלוט
פליט
פלייש
פרייד
פריידלנדר
צאק
קגן
קדוביץ
קון
קופר
קושנר
קירזנר
קירפיצניק
קלוויר
קלמן
קמבר
קמניץ
קפלן
קפר
קרביץ
קרבלניק
קרויץ
קרום
קריגר
רבינוביץ
רוטשטיין
רזובסקי
ריכטמן
שבח
שדוביץ
שוכמן
שולקין
שטיין
שידרוב
שיינקמן
שמייד
שניידר
שנייר
שנקמן
שר

Courtesy of Jon Seligman http://www.seligman.org.il/seduva_memorium.html

Nochum Berman – Writer of the Yiddish Letters

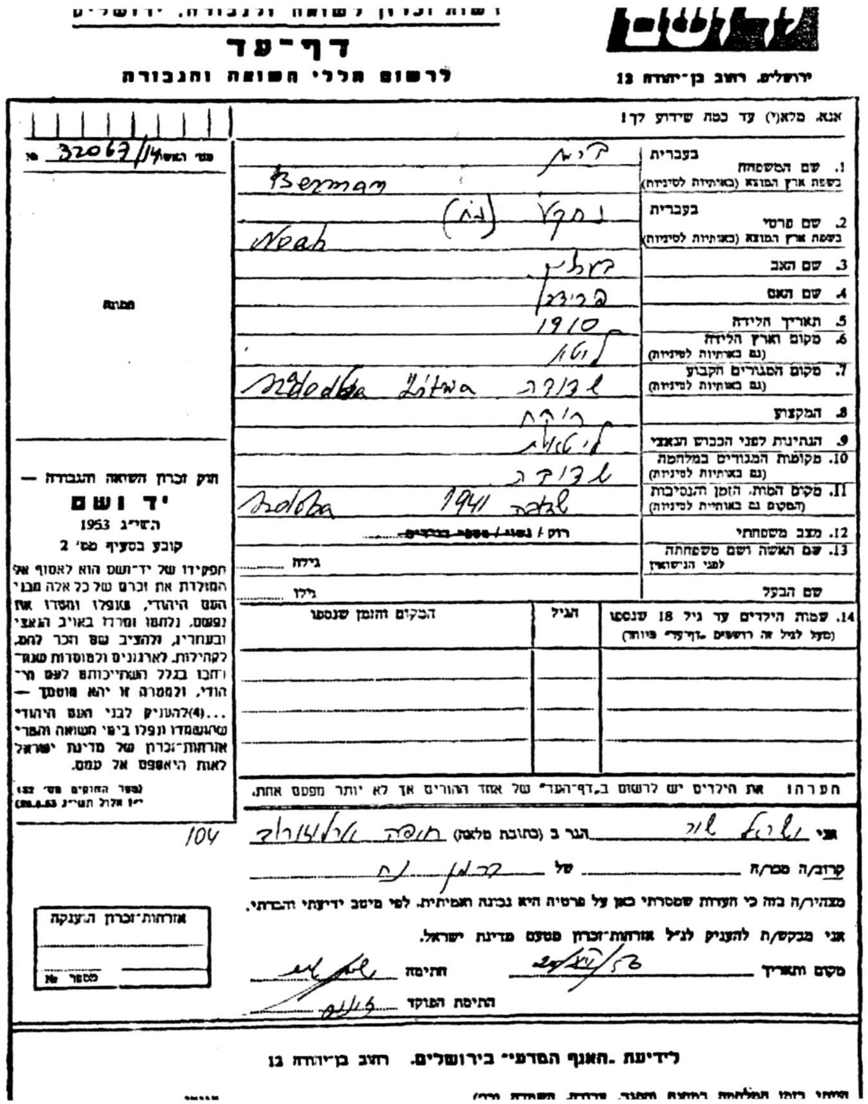
דף-עד

לרשום חללי השואה והגבורה

יד ושם

First Name	NOAKH
First Name	NOAH
First Name*	NEKHA
Mother's First Name	FRIDA
Sex	Male
Date of Birth	1910
Place of Birth	LITHUANIA
Marital Status	SINGLE
Permanent residence	SHADOV,PANEVEZYS,LITHUANIA
Profession	PHARMACIST
Place during the war	SHADOV,PANEVEZYS,LITHUANIA
Place of Death	SHADOV,PANEVEZYS,LITHUANIA
Date of Death	1941
Type of material	Page of Testimony
Submitter's Last Name	SHUR
Submitter's First Name	YISRAEL
Relationship to victim	RELATIVE
Registration date	20/12/1956

Nochum Berman – Writer of the Yiddish Letters

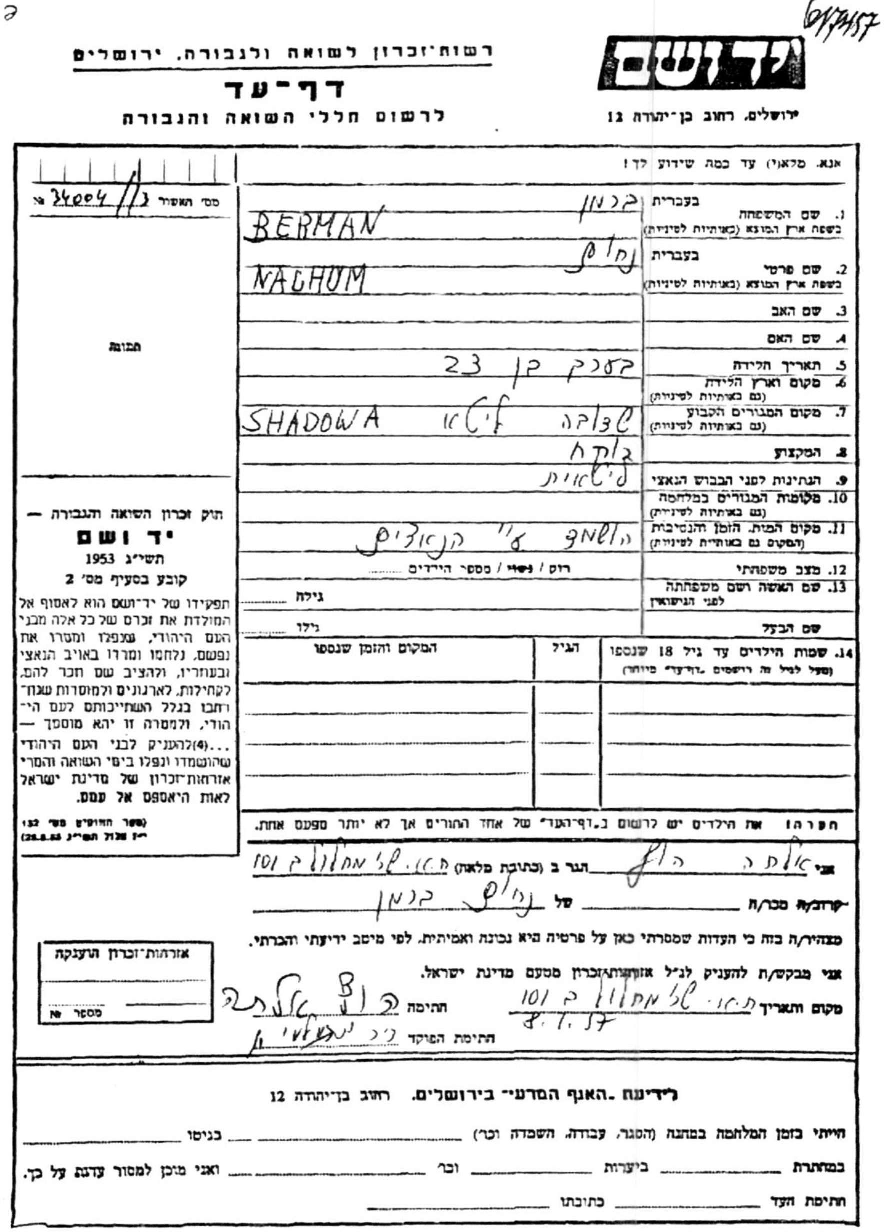

Source	Pages of Testimony
Last Name	BERMAN
First Name	NACHUM
First Name	NAKHUM
Sex	Male
Age	23
Marital Status	SINGLE
Permanent residence	SHADOWA,PANEVEZYS,LITHUANIA
Profession	PHARMACIST
Type of material	Page of Testimony
Submitter's Last Name	HOTZ
Submitter's First Name*	ALTE
Relationship to victim	ACQUAINTANCE
Registration date	08/01/1957

Freida Berman – Nochum's Mother

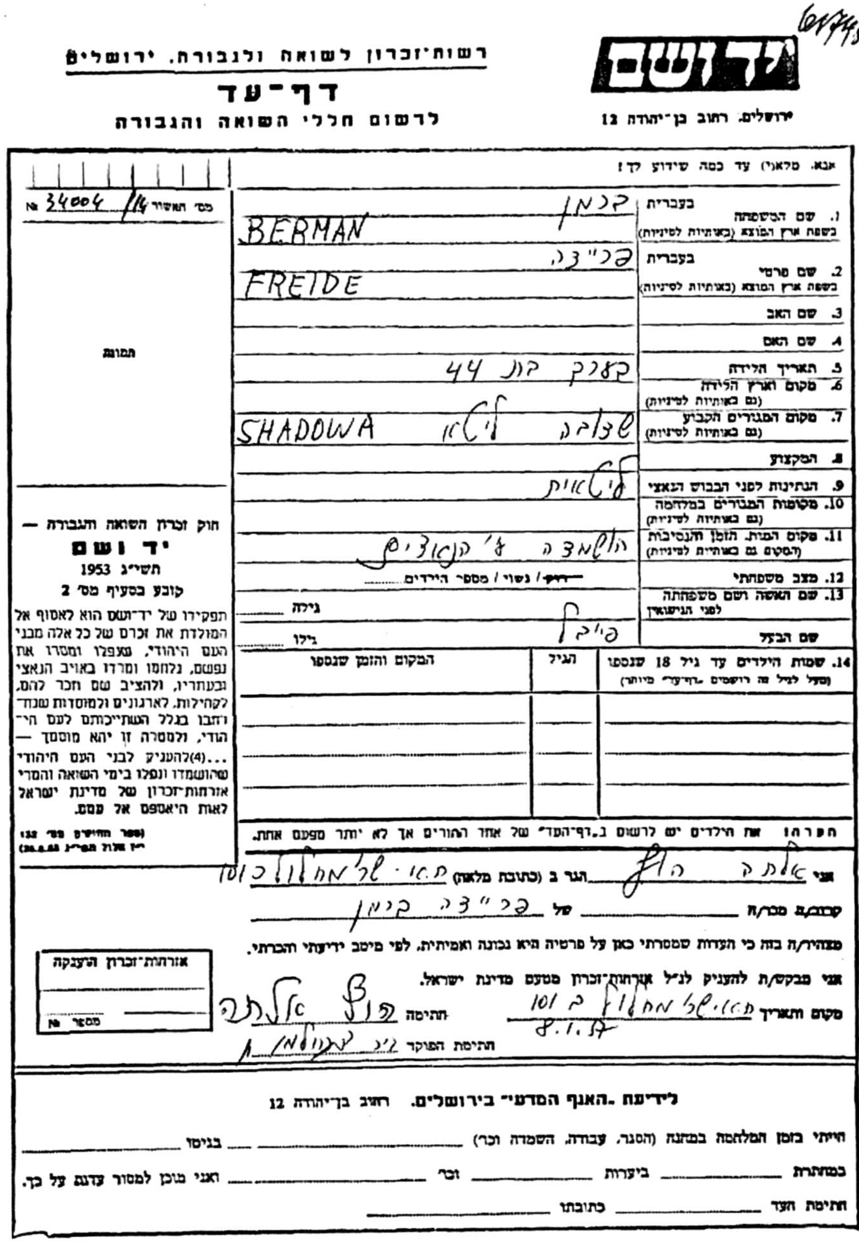

יד ושם

רשות־זכרון לשואה ולגבורה, ירושלים

דף־עד

לרשום חללי השואה והגבורה

6474458

34004/14

BERMAN

FREIDE

SHADOWA

Source	Pages of Testimony
Last Name	BERMAN
First Name	FRIDA
Sex	Female
Date of Birth	1885
Place of Birth	LITHUANIA
Permanent residence	SZADOW,PANEVEZYS,LITHUANIA
Place during the war	SZADOW,PANEVEZYS,LITHUANIA
Place of Death	SZADOW,PANEVEZYS,LITHUANIA
Date of Death	1941
Type of material	Page of Testimony
Submitter's Last Name	SHUR
Submitter's First Name	YISRAEL
Relationship to victim	RELATIVE
Registration date	20/12/1956

Frejda Berman – Nochum's Mother

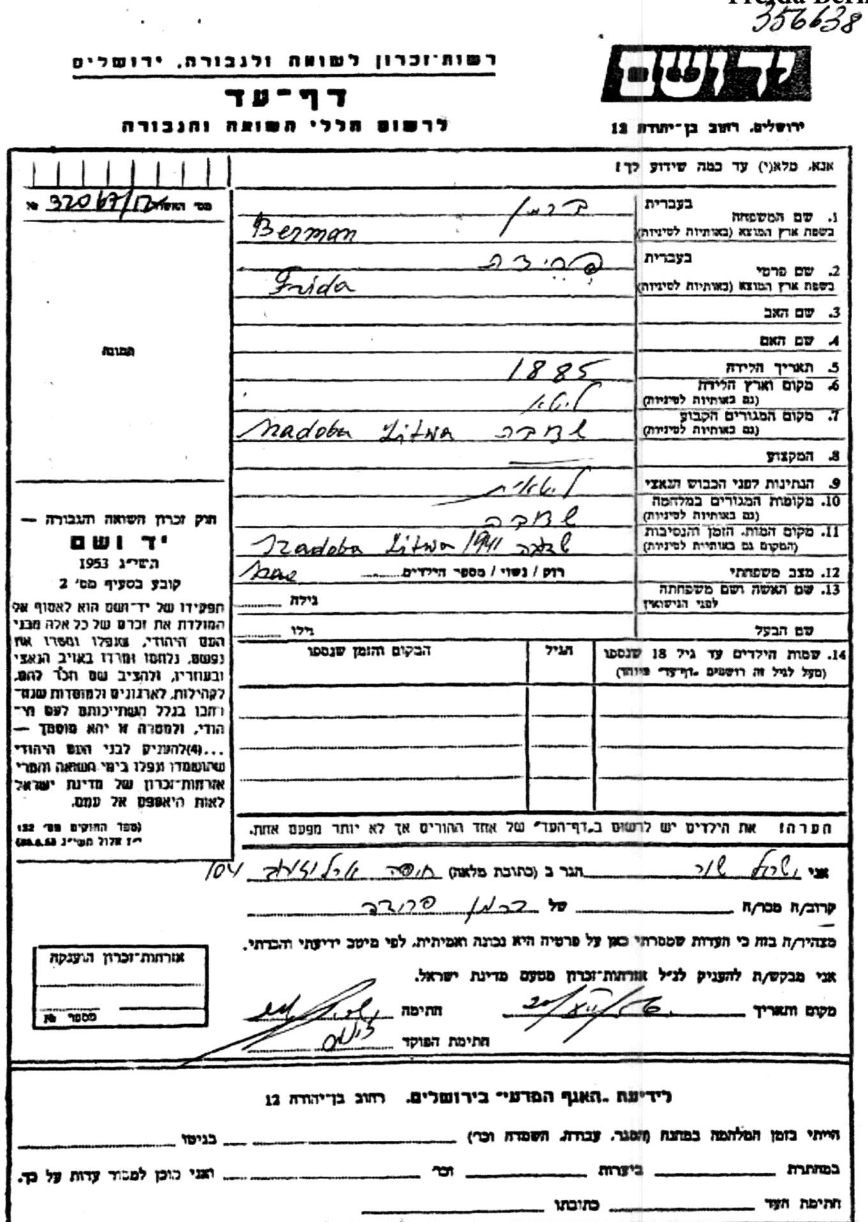
356638

רשות־זכרון לשואה ולגבורה, ירושלים
דף־עד
לרשום חללי השואה והגבורה

יד ושם
ירושלים, רחוב בן־יהודה 12

1. שם המשפחה	Berman / ברמן
2. שם פרטי	Frida / פרידה
5. תאריך הלידה	1885
6. מקום וארץ הלידה	ליטא
7. מקום המגורים הקבוע	Nadoba Litwa / שאדוב
9. התחנות לפני הכבוש הנאצי	
10. מקומות המגורים במלחמה	שאדוב
11. מקום המות, הזמן והנסיבות	Zzadoba Litwa 1941
12. מצב משפחתי	

Source	
Last Name	BERMAN
First Name	FRIDA
Sex	Female
Date of Birth	1885
Place of Birth	LITHUANIA
Permanent residence	SZADOW,PANEVEZYS,LITHUANIA
Place during the war	SZADOW,PANEVEZYS,LITHUANIA
Place of Death	SZADOW,PANEVEZYS,LITHUANIA
Date of Death	1941
Type of material	Page of Testimony
Submitter's Last Name	SHUR
Submitter's First Name	YISRAEL
Relationship to victim	RELATIVE
Registration date	20/12/1956

Faivel Berman – Nochum's Father

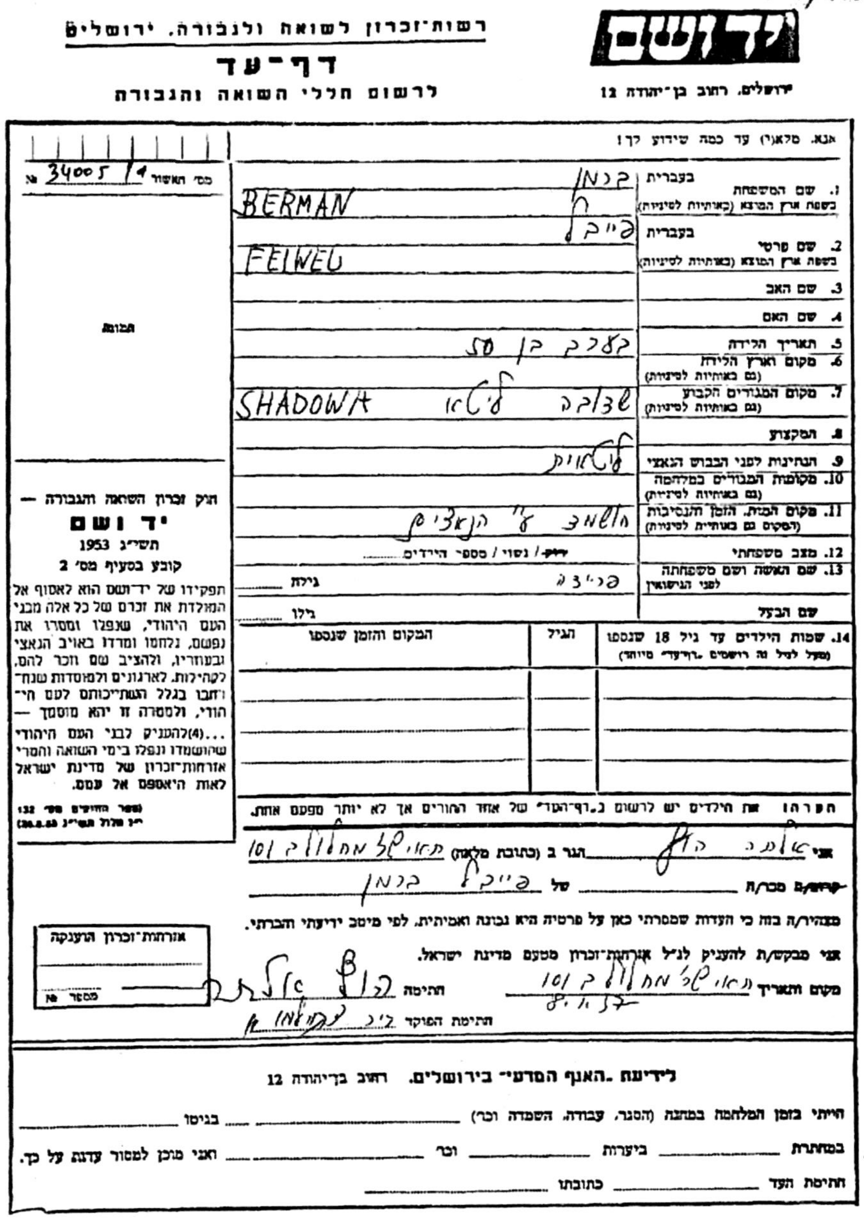
רשות־זכרון לשואה ולגבורה, ירושלים
דף־עד
לרשום חללי השואה והגבורה
יד ושם
ירושלים, רחוב בן־יהודה 12
34005
BERMAN
FEIWEL
SHADOWA

Source	Pages of Testimony
Last Name	BERMAN
First Name	FEIWEL
First Name	FAIVEL
Age	50
Marital Status	MARRIED
Spouse's First Name	FRIDA
Permanent residence	SHADOVA,PANEVEZYS,LITHUANIA
Type of material	Page of Testimony
Submitter's Last Name	HOF
Submitter's First Name*	ALTE
Relationship to victim	ACQUAINTANCE
Registration date	08/01/1957

Alchonan Zarchi, Hinda's Father

124560

YAD VASHEM
Martyrs' and Heroes' Remembrance Authority
P.O.B. 3477 Jerusalem, Israel

דף-עד
עדות-בלאט
A Page of Testimony

יד ושם
אינסטיטוט צום אנדענק פון אומקום און גבורה

THE MARTYRS' AND HEROES' REMEMBRANCE LAW, 5713–1953 determines in article No. 2 that –
The task of YAD VASHEM is to gather into the homeland material regarding all those members of the Jewish people who laid down their lives, who fought and rebelled against the Nazi enemy and his collaborators, and to perpetuate their NAMES and those of the communities, organisations, and institutions which were destroyed because they were Jewish.

דאס געזעץ אנדענק פון אומקום און גבורה - יד-ושם, תשי"ג 1953 שטעלט פעסט אין פאראגראף נומ׳ 2:
די אויפגאבע פון יד-ושם איז איינזאמלען אין היימלאנד דעם אנדענק פון אלע יידן, וואס זענען געפאלן, האבן זיך מוסר נפש געווען, געקעמפט און זיך אנטקעגנגעשטעלט דעם נאצישן שונא און זיינע ארויסהעלפער, און זיי אלעמען, די קהילות, די ארגאניזאציעס און אינסטיטוציעס, וועלכע זענען חרוב געווארן צוליב זייער אנגעהעריקייט צום יידישן פאלק — שטעלן א דענקמאל.
(געזעץ-בוך נומ׳ 231, י"ז אלול תשי"ג, 28.8.1953)

דאטען וועגן אומגעקומענעם: יעדן נאמען אויף א באזונדער בלאט, מיט קלארער שריפט
DETAILS OF VICTIM: INSCRIBE EACH VICTIM ON A SEPARATE PAGE, IN BLOCK LETTERS

בילד פון דעם אומגעקומענעם
שרייבט או דעם נאמען אויף דער ריקזייט פון דעם בילד
Victim's photo
write victim's name on back side please

1. Family name: ZARCH צרכ
2. First name: ALCHONON
3. Previous name: (nee for woman)
4. Birth date or appr. age: Died at app 52
5. Sex: MALE
6. Fam. status: MARRIED
7. Birth place and country: WIDZE, Russia – later Poland 1918

8. Victim's mother - First name: LIFSHA - Maiden name/nee:

9. Victim's father - First name: LEIB

10. Victim's spouse - First name: ESTHER CHANA - Maiden name/nee: KAGAN

11. Permanent residence place and country: WIDZE, Russia, Poland (pres. Bialoruss)

12. Wartime residence place and country: WIDZE, Poland

14. Date/year of death: 1941 | 13. Victim's profession: Business man

15. Death place: Circumstances of death: 1941 was shot with first group of men

Reported by:
I, the undersigned Hinda Zarkey Saul
Residing at (address) 3924 Eastway Rd. Cleveland, OH 44118 (USA)
Relationship to victim (family/other) Father

HEREBY DECLARE THAT THIS TESTIMONY IS CORRECT TO THE BEST OF MY KNOWLEDGE
Place and date Jerusalem 10/V/1995 Signature Hinda Zarkey Saul

"ונתתי להם בביתי ובחומותי יד ושם..אשר לא יכרת". ישעיהו נו ה
"...even unto them will I give in mine house and within my walls a place and a name...that shall not be cut off." Isaiah, lvi,5

Source	Pages of Testimony
Last Name	ZARCH
Last Name	ZARKH
Last Name	ZARKHI
First Name	ALCHONON
First Name	ELKHANAN
Father's First Name	LEIB
Mother's First Name	LIFSHA
Mother's First Name	LIFSHA
Sex	Male
Date of Birth	1889
Age	52
Place of Birth	WIDZE,BRASLAW,WILNO,POLAND
Marital Status	MARRIED
Spouse's First Name	ESTHER
Spouse's First Name	CHANA
Spouse's First Name	ESTER
Spouse's First Name	KHANA
Permanent residence	WIDZE,BRASLAW,WILNO,POLAND
Profession	BUSINESSMAN
Place during the war	WIDZE,BRASLAW,WILNO,POLAND
Place of Death	WIDZE,BRASLAW,WILNO,POLAND
Date of Death	1941
Type of material	Page of Testimony
Submitter's Last Name	SAUL
Submitter's Last Name	ZARKEY
Submitter's First Name	HINDA
Relationship to victim	SON

Chana Zarchi, Hinda's Mother

124557

YAD VASHEM
Martyrs' and Heroes' Remembrance Authority
P.O.B. 3477 Jerusalem, Israel

דף-עד
עדות-בלאט
A Page of Testimony

יד ושם

THE MARTYRS' AND HEROES' REMEMBRANCE LAW, 5713-1953 determines in article No. 2 that –
The task of YAD VASHEM is to gather into the homeland material regarding all those members of the Jewish people who laid down their lives, who fought and rebelled against the Nazi enemy and his collaborators, and to perpetuate their NAMES and those of the communities, organisations, and institutions which were destroyed because they were Jewish.

DETAILS OF VICTIM: INSCRIBE EACH VICTIM ON A SEPARATE PAGE, IN BLOCK LETTERS

Victim's photo write victim's name on back side please

1. Family name: ZARCH
2. First name: ESTHER CHANA
3. Previous name: (nee for woman) KAGAN
4. Birth date or appr. age: App. 52 yrs old when died
5. Sex: Female
6. Fam. status: Married
7. Birth place and country: WIDZE, Russia, Poland (Pres. Bialoruss)
8. Victim's mother - First name: / - Maiden name/nee: Dobe HIMELFARB KAGAN
9. Victim's father - First name: HIRSH (צבי) KAGAN
10. Victim's spouse - First name: ALCHONON ZARCH / - Maiden name/nee:
11. Permanent residence place and country: WIDZE, RUSSIA, POLAND (Pres. BIALORUSS)
12. Wartime residence place and country: WIDZE, Poland
13. Victim's profession: BUSINESS Woman
14. Date/year of death: April, 1943
15. Death place: WIDZE – ON WAY TO OVENS
Circumstances of death: JUMPED OFF THE TRAIN – WAS SHOT

Reported by:
I, the undersigned Hinda Zarkey Saul
Residing at (address) 3924 Eastway Rd. Cleveland, OH 44118, USA
Relationship to victim (family/other) Mother

HEREBY DECLARE THAT THIS TESTIMONY IS CORRECT TO THE BEST OF MY KNOWLEDGE
Place and date Jerusalem (Yad Vashem) 11/5/1995 Signature Hinda Z. Saul

"ונתתי להם בביתי ובחומותי יד ושם..אשר לא יכרת" ישעיהו נו ה
"...even unto them will I give in mine house and within my walls a place and a name...that shall not be cut off." isaiah, lvi,5

Source	Pages of Testimony
Last Name	ZARCH
Last Name	ZARKH
Last Name	ZARKHI
First Name	ESTHER
First Name	CHANA
First Name	ESTER
First Name	KHANA
Maiden Name	KAGAN
Father's First Name	HIRSH
Father's First Name	TZVI
Mother's First Name	DOBE
Mother's First Name	DOBA
Mother's Maiden Name	HIMELFARB
Sex	Female
Date of Birth	1891
Age	52
Place of Birth	WIDZE,BRASLAW,WILNO,POLAND
Marital Status	MARRIED
Spouse's First Name	ALCHONON
Spouse's First Name	ELKHANAN
Permanent residence	WIDZE,BRASLAW,WILNO,POLAND
Profession	BUSINESSMAN
Place during the war	WIDZE,BRASLAW,WILNO,POLAND
Place of Death	WIDZE,BRASLAW,WILNO,POLAND
Date of Death	1943
Type of material	Page of Testimony
Submitter's Last Name	SAUL
Submitter's Last Name	ZARKEY
Submitter's First Name	HINDA
Relationship to victim	DAUGHTER

Gita Zarchi, Hinda's Sister

124565

YAD VASHEM
Martyrs' and Heroes' Remembrance Authority
P.O.B. 3477 Jerusalem, Israel

דף-עד
עדות-בלאט
A Page of Testimony

יד ושם
אינסטיטוט צום אדענק
פון אומקום און גבורה

THE MARTYRS' AND HEROES' REMEMBRANCE LAW, 5713–1953 determines in article No. 2 that –
The task of YAD VASHEM is to gather into the homeland material regarding all those members of the Jewish people who laid down their lives, who fought and rebelled against the Nazi enemy and his collaborators, and to perpetuate their NAMES and those of the communities, organisations, and institutions which were destroyed because they were Jewish.

דאס געזעץ אנדענק פון אומקום און גבורה - יד-ושם, תשי"ג 1953 שטעלט פעסט אין פאראגראף נומ׳ 2:
די אויפגאבע פון יד-ושם איז איינזאמלען אין היימלאנד דעם אנדענק פון אלע יידן, וואס זענען געפאלן, האבן זיך מוסר נפש געווען, געקעמפט און זיך אנטקעגנגעשטעלט דעם נאצישן שונא און זיינע ארויסהעלפער, און זיי אלעמען, די קהילות, די ארגאניזאציעס און אינסטיטוציעס, וועלכע זענען חרוב געווארן צוליב זייער אנגעהעריקייט צום יידישן פאלק — שטעלן א דענקמאל.
(מעזעץ-בוך נומ׳ 231, י"ז אלול תשי"ג, 82.8.3591)

דאטען וועגן אומגעקומענעם: יעדן נאמען אויף א באזונדער בלאט, מיט קלארער שריפט
DETAILS OF VICTIM: INSCRIBE EACH VICTIM ON A SEPARATE PAGE, IN BLOCK LETTERS

בילד פון דעם אומגעקומענעם
שרייבט אן דעם נאמען אויף דער ריקזייט פון דעם בילד
Victim's photo write victim's name on back side please

1. Family name: ZARCH — פאמיליע-נאמען:
2. First name: GITA — פארנאמען:
3. Previous name: (nee for woman) — פאמיליע-נאמען פאר דער חתונה (פאר א פרוי):
4. Birth date or appr. age: 19 yrs. old at time of death — געבורטס-דאטע (ווי אלט)
5. Sex: FEMALE — מין:
6. Fam. status: SINGLE — פארהייראט:
7. Birth place and country: Panevėžys — פאנעוועזשיס — ארט פון געבורט (שטאט, לאנד):

8. Victim's mother - First name: ESTHER CHANA - Maiden name/nee: KAGAN — מוטער פון דעם אומגעקומענעם - פארנאמען: - מיידלשע-פאמיליע:
9. Victim's father - First name: ALCHONON ZARCH — פאטער פון דעם אומגעקומענעם - פארנאמען:
10. Victim's spouse - First name: - Maiden name/nee: — מאן/פרוי פון דעם אומגעקומענעם - פארנאמען: - מיידלשע-פאמיליע:
11. Permanent residence place and country: WIDZE, POLAND (Pres. BIALORUSS) — סטאבילער וואוינארט (שטאט, לאנד):
12. Wartime residence place and country: WIDZE, POLAND — וואוינערטער בעת דער מלחמה (שטאט, לאנד):
14. Date/year of death: April or May, 1943 — צייט פון טויט:
13. Victim's profession: — בערוף אדער פאך:
15. Death place: Circumstances of death: ON WAY FROM WIDZE TO Destruction jumped off the train together with mother and younger Sister – all were shot — ארט און אומשטענדן פון טויט:

Reported by: — געשריבן פון:
I, the undersigned Hinda Zarkey Saul — איך, דער אונטערגעשריבענער
Residing at (address) 3924 Eastway Rd. Cleveland, OH 44118 U.S.A. — וואס וואוינט (אדרעס)
Relationship to victim (family/other) Sister — קרובישאפט

דערקלער דערמיט, אז די עדות מיט אלע פרטים איז א ריכטיקע לויט מיין בעסטען וויסן
HEREBY DECLARE THAT THIS TESTIMONY IS CORRECT TO THE BEST OF MY KNOWLEDGE

Place and date Jerusalem 10/5/1995 — ארט און דאטע   Signature Hinda Saul — אונטערשריפט

"...ונתתי להם בביתי ובחומותי יד ושם..אשר לא יכרת". ישעיהו נו ה
"...even unto them will I give in mine house and within my walls a place and a name...that shall not be cut off." isaiah, lvi,5

Source	Pages of Testimony
Last Name	ZARCH
Last Name	ZARKH
Last Name	ZARKHI
First Name	GITA
Father's First Name	ALCHONON
Father's First Name	ELKHANAN
Mother's First Name	ESTHER
Mother's First Name	CHANA
Mother's First Name	ESTER
Mother's First Name	KHANA
Mother's Maiden Name	KAGAN
Sex	Female
Date of Birth	1924
Age	19
Place of Birth	PANEVEZYS,PANEVEZYS,LITHUANIA
Marital Status	SINGLE
Permanent residence	WIDZE,BRASLAW,WILNO,POLAND
Place during the war	WIDZE,BRASLAW,WILNO,POLAND
Place of Death	POLAND
Date of Death	1943
Type of material	Page of Testimony
Submitter's Last Name	SAUL
Submitter's Last Name	ZARKEY
Submitter's First Name	HINDA
Relationship to victim	SISTER

Leah Zarchi, Hinda's Sister

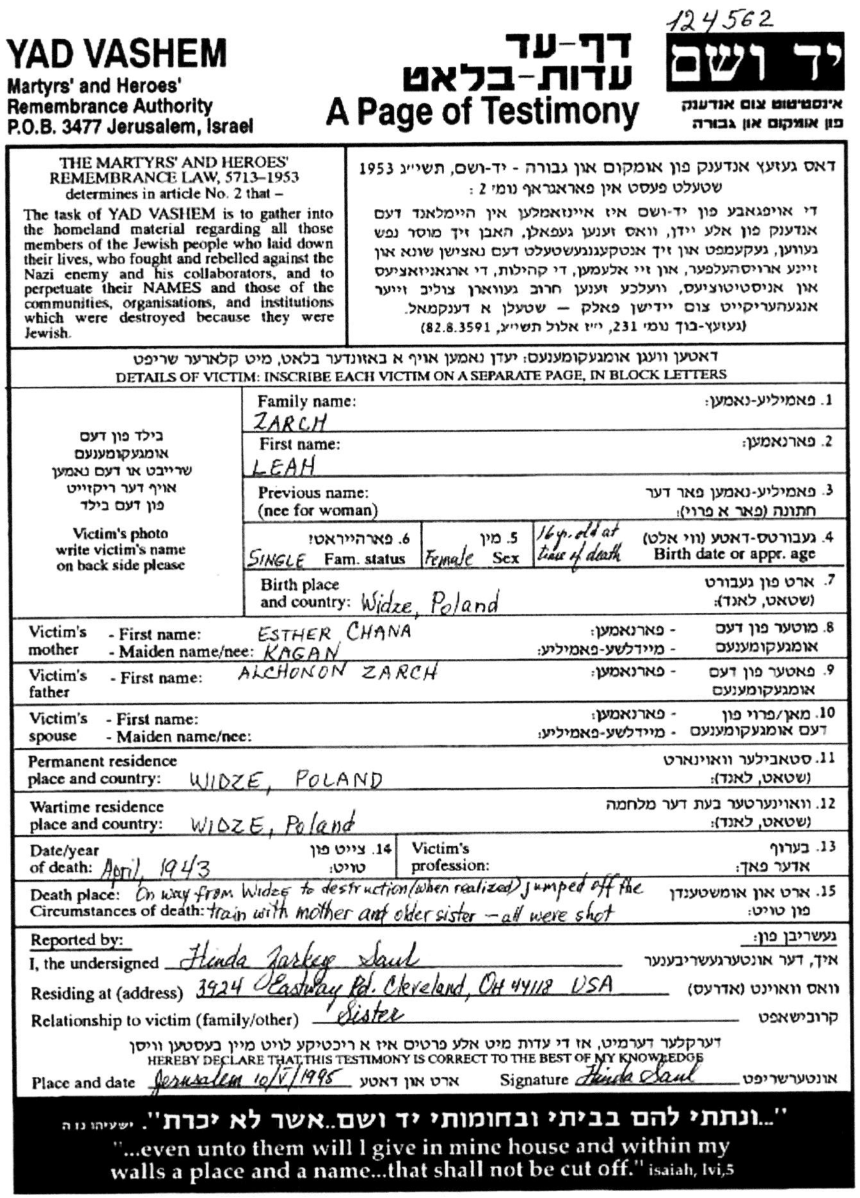

124562

YAD VASHEM
Martyrs' and Heroes' Remembrance Authority
P.O.B. 3477 Jerusalem, Israel

דף-עד
עדות-בלאט
A Page of Testimony

יד ושם
אינסטיטוט צום אנדענק
פון אומקום און גבורה

THE MARTYRS' AND HEROES' REMEMBRANCE LAW, 5713–1953 determines in article No. 2 that –
The task of YAD VASHEM is to gather into the homeland material regarding all those members of the Jewish people who laid down their lives, who fought and rebelled against the Nazi enemy and his collaborators, and to perpetuate their NAMES and those of the communities, organisations, and institutions which were destroyed because they were Jewish.

דאס געזעץ אנדענק פון אומקום און גבורה - יד-ושם, תשי״ג 1953 שטעלט פעסט אין פאראגראף נומ׳ 2:
די אויפגאבע פון יד-ושם איז איינזאמלען אין היימלאנד דעם אנדענק פון אלע יידן, וואס זענען געפאלן, האבן זיך מוסר נפש געווען, געקעמפט און זיך אנטקעגנגעשטעלט דעם נאציש שונא און זיינע ארויסהעלפער, און זיי אלעמען, די קהילות, די ארגאניזאציעס און אינסטיטוציעס, וועלכע זענען חרוב געווארן צוליב זייער אנגעהעריקייט צום יידישן פאלק — שטעלן א דענקמאל.
(געזעץ-בוך נומ׳ 231, י״ז אלול תשי״ג, 28.8.1953)

דאטען וועגן אומגעקומענעם: יעדן נאמען אויף א באזונדער בלאט, מיט קלארער שריפט
DETAILS OF VICTIM: INSCRIBE EACH VICTIM ON A SEPARATE PAGE, IN BLOCK LETTERS

בילד פון דעם אומגעקומענעם שרייבט אז דעם נאמען אויף דער ריקזייט פון דעם בילד
Victim's photo write victim's name on back side please

1. Family name: ZARCH — פאמיליע-נאמען:
2. First name: LEAH — פארנאמען:
3. Previous name: (nee for woman) — פאמיליע-נאמען פאר דער חתונה (פאר א פרוי):
4. Birth date or appr. age: 16 yr. old at time of death — געבורטס-דאטע (ווי אלט)
5. Sex: Female — מין
6. Fam. status: SINGLE — פארהייראט?
7. Birth place and country: Widze, Poland — ארט פון געבורט (שטאט, לאנד):
8. Victim's mother - First name: ESTHER CHANA - Maiden name/nee: KAGAN — מוטער פון דעם אומגעקומענעם - פארנאמען: - מיידלשע-פאמיליע:
9. Victim's father - First name: ALCHONON ZARCH — פאטער פון דעם אומגעקומענעם - פארנאמען:
10. Victim's spouse - First name: - Maiden name/nee: — מאן/פרוי פון דעם אומגעקומענעם - פארנאמען: - מיידלשע-פאמיליע:
11. Permanent residence place and country: WIDZE, POLAND — סטאבילער וואוינארט (שטאט, לאנד):
12. Wartime residence place and country: WIDZE, Poland — וואוינערטער בעת דער מלחמה (שטאט, לאנד):
13. Victim's profession: — בערוף אדער פאך:
14. Date/year of death: April, 1943 — צייט פון טויט:
15. Death place: Circumstances of death: On way from Widze to destruction (when realized) jumped off the train with mother and older sister — all were shot — ארט און אומשטענדן פון טויט:

Reported by: — געשריבן פון:
I, the undersigned Hinda Zarkey Saul — איך, דער אונטערגעשריבענער
Residing at (address) 3924 Eastway Rd. Cleveland, OH 44118 USA — וואס וואוינט (אדרעס)
Relationship to victim (family/other) Sister — קרובשאפט

דערקלער דערמיט, אז די עדות מיט אלע פרטים איז א ריכטיקע לויט מיין בעסטען וויסן
HEREBY DECLARE THAT THIS TESTIMONY IS CORRECT TO THE BEST OF MY KNOWLEDGE

Place and date Jerusalem 10/V/1995 — ארט און דאטע
Signature Hinda Saul — אונטערשריפט

״...ונתתי להם בביתי ובחומותי יד ושם..אשר לא יכרת״. ישעיהו נו ה
"...even unto them will I give in mine house and within my walls a place and a name...that shall not be cut off." isaiah, lvi,5

Source	Pages of Testimony
Last Name	ZARCH
Last Name	ZARKH
Last Name	ZARKHI
First Name	LEAH
First Name	LEA
Father's First Name	ALCHONON
Father's First Name	ELKHANAN
Mother's First Name	ESTHER
Mother's First Name	CHANA
Mother's First Name	ESTER
Mother's First Name	KHANA
Mother's Maiden Name	KAGAN
Sex	Female
Date of Birth	1927
Age	16
Place of Birth	WIDZE,BRASLAW,WILNO,POLAND
Marital Status	CHILD
Permanent residence	WIDZE,BRASLAW,WILNO,POLAND
Profession	PUPIL
Place during the war	WIDZE,BRASLAW,WILNO,POLAND
Place of Death	POLAND
Date of Death	1943
Type of material	Page of Testimony
Submitter's Last Name	SAUL
Submitter's Last Name	ZARKEY
Submitter's First Name	HINDA
Relationship to victim	SISTER

Milke Bret, Hinda's Friend

847188

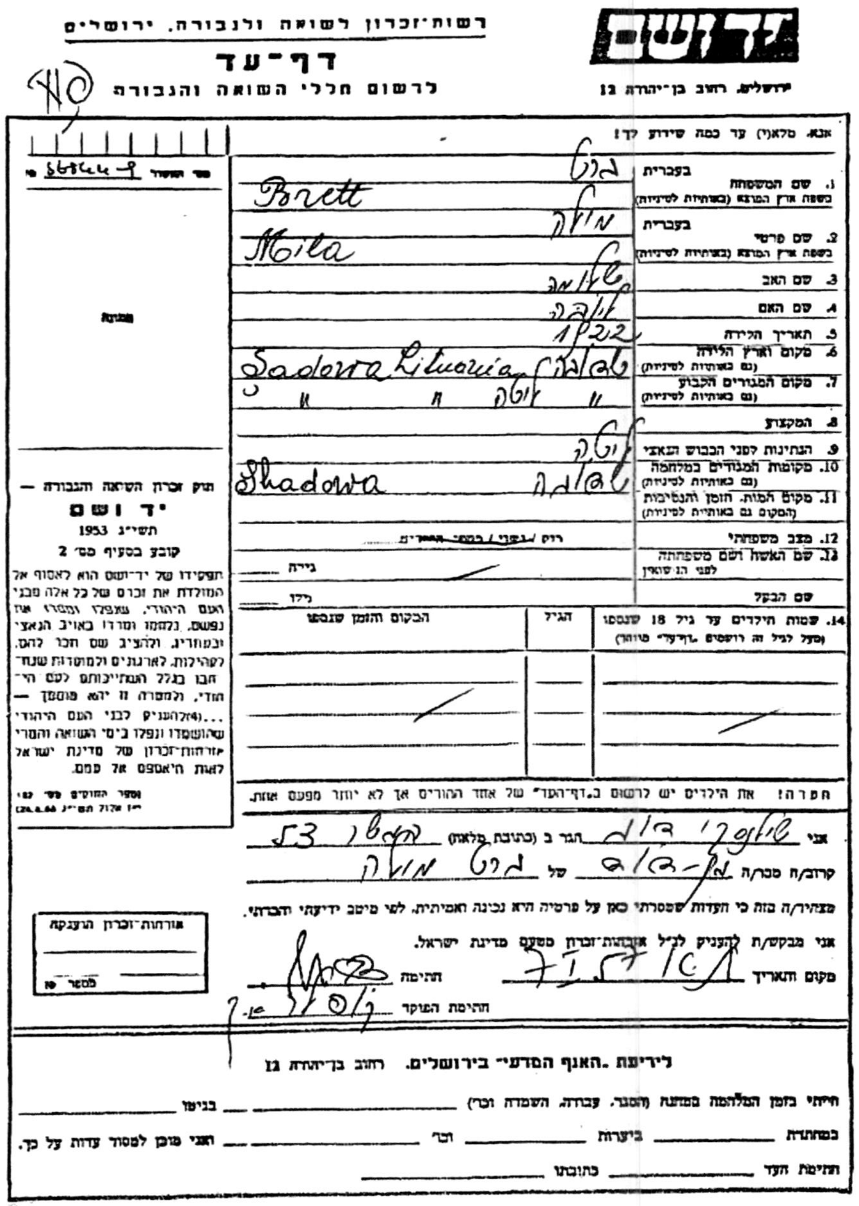
רשות־זכרון לשואה ולגבורה, ירושלים
דף־עד
לרשום חללי השואה והגבורה
יד ושם
ירושלים, רחוב בן־יהודה 12
1. שם המשפחה — Brett
2. שם פרטי — Mila
3. שם האב
4. שם האם
5. תאריך הלידה — 1922
6. מקום וארץ הלידה — Sadowa Lituania
7. מקום המגורים הקבוע
8. המקצוע
9. הנתינות לפני הכבוש הנאצי
10. מקומות המגורים במלחמה — Shadowa
11. מקום המות, הזמן והנסיבות
12. מצב משפחתי
13. שם האשה ושם משפחתה לפני הנשואין
14. שמות הילדים עד גיל 18 שנספו

Source	Pages of Testimony
Last Name	BRETT
Last Name	BART
First Name	MILA
Father's First Name	SHLOMO
Mother's First Name	LIUBA
Sex	Female
Date of Birth	1922
Place of Birth	SHADOWA,PANEVEZYS,LITHUANIA
Marital Status	SINGLE
Permanent residence	SHADOWA,PANEVEZYS,LITHUANIA
Place during the war	SHADOWA,PANEVEZYS,LITHUANIA
Type of material	Page of Testimony
Submitter's Last Name	SHILANSKI
Submitter's First Name	DOV
Submitter's First Name*	BER
Relationship to victim	COUSIN
Registration date	07/01/1957

Sioma Davidowitz, Hinda's Friend

רשות־זכרון לשואה ולגבורה, ירושלים

יד ושם
ירושלים, רחוב בן־יהודה 12

דף־עד

לרשום חללי השואה והגבורה

מס׳ האישור 34005

אנא, מלא(י) עד כמה שידוע לך!

1. שם המשפחה — בעברית: דוידוביץ — בשפת ארץ המוצא (באותיות לטיניות): DAVIDOWICZ
2. שם פרטי — בעברית: שמקה — בשפת ארץ המוצא (באותיות לטיניות): SHAMKE
3. שם האב
4. שם האם
5. תאריך הלידה — צעיר בן 19
6. מקום וארץ הלידה (גם באותיות לטיניות)
7. מקום המגורים הקבוע (גם באותיות לטיניות) — שדובה ליטא SHADOWA
8. המקצוע — תלמיד
9. הנתינות לפני הכבוש הנאצי — ליטאית
10. פעולות המגורים במלחמה (גם באותיות לטיניות)
11. מקום המות, הזמן והנסיבות (המקום גם באותיות לטיניות) — הושמד ע״י הנאצים
12. מצב משפחתי — רוק / נשוי / מספר הילדים
13. שם האשה ושם משפחתה לפני הנישואין — גילה
שם הבעל — גילו

14. שמות הילדים עד גיל 18 שנספו (שמל לגיל זה רושמים „דף־עד״ מיוחד)	הגיל	המקום והזמן שנספו

תבונה

חוק זכרון השואה והגבורה — יד ושם תשי״ג 1953 קובע בסעיף מס׳ 2

תפקידו של יד־ושם הוא לאסוף אל המולדת את זכרם של כל אלה מבני העם היהודי, שנפלו ומסרו את נפשם, נלחמו ומרדו באויב הנאצי ובעוזריו, ולהציב שם וזכר להם, לקהילות, לארגונים ולמוסדות שנחרבו בגלל השתייכותם לעם היהודי, ולמטרה זו יהא מוסמך — ...(4)להעניק לבני העם היהודי שהושמדו ונפלו בימי השואה והמרי אזרחות־זכרון של מדינת ישראל לאות היאספם אל עמם.

(ספר החוקים מס׳ 132 י״ז אלול תשי״ג 28.8.53)

הערה: את הילדים יש לרשום ב„דף־העד״ של אחד ההורים אך לא יותר מפעם אחת.

אני אלטה הוץ הגר ב (כתובת מלאה) תל־אביב שלמה ... 101
קרוב/ה מכר/ה של שמקה דוידוביץ

מצהיר/ה בזה כי העדות שמסרתי כאן על פרטיה היא נכונה ואמיתית, לפי מיטב ידיעתי והכרתי.

אני מבקש/ת להעניק לנ״ל אזרחות־זכרון מטעם מדינת ישראל.

מקום ותאריך: תל־אביב ... 101 8.1.57 — חתימה: הוץ אלטה

חתימת הפוקד

אזרחות־זכרון הוענקה
מספר

לידיעת „האגף המדעי״ בירושלים, רחוב בן־יהודה 12

הייתי בזמן המלחמה במחנה (הסגר, עבודה, השמדה וכו׳) ______ בגיטו ______
במחתרת ______ ביערות ______ וכו׳ ______ ואני מוכן למסור עדות על כך.
חתימת העד ______ כתובתו ______

Source	Pages of Testimony
Last Name	DAVIDOWICZ
Last Name	DAVIDOVITZ
First Name	SHAMKE
Sex	Male
Age	19
Marital Status	SINGLE
Permanent residence	SHADOWA,PANEVEZYS,LITHUANIA
Profession	PUPIL
Type of material	Page of Testimony
Submitter's Last Name	HOTZ
Submitter's First Name*	ALTE
Relationship to victim	ACQUAINTANCE
Registration date	08/01/1957

Hinda Zarkey, Recipient of the Letters

Nochum Berman, Writer of the Letters

Top with outstretched arms: Hinda Zarkey, Sioma Davidowitz

From left around table: Samuel Bardon, Dr. Blumberg, Raisa Payim, Mr. Kellman (teacher), Miss Ulfsky (teacher), Krieger sister, Unknown, Mrs. Rabinowitz, Mr. Fish (principal), Krieger sister, Mrs. Davidowitz, Unknown, Mr. Davidowitz, Goda Bardon

Nechama Hak

Elke Friedlander, Kaunas, 1940

Lola Mellman, 1937

Gnessa Yosem

Šeduva Class Picture

Teachers Mr. Kellman, Miss Ulfsky, Principal Fish

Class Trip to Panevėžys, with Teacher, Mr. Grinis

Middle of circle: Hinda Zarkey; Clockwise from top: Gnessa Yosem, Hadassah, Milke Bret, Freidele Mel, Malke Kaplan, Nechama Hak, Elke Friedlander

Alchonan Zarchi (Zarkey), Hinda's Father

Chana Zarchi (Zarkey), Hinda's Mother

Gita and Leah Zarchi (Zarkey), Hinda's Sisters

Leah, Gita and Hinda Zarchi (Zarkey)

Endnotes

Introductory Sections

1 According to the Lithuanian census of 1923, there were 19,147 people in Panevėžys, among them 6,845 Jews (36%). In Yiddish, the town's name was transliterated as Ponevezh. (Web address: http://en.wikipedia.org/wiki/Panev%C4%97%C5%BEys. Last accessed June 26, 2011)

2 Jewish Gen, Inc.'s online *Glossary of Yizkor Book Terms* defines the Yiddish word *shtetl* (plural is *shtetlekh*) as "a small town or village, usually used to refer to a small Jewish community; often used (as in Yizkor Book Database) to refer to a Jewish community of any size." (Web address: http://www.jewishgen.org/Yizkor/yizterms.html. Last accessed June 25, 2011)

3 Anne Frank was a young Jewish girl whose family went into hiding in Holland during World War II. Her diary has become world-famous. Detailed information about her, her life, family, and diary can be found at the Anne Frank Stichting website. (Web address: http://www.annefrank.org/en. Last accessed June 26, 2011)

4 Winer, G. *Widze Memorial Book.* Pages 1-14 are in English and the stories on those pages provide a good historical overview of the city and how it was affected by the many different wars.

5 Yad Vashem's Untold Stories website includes a brief description of Šeduva and is the source for the statistics listed. (Web address: http://www1.yadvashem.org/untoldstories/database/index.asp?cid=276. Last accessed June 25, 2011)

6 Spector, S. *The Encyclopedia of Jewish Life Before and During the Holocaust.* Volume II. pages 1156-1157.

7 Gartner, Lloyd P. *History of the Jews of Cleveland.* page 267.

8 Stein, J. *Fiddler on the* Roof, Act 2, Scene 5, includes a scene where people in the small Russian village, Anatevka, visit Motel Kamzoil, a tailor, when he gets a new sewing machine. pages 88-93.

9 Brigadoon is described as "...the story of a mysterious Scottish village that appears for only one day every hundred years, though to the villagers, the passing of each century seems no longer than one night. The enchantment is viewed by them as a blessing rather than a curse, for it saved the village from destruction. According to their covenant with God, no one from Brigadoon may ever leave, or the enchantment will be broken and the site and all its inhabitants will disappear into the mist forever. Two American tourists, lost in the Scottish Highlands, stumble upon the village just as a wedding is about to be celebrated, and their arrival has serious implications for the village's inhabitants." (Web address: http://en.wikipedia.org/wiki/Brigadoon. Last accessed June 25, 2011)

10 The *List of residents*, compiled by Yehuda Grodnik, Baruch Gofer and Alter Kaplan and the Hebrew version (courtesy of Pnina Gofer, Baruch Gofer's widow) has been reproduced in a number of places including the Šeduva Yizkor Book website, hosted by Dora Boom, and submitted by Nava Shulkin. Baruch Gofer recorded their names on the witness pages of "Yad Vashem." "This is probably a partial list—an unfinished job. I have nobody to ask..." "Arranged and printed by Pnina Gofer, widow of Baruch. Translated into English—*Anat* and *Eitan Rosen*." (Web address: http://www.shtetlinks.jewishgen.org/Seduva/descendants/nava/framesetnava.htm. Last accessed June 25, 2011.)

11 *A Memory of a Shtetl* is a section of Jon Seligman's Shadova—Šeduva website. "In 1990 three former natives of Shadova—Šeduva, Yehuda Grodnik, Baruch Gofer and Alter Kaplan, compiled a list of the names of the Jewish residents of the town before the Shoah. To ease their memory they listed the names street-by-street and home by home... We learn of the layout of the town, the division between the Jewish and gentile residents, the professions and trades practiced and even get to hear about some of the more colourful members of the community." (Web address: http://www.

seligman.org.il/seduva_residences.html. Last accessed June 25, 2011)

Letters

1937

12 **Letter 1**—May 3, 1937—3 weeks after Hinda left for the United States

13 Hinda Zarkey ("Hindalla" is a diminutive and endearing), the recipient of all letters, is the oldest of three daughters of Alchonon Zarchi and Chana Esther Kagan Zarchi. Both parents were born in Vidz, at that time part of Russia. When World War I started many residents of Vidz fled to nearby cities, as they anticipated fighting in Vidz. Her parents fled to Ponevezh, where they spent the World War I years. In 1925, they returned to Vidz, their home, which by that time had become part of Poland, and the small town's name was changed to Widze. Hinda lived there until 1935 when she went to live with her Aunt and Uncle, Goda and Samuel Bardon, in Šeduva, Lithuania, in order to attend junior high school, there (Widze only had an elementary school and no junior or high school.)

14 The girlfriends in Šeduva included: Lola Mellman, Elke Friedlander, Nechama Hak, and Malke Kaplan.

15 His mother's name was Freida Berman.

16 Kovno (Kaunas in Lithuanian) is a city in Lithuania. At the time this letter was written, it was the largest city in Lithuania and was also the temporary capital when Vilno (Vilnius in Lithuanian) became part of Poland. Kovno also had the largest Jewish population.

17 The first time refers to when Hinda left her parents, in Widze, Poland, to live with her maternal Aunt and Uncle (Goda and Samuel Bardon) in Šeduva, so she could attend junior high school. The second time refers to her leaving for America with this same Aunt and her Aunt's young daughter, and starting a new life there.

18 Hinda's Aunt Goda owned the pharmacy where Berman worked as a pharmacist. When Goda left for America, Berman became the manager.

19 The Provinces refer to the smaller towns around the countryside.

20 Berman's father, Faiva Berman, was a bank manager.

21 First wages were 200.00 litas.

22 Miss Kotzin was a pharmacy intern.

23 The pharmacy was in a position to pay for a pharmacy intern, but not in a position to hire additonal pharmacists at pharmacist wages. When Miss Kotzin completed her internship she was then able to look for a job as a pharmacist. The pharmacy in Seduva wouldn't have been able to afford to hire her in that capacity.

24 **Letter 2**—June 5, 1937—dated one month after Letter 1

25 *The Sorrows of Young Werther* (originally published as *Die Leiden des jungen Werther*) is an epistolary and loosely autobiographical novel by Johann Wolfgang von Goethe, first published in 1774. (Web address: http://en.wikipedia.org/wiki/The_Sorrows_of_Young_Werther. Last accessed: June 29, 2011)

26 Syme, D. *The Jewish Home: A Guide for Jewish Living*. Shavuot is a Jewish holiday which celebrates the giving of the Torah on Mount Sinai. It falls on the sixth and seventh days of the Hebrew month of Sivan. page 43.

27 Telshe Yeshiva was founded in 1875 in the Lithuanian town of Telshiai to provide Jewish religious education to men in the area. After World War II, the yeshiva relocated to Wickliffe, Ohio, in the

United States, where it currently resides. The Slabodka Yeshiva was located in the Lithuanian town of Slabodka, adjacent to Kovno. It functioned from the late 19th century until World War II.

28 Aunt Goda Bardon was still the owner of the pharmacy in Šeduva where Berman was the manager. She did not want to sell the pharmacy, even though she was living in America. She corresponded periodically with Berman who would keep her abreast of the finances and changes.

29 **Letter 3**—June 28, 1937—dated 3 weeks after Letter 2

30 Sholem Asch (1880-1957) was born in Kutno, Poland, and died in London, He became a naturalized United States citizen in 1920. He initially wrote in Hebrew, but later switched to Yiddish. He wrote *Der Thilim Yid* in 1934, and it was translated into English as *Salvation.*

31 Mrs. Davidowitz was a friend of Goda's and the mother of Sioma, who later became a pharmacy intern.

32 Mr. Katz leased the pharmacy from Goda Bardon during this time.

33 Young men were drafted into the Lithuanian service. Berman was 25 years old and single.

34 It was common for students to use a tutor to help prepare them for future exams. Berman likely tutored math, Latin, and science.

35 The teacher who took no money for lessons was Mrs. Elisa Myers. She was an elderly lady who originally came from Germany and had a heavy German accent. She taught elderly people to help them pass their citizenship exams. Hinda was by far her youngest student and she enjoyed teaching her, and hence, did not charge.

36 Yvette is Hinda's cousin - the daughter of Goda and Samuel Bardon. It was her 6th birthday.

37 Miss Kotzin frequently enclosed a few words to Hinda with Berman's letters.

38 **Letter 4**—August 6, 1937—dated 6 weeks after Letter 3

39 Hinda sent Berman a picture she made of a young girl dressed in clothes made of scraps of silk, lace and other materials. Hinda was artistic and her hope was to study art as a career.

40 This quote is from *Childhood* (1852) the first novel in Leo Tolstoy's (1828-1910) autobiographical trilogy.

41 Alytus is in southern Lithuania. It is 70km from Kaunas and 105 km to Vilnius.

42 Registration was for the opening position of pharmacy internship, after the previous intern left.

43 Sioma Davidowitz became the new pharmacy intern.

44 Shavl Street was one of the major streets in Šeduva.

45 The Baers were a family in Šeduva.

46 Shaya and Chava (a dentist) Mellman were friends of Goda and Samuel Bardon. Their daughter Lola was a schoolmate and special friend of Hinda's.

47 David Bergelson (1884-1952) was Ukranian-born and wrote in Yiddish. *Baym Dnieper* (*At the Dneiper*) was written in 1932.

48 Leon Kobrin (1873-1946) wrote short stories and novels for the Yiddish theater. Many of his themes dealt with assimilation of immigrant Jews in America, Jewish tradition, and the first generation of American-born Jews.

49 **Letter 5**—September 8, 1937—dated one month after Letter 4

50 Syme, D. *The Jewish Home: A Guide for Jewish Living.* Rosh Hashanah is the Jewish New Year, celebrated on the first day of the Hebrew month of Tishrei. page 28.

51 Sholem Asch (1880-1957) was born in Kutno, Poland. He wrote *Der Thilim Yid* (translated as *Salvation*) in 1934.

52 Sholem Asch wrote *Der veg tsu zikh* (translated as *The Way to Oneself*) in 1917.

53 Syme, D. *The Jewish Home: A Guide for Jewish Living.* Succot is the Jewish holiday which gives thanks for the fall harvest and commemorates the forty years of Jewish wandering in the desert. page 49.

54 "The matter started last year" refers to his trying to get out of the military service.

55 Bassia Ulfsky was a teacher at the Hebrew School in Šeduva.

56 Kibbutz Mizrahi was a young Zionist group.

57 Garshviene was the Bardon family's maid.

58 Ponevezh (Panevezys in Lithuanian) is located halfway between Vilnius and Riga. It is about 25 miles east of Šeduva.

59 Shavl (Siauliai in Lithuanian) was the second largest city in Lithuania. At the time of this letter, 25% of the population was Jewish.

60 If you passed all your exams you received a diploma stating that you graduated from junior high school. If you wanted a high school diploma, you had to apply to a larger city where they had a high school. Šeduva had no high school. Or, you could live at home and find a tutor to prepare you for the exams each year. You had to pass each subject separately. If you failed a subject you could try again until you passed.

61 **Letter 6**—October 8, 1937—dated one month after Letter 5

62 The method he mentioned was to find a way not to go into the service. The way he did it was to diet and lose weight. Since he was of slight built and short in stature, he was able to lose enough weight to be disqualified by being below the required weight.

63 The rejection refers to being disqualified from entering the service.

64 H. Lei Vick (pseudonym of Levi Helper) (1886-1962) wrote the poem *Abelard and Heloise* based on their love affair and tragedy.

65 *Yidel Mitn Fidel* (*Yiddle with his Fiddle*) was released in 1936 and starred Molly Picon. It was filmed in Kazimierz, Poland and used shtetl residents as extras.

66 *The Good Earth* was published in 1931 and was written by Pearl Buck (1892-1973). The book was awarded the Pulitzer Prize for the Novel, in 1932. "The novel described a non-Caucasian culture in detail and helped prepare Americans of the 1930s to consider Chinese as allies in the coming war with Japan." (Web address: http://en.wikipedia.org/wiki/The_Good_Earth. Last accessed June 29, 2011.)

67 *Madame Butterfly* is a three-act opera by Giacomo Puccini.

68 This was a different Yvette Bardon, who was Uncle Samuel Bardon's niece. She was the same age as Hinda and they were in the same grade at school and became good friends.

69 Since Berman and Aunt Goda had a business relationship, they would correspond periodically.

70 **Letter 7**—November 8, 1937—dated 1 month after Letter 6

71 Ivan Andreyevich Krylov (1769-1844) is Russia's best-known fablist.

72 His description of life in America compared to that in Šeduva; it was a realistic comparison of a large city to a small town.

73 *The Garden of Allah* was a movie based on the novel by Robert Smythe Hichens, an English novelist.

74 *A Doll's House* was an 1879 play by the Norwegian author, Henrik Ibsen (1828-1906).

75 **Letter 8**—December 16, 1937—dated 5 weeks after Letter 7

76 Berman's plans were to go to Russia for his vacation.

77 Berman was trying to study English by himself in preparation, and in hopes, of his eventually coming to America.

78 Dr. Blumberg was one of the two doctors in Šeduva. He was a bachelor and was very popular with the young ladies in Šeduva. However, he had a girlfriend in Kovno who was an attorney, but that didn't stop the young girls from going after him. He was a personal friend of Aunt Goda and Uncle Samuel. He was also a friend to Hinda; whenever he went to Kovno (by train) he would think up some algebra problems for her and she was always happy to work them out.

1938

79 **Letter 9**—January 18, 1938—dated 1 month after Letter 6

80 Lastauskiene was the landlady of the pharmacy and the attached living quarters where the Bardon family lived (along with Hinda). The attached living quarters was a necessity since very few people had telephones; if someone got sick during the night, they rang the bell of the pharmacy. This would awaken the pharmacist in the attached apartment, who would listen to the complaint and could then immediately dispense the proper medication. If it was necessary to see the doctor, the pharmacist advised and the patient would see the doctor in the morning.

81 The Efraimsons were friends of the Bardons.

82 "The Scout movement in Lithuania began in 1918, when the first Scout troop was founded in Vilnius by Scouter Kostas Jurgela." They often entertained at a New Year's Ball; sometimes they put on plays. (Web address: http://en.wikipedia.org/wiki/Lietuvos_Skautija. Last accessed June 29, 2011)

83 *Columbia Encyclopedia.* Founded in 1917 in Moscow by Nahum Zemach and at first affiliated with the Moscow Art Theatre, The Habima Theater was one of the first Hebrew-language theaters. In 1926 the company left the Soviet Union and toured extensively for several years before settling in Palestine in 1931. Among its best-known productions were *The Dybbuk*, *The Golem*, and *Oedipus Rex*. (Web address: http://www.encyclopedia.com/doc/1E1-HabimaTh.html. Last accessed June 29, 2011)

84 Shloyme Zanvl Rappoport (1863-1920) was a Yiddish author, and better known by the pseudonym S. Ansky. *The Dybbuk* (translated as *Between Two Worlds*) was written in 1914. It is the story of a young bride possessed by a dybbuk (a malicious possessing spirit believed to be the dislocated soul of a dead person) on the eve of her wedding.

85 Released in 1936, *Mazurka* is a German melodrama that was directed by Willi Forst and starred Pola Negri.

86 Lola Mellman was a classmate and good friend of Hinda's.

87 **Letter 10**—February 26, 1938—dated 5 weeks after Letter 9

88 *Sons* is a sequel to *The Good Earth.* According to goodreads.com, "Second in the trilogy that began with *The Good Earth*, Buck's classic and starkly real tale of sons rising against their honored fathers tells of the bitter struggle to the death between the old and the new in China. Revolutions sweep the vast nation, leaving destruction and death in their wake, yet also promising emancipation to China's oppressed millions who are groping for a way to survive in a modern age."

89 *The House Divided* is the third and final volume of the Pearl S. Buck trilogy, following, *A Good Earth* and *Sons.* It centers around the third generation of Wang Lung's family.

90 *The Voice* refers to the daily Lithuanian newspaper.

91 *Der Purimspiler* starring Hymie Jacobson and Zygmond Turkov was filmed on location in Warsaw and Krakow. The movie takes place in a circus atmosphere and culminates with the Purim holiday.

92 Apparently this was very important, as Berman assumed Hinda had read about it in American papers; however, she had not read about it. Apparently it concerned the pharmacists and also the tighter requirements regarding promotions from one grade to the next.

93 **Letter 11**—March 31, 1938—dated 1 month after Letter 10

94 Lola Mellman and her father, Shaya, came to Gary, Indiana and lived with an aunt. Her mother, Chava, and younger sister, Ania, planned to follow after Lola and her father were established. However, within a year, Mr. Mellman became ill and died. Lola later married Myron Friedman and moved to Morristown, New Jersey. She and Hinda continue to regularly stay in touch. Ania and Chava remained in Šeduva.

95 Berman would enclose a coupon towards the postage stamp, which was equivalent to $1.00 This would assure him that Hinda would answer his letter, prepaid.

96 **Letter 12**—May 8, 1938—dated 5 weeks after Letter 11

97 Hinda's 2nd cousin (Rachmiel Gordon) came to visit from New Jersey with his wife and their two children, Ralph and Gloria. Rachmiel's mother was Hinda's father's sister.

98 The Vilna Troupe, a Yiddish theater company was founded in Vilna in 1915.

99 Yonas Turkov was a Yiddish actor.

100 Yankev Shternberg (1890-1973) was a Yiddish theater director, teacher of theater, playwright, *avant-garde* poet and short-story writer, best known for his theater work in Romania between the two world wars. At one time he was the Director of the Vilna Troupe.

101 Moscow was the capital of the Soviet Union, in 1938. Under the Communist system, May 1st was International Worker's Solidarity Day. It later became known as the "Holiday of Spring and Labor," "Labor Day," "May Holiday," or "Worker's Day."

102 **Letter 13**—June 8, 1938—dated 1 month after Letter 12

103 Memel (also known as Klaipeda) is in western Lithuania on the Baltic Sea.

104 Berman's main complaint about being a pharmacist in Šeduva was that it was a small town and he always tried to find a similar position in a larger city where there would be more cultural events. He had many interests and the small town did not provide all he had wanted. He also may have had a clause in his contract requiring him to find a permanent replacement before he could leave his position in Šeduva. He tried several times, but it never happened.

105 This shows that something is starting to happen in Šeduva…

106 **Letter 14**—July 17, 1938—dated 5 weeks after Letter 13. Imatra is a town in Finland, near the Russian border.

107 Helsinki, the largest city in Finland, is 230 km from Imatra.

108 **Letter 15**—August 2, 1938—dated 2 weeks after Letter 14

109 A dacha is "…a Russian word for seasonal or year-round second homes located in the exurbs of Soviet and Russian cities. In some cases it is occupied part of the year by its owner or rented out to urban residents as a summer retreat. Dachas are very common in Russia…" (Web address: http://en.wikipedia.org/wiki/Dacha. Last accessed June 29, 2011)

110 Stockholm is Sweden's capital and largest city. It is on the east coast, on the Baltic Sea.

111 Antanas Vienuolis (1882-1957) was born Antanas Zukauskas. He was a pharmacist's assistant prior to becoming a writer and dramatist.

112 At the time of this letter, Vipuri, was the second largest city in Finland.

113 Lake Ladoga is a freshwater lake.

114 Valaam is the largest island in the Valaam archipelago ("Valamo" in Finnish).

115 It would be logical because Russia had better relations with Czechoslovakia than with Lithuania.

116 "The Vuoksi River (Russian: Вуокса; Finnish: Vuoksi; Swedish: Vuoksen) runs in the northernmost part of the Karelian Isthmus from Lake Saimaa in southeastern Finland to Lake Ladoga in northwestern Russia." (Web address: http://en.wikipedia.org/wiki/Vuoksi_River. Last accessed June 29, 2011)

117Helsinki is the capital and largest city in Finland.

118Tallinn (historically known as Reval and Rewel) is on the Gulf of Finland. It is the capital and largest city in Estonia.

119 Dorfat, also known as Tartu, is 186 km southeast of Tallin, and is home to Estonia's oldest university, which was established in 1632.

120Riga, the capital of Latvia, is on the Baltic Sea.

121August 1st 1938 would be Berman's 26th birthday.

122**Letter 16**—August 28, 1938—dated 4 weeks after Letter 15

123Israel Joshua Singer (1893-1944) was a Polish-born Yiddish novelist. *Steel and Iron* was his first novel, written in 1927. *The Brothers Ashkenazai* was written in 1937. He was the brother of the author Isaac Bashevis Singer and the novelist Esther Kreitman.

124 The Fifth Zionist Congress in Basel, 1901 decided to establish Keren Kayemeth LeIsrael-Jewish National Fund KKL-JNF, as proposed by Professor Zvi (Hermann) Schapira, in order to purchase land in Eretz Israel for the Jewish People (Web address: http://www.kkl.org.il/KKL/SBMANAGE/showcontent.aspx?id=15909. Last accessed June 29, 2011)

125 From Nationmaster.com: World Agudath Israel was established in 1912 after the Tenth World Zionist Congress defeated a motion for funding yeshivas. Its aim was to mobilize Torah-loyal Jews for the perpetuation of authentic Judaism. They operated a number of Jewish educational institutions throughout Europe.

126 Malke Kaplan was a student and a year younger than Hinda.

127 **Letter 17**—October 4, 1938—dated 5 weeks after Letter 16

128 "Chronology of International Events, March 1938 to December 1941 issued by the Department of State, December 18, 1941" (Web address: http://www.ibiblio.org/pha/events/events.html. Last accessed July 23, 2011)

129 Stefan Zweig (1881-1942) was an Austrian-born writer. *Marie Antoinette: The Portrait of an Average Woman* was written in 1932.

130 Joseph Opatoshu (Yosef Meir Opatowski) (1886-1954) was a Polish-born Yiddish writer.

131 **Letter 18**—November 14, 1938—dated 6 weeks after Letter 17

132 This letter is a premonition of things to come. It is sad to see it coming and to not be able to do anything about it. The government didn't let anyone leave and people were trapped. Berman's dreams of further study vanished, but, still, not giving up that it will all pass and better days will follow. Hope and courage!

133 "...The Jewish Question referred to the sense that the existence of Jews in Germany posed a problem for the state. ...Upon achieving power in 1933, Hitler and the Nazi state began to implement increasingly radical measures aimed at segregating and ultimately removing the Jewish people from Germany and (eventually) all of Europe..."(Web address: http://en.wikipedia.org/wiki/Jewish_question. Last accessed August 2, 2011)

134 Joseph Opatoshu (born Yosef Meir Opatowski) (1886-1954) was a Polish-born Yiddish novelist and short story writer. (Web address: http://en.wikipedia.org/wiki/Joseph_Opatoshu. Last accessed June 29, 2011)

135 *Tkias Kaf* (translated as *Contract* or *Agreement*) is a Yiddish-language play, written in 1907 by Peretz Hirschbein (1880-1948), a Yiddish-language playwright.

136 *Maytime* is a 1937 MGM musical romance, directed by Robert Z. Leonard, starring Jeanette MacDonald and Nelson Eddy.

137 **Letter 19**—December 20, 1938—dated 5 weeks after Letter 18

138 Mail to the United States from Poland and Lithuania was irregular. In Poland, Hinda left behind her parents, two sisters, two paternal grandparents and one maternal grandfather (her maternal grandmother had already died) in addition to two very close girlfriends with whom she tried to correspond.

1939

139 **Letter 20**—February 25, 1939—2 months after Letter 19

140 Wordlanguage.com. *Green Fields*, directed by Edgar G. Ulmer is a romance film which was based on Peretz Hirschbein's story of a young student who leaves the Yeshiva in search of "true Jews." (Web address: http://www.worldlanguage.com/Products/Green-Fields-4861.htm. Last accessed June 29, 2011)

141 Ajzyk (Isaac) Samberg was one of the leads in the 1937 movie adaptation of *The Dybbuk*.

142 *Yoshe Kalb* was written in 1932 by Israel Joshua Singer, between *Steel and Iron* (1927) and *The Brothers Ashkenazi* (1937).

143 Maurice Schwartz (1890-1960) founded the Yiddish Art Theatre, in New York City, in 1926.

144 Sholom Aleichem (1859-1916) was a Jewish author of Yiddish literature. He was the first to write children's literature in Yiddish.

145 *Yankel der Schmid* (also known as *Jacob the Blacksmith* and *The Singing Blacksmith*) was an American film, and was released in 1938. It is about a young blacksmith who is tempted to stray from his marriage vows. The lead was played by Herschel Bernardi, in his film debut. The movie was based on a book written in 1909 by David Pinski (1872-1959), a Yiddish language writer.

146 **Letter 21**—April 29, 1939—2 months after Letter 20

147 The snow and early spring remind him of when Hinda left Šeduva, in March.

148 This is the fourth year he had been working in the same pharmacy in Šeduva; he could see this tree from the pharmacy window.

149 The 1939-40 New York World's Fair was the biggest international event since World War I. Over 44 million people attended. The grand opening was April 30, 1939 and it closed on October 27, 1940. It was open from April through October of each year.

150 *Otello* is a four-act opera by Giuseppe Verdi, based on Shakespeare's play, *Othello*.

151 Milke Bret and Freidele Mel were good friends and were a year younger than Hinda.

152 Henryk Vogler (1911-2005) was a Polish-Jewish writer from Krakow.

153 Hinda organized a social club for Glenville High School students who arrived in America from different parts of Europe.

154 The school play was at Glenville High School and was part of a class covering the subject of stage design.

155 Imbd.com. *Professor Mamlok* was released in 1938. "A Jewish surgeon, a war veteran, brilliant scientist and respected citizen becomes a victim of the mad anti-semitic purge and is stripped of all his possessions and discarded by the hospital. He is pressed back into service to perform an operation on a Nazi leader, and then machine-gunned as a reward." (Synopsis written by Les Adams). (Web address: http://www.imdb.com/title/tt0163797/. Last accessed June 29, 2011)

156 **Letter 22**—June 1, 1939—1 month after Letter 21

157 *Noah Pandre* was written by Zalman Shneour (1887-1959), a poet and novelist. The multi-volume novel described Jewish life in White Russia.

158 This package was never received by Hinda.

159 His American relatives would probably have been Aunt Goda, though Hinda knew nothing of her plan, or how Aunt Goda was going to document how Goda and Berman were related.

160 Every small town had a market day. In Widze, Hinda's home town in Poland, the big market day was Tuesday and a smaller market day was Friday. In Šeduva the market was in a large place at the center of town where much merchandise was brought in. Farmers brought fresh vegetables, seasonal fruit, fresh eggs, chickens, geese, ducks, cows, milk and milk products. Horses were also sold and traded. In addition, merchants would bring samples for sale. These were busy days for buying and selling.

161 **Letter 23**—June 18, 1939—2 weeks after Letter 22

162 Rachel Kagan is Hinda's Aunt, a sister to both Hinda's mother and to Goda. She was a schoolteacher.

163 Goda filed papers on Berman's behalf which would allow him to come to America. She also filed papers for Hinda's parents, hoping they, too, would come to America. Hinda was not yet 18 years old, so she was not yet a United States citizen. Until she became a citizen she could not send for anyone.

164 *Drei Kameraden* (*Three Comrades*) was published in 1837. It was written by Erich Maria Remarque (1898-1970).

165 Erich Maria Remarque's (1898-1970) most famous work was *All Quiet on the Western Front*. "In 1933, the Nazis banned and burned Remarque's works, and issued propaganda stating that he was a descendant of French Jews and that his real last name was Kramer, a Jewish-sounding name, and his original name spelled backwards. This is still listed in some biographies despite the complete lack of evidence." (Web address: http://en.wikipedia.org/wiki/Erich_Maria_Remarque. Last accessed June 29, 2011)

166 *A Doll's House* was written by Henrik Ibsen.

167 **Letter 24**—July 30, 1939—6 weeks after Letter 23

168 A distant relative of Uncle Samuel owned a candy store in a poor neighborhood. He asked if Hinda would be willing to work every Sunday from noon to 10:00 pm so he and his wife could have a day off. It paid $1.00. Even though Hinda didn't really enjoy the work (she shared the shift with another girl) it was the first money she had earned.

169 Fantasticfiction.co.uk. "This swift and timely story covers the events of twelve years. It begins with

the revolution sweeping down the Yangtze, when young students, fired with new patriotism, went singing to jail or to the beheading ground. It ends in the mountains of inner China, where driven back again and again by the invader, students and peasants, old war lords and young guerilla alike, stand in a united front and fight on." (Web address: http://www.fantasticfiction.co.uk/b/pearl-s-buck/patriot.htm. Last accessed June 29, 2011)

170 *Marie Stuart* was written in 1936 by Stefan Zweig (1881-1942) an Austrian, Jewish novelist, playwright, journalist and biographer.

171 August Gailit (1891-1960) was an Estonian writer.

172 A postal receipt documented the papers he had received from Hinda's Aunt Goda.

173 Yvette's birthday was July 23rd.

174 Rosalimas is a resort town where Hinda's Aunt Rachel (a sister to Hinda's Aunt Goda and Hinda's mother) spent her vacation.

175 **Letter 25**—August 20, 1939—3 weeks after Letter 24

176 Books.google.com, "Marie Sklodowska Curie (1867–1934) was the first woman scientist to win worldwide acclaim and was, indeed, one of the great scientists of the twentieth century." In 1937, her daughter, Eve Curie Labouisse wrote, *Madame Curie: A Biography*. It is likely this is the book he was reading. Hinda sent this to Berman for his birthday, August 1st.

177 **Letter 26**—October 27, 1939—2 months after Letter 25

178 There was no gasoline because of the war.

179 **Letter 27**—December 6, 1939—6 weeks after Letter 26

1940

180 **Letter 28**—January 21, 1940—6 weeks after Letter 27

181 The letter was received two months after it was sent.

182 Hinda's sisters were Gita (born in 1925) and Leah (born in 1928).

183 Ilya Ilf and Eugene Petrov's book was written in Russian. It was translated into English by Charles Malamuth and titled, *Little Golden America:Two famous Soviet Humorists Survey These United States*. The original Russian title of this books is: *Odnoetazhnaya Amerika (One-Storied America).*

1959

184 This letter, dated July 11, 1959, was written from Mrs. Mellman to her daughter, Lola. Lola gave it to Hinda.

Epilogue

185 Aron Bank moved to the United States, remarried, and had a place in the Catskills (a resort area in New York) which was a *kochaleyn*. Rosten, *The New Joys of Yiddish* defines a *kochaleyn* as "a room or bungalow, in a summer colony, with cooking facilities." He and Hinda continued to stay in touch. Additionally, various resources accessible through www.ancestry.com (accessed on April 24, 2011) confirm Aron Bank was born in 1905 in Widze, came to the United States in 1946, and died in June, 1973.

186 Guzenberg, I. *The Ghettos of Oshmyany, Svir, Švenčionys Regions: Lists of Prisoners 1942.* There is a picture of the seventh-grade students from Widze, which includes Hinda's sister, Gita, dated 1940. page 628.

187 Winer, G. *Widze Memorial Book.*

188 Guzenberg, I. *The Ghettos of Oshmyany, Svir, Švenčionys Regions: Lists of Prisoners 1942.* It is stated

that the Germans occupied Widze in the first week of the war and during the first days of the occupation the Nazis executed 50 Jews by the Widze lake. Alchonon was likely one of them. page 104.

189 Guzenberg, I. *The Ghettos of Oshmyany, Svir, Švenčionys Regions: Lists of Prisoners 1942.* The Widze ghetto was established in the fall of 1941. page 104. Chana, Gita and Leah's living quarters assignments in the Widze ghetto are documented on page 592. They were three of the 1224 Jews in the ghetto. The absence of Alchonan's name in the census implies he already had been killed.

190 Guzenberg, I. *The Ghettos of Oshmyany, Svir, Švenčionys Regions: Lists of Prisoners 1942.* The Widze ghetto was terminated in the summer of 1942 and the Jews were transferred to the ghetto in Švenčionys. pages 92-93.The ghetto of Švenčionys became crowded and an outbreak of typhus developed but it still existed at the end of 1942. On April 4, 1943, Jews that had not previously been reassigned to ghettos in Vilnius or Kaunas were put on a train and were told they were going to Kaunas. When the train stopped in Ponar, many realized this was an extermination site, and tried, unsuccessfully, to escape. This is likely when Chana, Gita and Leah tried, also unsuccessfully, to survive—by jumping off the train. The Widze residents were murdered in Ponar on April 5, 1943.

191 Guzenberg, I. *The Ghettos of Oshmyany, Svir, Švenčionys Regions: Lists of Prisoners 1942.*

192 Schoenburg, N. *Lithuanian Jewish Communities.* This source states that this meeting was able to take place twice a year—on Tisha B'Av and the Fast of Gedaliah. In 1938, Lithuania stopped issuing permits and visits were no longer possible. page 175.

193 Yad Vashem, 2009. *Untold Stories - Šeduva.*

194 *International Jewish Cemetery Project.* (Web address: http://www.iajgsjewishcemeteryproject.org// lithuania/Šeduva/print.html Last accessed May 4, 2011)

195 Margol, H. *Jewish Heritage Trip to Lithuania.* (Web address for current trip: http://www.litvaktrip.peggyspage.org/index.html)

196 Yad Vashem. "In 1940 and 1941 the Soviet government dug large pits at Ponar for fuel storage tanks, but they evacuated before they could complete the project. When the Germans occupied Lithuania in mid-1941, they used the pits for the mass murder of Jews from Vilna and the surrounding area, Soviet prisoners of war, and other enemies of the Nazis. Tens of thousands of victims were brought to Ponar, by foot, truck, and train. SS men, German police, and Lithuanian collaborators then shot them to death in the pits." Ponar is located 6.2 miles from Vilnius. It is estimated that 70,000-100,000 people were murdered there, mostly Jews. (Web address: http://www.yadvashem.org Last accessed July 22, 2011)

197 Yad Vashem. "The Central Database of Shoah Victims' Names" is a unique international undertaking led by Yad Vashem, from Jerusalem. It is the endeavor to recover the names and reconstruct the life stories of each individual Jew killed in the Shoah. Since 1955, Yad Vashem has worked to fulfill its mandate to preserve the memory of the six million Jews who were murdered in the Holocaust by collecting their names, the ultimate representation of a person's identity. The Shoah Victims' Names Recovery Project aims to memorialize each individual Jew who perished in the Holocaust by recording their names, biographical details and photographs on special forms created by Yad Vashem, called Pages of Testimony." (Web address: http://www.yadvashem.org Last accessed July 22, 2011)

Sources and Other References

Websites:

American Jewish Joint Distribution Committee. *Belarus.* http://www.jdc.org/jdc-worldwide-programs/former-soviet-union/belarus.aspx (accessed May 6, 2011).

American Jewish Joint Distribution Committee. *Lithuania.* http://www.jdc.org/jdc-worldwide-programs/europe/lithuania.aspx (accessed May 7, 2011).

Ancestry.com. http://www.ancestry.com (accessed April 25, 2011).

Anne Frank Stichting. http://www.annefrank.org/en/ (accessed June 26, 2011).

Boom, Dora, ed. *Shtetlinks: Seduva. JewishGen.* 2008. http://www.shtetlinks.jewishgen.org/Seduva/descendants/nava/framesetnava.htm (accessed July 2, 2011).

Columbia Encyclopedia. 6th ed. 2008. *http://www.encyclopedia.com* (accessed June 29, 2011).

Department of State. *Chronology of International Events, March 1938 to December 1941. (Department of State, Bulletin, December 27, 1941,* p. *590)* http://www.ibiblio.org/pha/events/events.html (accessed July 23, 2011).

Fantastic Fiction. http://www.Fantasticfiction.co.uk (accessed June 29, 2011).

Glossary of Yizkor Book Terms. http://www.jewishgen.org/Yizkor/yizterms.html (accessed April 24, 2011).

Goodreads, Inc. http://www.goodreads.com. (accessed August 2, 2011).

*Google Books htt*p://books.google.com. (accessed June 26, 2011).

International Jewish Cemetery Project. http://www.iajgsjewishcemeteryproject.org/lithuania/Šeduva/print.html (accessed May 4, 2011).

Internet Movie Database. http://www.imdb.com (accessed June 29, 2011).

Jewish Family History Foundation. http://www.jewishfamilyhistory.org/ (accessed July 2, 2011).

Jewish Joint Distribution Committee. http://www.jdc.org (accessed May 7, 2011).

Jewish Web Index. http://jewishwebindex.com/lithuania.htm (accessed July 2, 2011).

JewishGen. http://www.jewishgen.org (accessed July 2, 2011).

Katz, Dovid. http://www.dovidkatz.net (accessed August 31, 2011).

Lasky, Steven. *Museum of Family History.* http://www.museumoffamilyhistory.com/ (accessed August 31, 2011).

Levitan, Eilat Gordin. *Vidzy.* http://www.eilatgordinlevitan.com/vidzy/vidzy.html (accessed July 2, 2011).

LitvakSig. Jewish-Lithuanian Special Interest Group. http://litvaksig.org/ (accessed July 2, 2011).

Margol, Howard, and Peggy Freedman. *Jewish Heritage Trip to Lithuania.* http://www.litvaktrip.peggyspage.org/index.html (accessed May 30, 2011).

Nationmaster.com. http://www.nationmaster.com (accessed 2011).

Seligman, Jon, ed. *A Memory of the Shtetl.* 2009. http://www.seligman.org.il/seduva_residences.html (accessed 2011).

Turner Classic Movies. http://www.tcm.com (accessed August 23, 2011)

United States Holocaust Memorial Museum. http://www.ushmm.org/ (accessed August 19, 2011).

Wikipedia. Wikimedia Foundation. http://en.wikipedia.org (accessed 2011).

Woolf, Joe. *The Holocaust in 21 Lithuanian Towns.* http://www.jewishgen.org/yizkor/lithuania3/lit3_003.html (accessed July 2, 2011).

World Language. http://www.worldlanguage.com (accessed June 29, 2011).

Yad Vashem. *The Holocaust Martyrs' and Heroes' Remembrance Authority.* http://yadvashem.org (accessed June 25, 2011).

Yad Vashem. *Untold Stories—Šeduva.* 2009. http://www1.yadvashem.org/untoldstories/database/index.asp?cid=276 (accessed May 29, 2011).

Books:

Bubnys, Arūnas. "The Fate of the Jews of Švenčionys, Oshmyany and Svir Regions." In: *The Ghettos of Oshmyany, Svir, Švenčionys Regions: Lists of Prisoners 1942,* by Irina Guzenberg, Olga Movsovic and Jevgenija Sedova. Vilnius, Lithuania:

Valstybinis Vilniaus Gaono žydų muziejus, 2009.

Bubnys, Arūnas. *The Holocaust in Lithuania between 1941 and 1944.* Vilnius, Lithuania: Genocide and Resistance Research Centre of Lithuania, 2008.

Dawidowicz, Lucy S. *From that Place and Time: A Memoir 1938-1947.* New York, NY: Bantam Books, 1991.

Faitelson, Alex. *Heroism & Bravery in Lithuania, 1941-1945.* Jerusalem, Israel: Gefen, 1996.

Fishman, David E. *Embers Plucked from the Fire: The Rescue of Jewish Cultural Treasures in Vilna.* New York, NY: YIVO Institute for Jewish Research, 1995.

Gartner, Lloyd P. *History of the Jews of Cleveland.* [Cleveland, OH]: Western Reserve Historical Society and Jewish Theological Seminary of America, 1978.

Gitelman, Zvi. *Bitter Legacy: Confronting the Holocaust in the USSR.* Bloomington, IN: Indiana University Press, 1997.

Gordon, Harry. *The Shadow of Death: The Holocaust in Lithuania.* Lexington, KY: University Press of Kentucky, 1992.

Greenbaum, Masha. *The Jews of Lithuania: A History of a Remarkable Community 1316-1945.* New York, NY: Gefen Books, 1995.

Guzenberg, Irina, Olga Movsovic, and Jevgenija Sedova. *The Ghettos of Oshmyany, Svir, Švenčionys Regions: Lists of Prisoners 1942.* Vilnius, Lithuania: Valstybinis Vilniaus Gaono žydų muziejus, 2009.

Katz, Dovid. *Lithuanian Jewish Culture.* Vilnius, Lithuania: Central European University Press, 2010.

Kostanian, Rachel. *The Jewish State Museum of Lithuania.* Vilnius, Lithuania: The Jewish State Museum of Lithuania, 1996.

Leidykla, R. Paknio. *Sounds of Silence: Traces of Jewish Life in Lithuania.* Vilnius, Lithuania: R. Paknio Leidykla, 2009.

Lerer-Cohen, Rose and Saul Issroff. *The Holocaust in Lithuania 1941-1945: a Book of Remembrance.* 4 vols. Jerusalem, Israel: Gefen, 2002.

Levin, Dov. *Baltic Jews under the Soviets 1940-1946.* Jerusalem, Israel: Hebrew University of Jerusalem, 1994.

Levin, Dov. *Fighting Back: Lithuanian Jewry's Armed Resistance to the Nazis, 1941-1945.* New York, NY: Holmes & Meier, 1997.

Levin, Dov. *The Litvaks: A Short History of the Jews in Lithuania.* Jerusalem: Yad Vashem, 2000.

Nikžentaitis, Alvydas, Stefan Schreiner, and Darius Staliūnas. *The Vanished World of Lithuanian Jews.* Amsterdam, Netherlands: Rodopi, 2004.

Rosin, Josef. *Protecting our Litvak Heritage: A History of 50 Jewish Communities in Lithuania.* Coral Gables, FL: The Friends of the Yurburg Jewish Cemetery, Inc., 2009.

Rosten, Leo. *The New Joys of Yiddish.* New York, NY: Three Rivers Press, 2001.

Schoenburg, Nancy, and Stuart Schoenburg. *Lithuanian Jewish Communities.* Northvale, NJ: Jason Aronson, Inc, 1996.

Spector, Shmuel. *The Encyclopedia of Jewish Life Before and During the Holocaust.* Jerusalem, Yad Vashem; Washington Square, NY: New York University Press, 2001.

Stein, Joseph. *Fiddler on the Roof.* New York, NY: Crown, 1964.

Sutton, Karen. *The Massacre of the Jews of Lithuania: Lithuanian Collaboration in the Final Solution 1941-1944.* New York, NY: Gefen Books, 2008.

Syme, Daniel B. *The Jewish Home: A Guide for Jewish Living.* New York, NY: UAHC Press, 1988.

Winer, Gershon. "Kaddish for our Shtetl." In: *Widze Memorial Book*, by Gerhson Winer and Yizhak Alperovitz. Tel Aviv, Israel: Widze Association in Israel, 1997.

Winer, Gershon. *Widze Memorial Book.* Tel Aviv, Israel: Widze Association in Israel, 1997.

Contributors

Hinda Zarkey Saul was born in Panevėžys, Lithuania, in 1922, and emigrated to the United States in 1937. She has lived in South Euclid, Ohio, for the past 58 years. She speaks seven languages and still teaches Yiddish for her synagogue's sisterhood. Over the years her artistic talents have been utilized in many ways: calligraphy on invitations, drawings on announcements, embroidery on linens, and needlepoint on wall hangings and pillows. Her husband Jack, to whom she was married for 63 years, passed away in 2009. They have three children and four grandchildren.

Marlene Saul Englander was born in Cleveland, Ohio, in 1952. Since receiving her master's degree in Library Science in 1976, she has worked as a medical librarian, currently at the Cleveland Clinic. In her spare time she is a flutist in a number of orchestral and wind ensembles, and also spends time working on the mysteries of her family's genealogy. She and her husband Jon currently live in Shaker Heights, Ohio, where they raised their children.

Nochum Berman was born in Šeduva, Lithuania, in 1912. He received his pharmacy education in Kaunas, Lithuania, and worked as a pharmacist in Šeduva at the time these letters were written. His letters to Hinda can now help us understand what life was like during pre-Holocaust years.